man, land & myth
IN NORTH AUSTRALIA
the gunwinggu people

man, land & myth
IN NORTH AUSTRALIA
the gunwinggu people

by RONALD M. BERNDT
and CATHERINE H. BERNDT

MICHIGAN STATE
UNIVERSITY PRESS,
EAST LANSING

Contents

CONTENTS

CONTENTS

Illustrations

FIGURES

TABLES

man, land & myth
IN NORTH AUSTRALIA
the gunwinggu people

Preface

WE FIRST MET Gunwinggu-speaking people in 1945, when we were carrying out anthropological research in Army-controlled Aboriginal settlements in the Northern Territory. Later we met others after civilian control was restored, in Darwin, and at Goulburn Island in 1946 on our way to Yirrkalla in eastern Arnhem Land. (Unless we note otherwise, by 'Goulburn Island' we mean 'South Goulburn Island'.) In 1947 we first visited Oenpelli, and we went back for a longer stay from the end of 1949 until the middle of 1950. After that, we revisited Goulburn Island. We returned to Oenpelli for a short visit in 1958, called there in 1961 on our way to Goulburn Island, revisited Goulburn Island in 1964, and went back to Oenpelli and to Croker Island for further short visits early in 1966 and again in 1968.

Over that period, one kind of data we were collecting was basic census and genealogical material. This includes information on births, betrothals, marriages, dissolution of marriages, and deaths. It also includes information on where people are located at a given time, their reasons for being there, and how they make a living, as well as case-history material from both men and women. Another kind of data highlights two themes that, as these people made clear to us quite early, were particularly important to them. One is the way they know their own land, intimately and personally, with a mixture of practical hard-headedness and intense emotional attachment. The other is their confident assurance of their own place in their traditional world in a more general sense. Both of these are really aspects of *one* theme, which is the dominating influence of religion, especially through the linkage of myth.

Any of these topics could be the starting point for a great deal of discussion. We have tried to be ruthless in restricting this, because what we want to do here is to provide an overview, although one that centres on the three linked aspects of people, land and religion, especially myth. But we have also tried to leave in enough detail for several purposes. One is to show not only the rules, the formulas for living, but also something of the actuality. Another is to suggest the sort of material that a research worker on these topics is likely to be faced with, even now. A third purpose is to avoid that over-simplified presentation which can gloss over too many of the difficulties and complexities and reinforce the still-popular stereotype of Australian Aborigines, including Gunwinggu, as lovable but simple characters whose way of life can be summed up in a few words. A fourth purpose is to pave the way to an appreciation of these people and the realities of their life, for understanding is more likely to come from knowing something about content as well as form.

When we were nearly halfway through the first draft of this volume, we found we had embarked on a demographic study. What we intended to be a preliminary part of the volume was becoming its totality. At that point we called a halt and started again. We decided, then, that such material obviously belongs in a separate study, because it covers not only Gunwinggu but other language units of western Arnhem Land – population on the one hand, territorial affiliations on the other. Our quantitative assessments of other aspects, too, involve this wider span of 'tribal' groupings, especially in the fields of betrothal and marriage, and breaches of the peace. A partial presentation that showed only the Gunwinggu data would give a distorted picture. However, we have included a list of territorial groups without going into details about them. And although the three genealogical diagrams (Figs 13, 14 and 20) we include are quite small, we have added some extra information for readers who would like to extend these for themselves. In the main part of the volume we concentrate almost entirely on the Gunwinggu and their neighbours, with a minimum of references to other writers and to other Australian Aboriginal material. In the final chapter, however, we take up a few points from the Gunwinggu situation, and look at them in relation to the broader picture.

We have not included archaeological material – principally because systematic archaeological research in western Arnhem Land is a fairly new development, and the implications of specific

Fig. 1 *Map of western Arnhem Land, showing the limits of Gunwinggu and associated group territories.*

ARAFURA SEA

Croker I.

De Courcy Head

Bowen Str.

Port Essington

Cobourg
Peninsula

Brogden Pt

Marganala Plain

Salt
Water
Creek

Van
Diemen
Gulf

Sandy Creeks

Tor Rock

Cooper's Creek

Nimbu

East
Alligator River

Oenpelli

Gur

Buffalo country

Mel

Bath

A

Gou

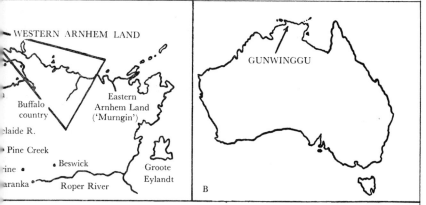

WESTERN ARNHEM LAND

Buffalo
country

Eastern
Arnhem Land
('Murngin')

laide R.

Pine Creek

ine •   • Beswick

aranka •   Roper River

Groote
Eylandt

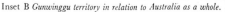

GUNWINGGU

B

et A *Arnhem Land and environs.*   Inset B *Gunwinggu territory in relation to Australia as a whole.*

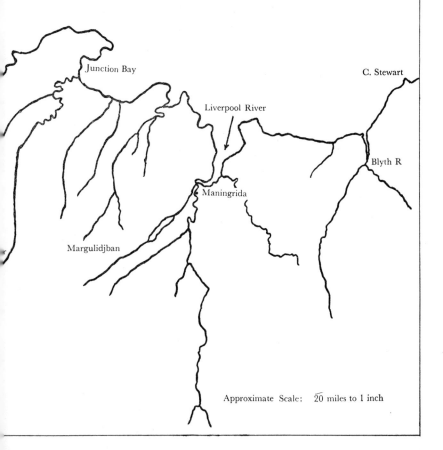

Junction Bay

C. Stewart

Liverpool River

Blyth R

Maningrida

Margulidjban

Approximate Scale: 20 miles to 1 inch

finds have not been entirely clear. When this volume was in the press, however, we learnt that the carbon dating of a polished stone axe found at Oenpelli by Dr Carmel White showed it to be of very early origin indeed – approaching 30,000 years. In other words, whatever the language and territorial affiliation of groups then living in and around Oenpelli, the region has certainly been inhabited, spasmodically or otherwise, for a very long time.

As regards orthography: in Gunwinggu words in italics and in kinship and subsection terms (Chapters 4 and 5), (j) is equivalent to 'y'; 'u' is pronounced as in 'put'; ʔ is a glottal stop; and 'ng' more often than not stands for a single sound, as in 'sing', except (for example) where 'g' follows the prefix *man-* or *gun-*. References to our own work are abbreviated as R. B. (or R.M.B.) and C. B. (or C.H.B.).

Our gratitude to various people and institutions cannot be compressed into so small a space: but, predominantly, we thank the Northern Territory Administration; the Methodist and Church Missionary Society missions; the Australian National Research Council, Professor A. P. Elkin, and the University of Sydney, under whose auspices we first carried out research in western Arnhem Land; the University of Western Australia, which supported later research and provided typing funds; the Australian Institute of Aboriginal Studies, which financed our 1966 trip; and the Australian Universities Commission, for help in 1967-8.

Above all, of course, this is a *Gunwinggu* book. Except for its shortcomings, it is their book and not ours. Those of them who eventually read it may be disappointed not to find in it all the information they would like to see. We would remind them, and others as well, that we have had to be selective even in outline. And in honesty we should add that, as our Maung and Gunbalang friends know, where western Arnhem Land is concerned one of us has a 'Gunwinggu bias'. But we hope they will all like this book, and that what we have said here will make other people want to know more about them, and also appreciate some of the problems that are facing them today.

RONALD M. BERNDT
CATHERINE H. BERNDT

Department of Anthropology,
University of Western Australia.

Chapter One

A Question of Identity

THIS IS NOT a picture of Australian Aborigines in a pristine state. Many of the people of this northern coast facing the Arafura Sea have a long history of contact with others – indirect to begin with, but affecting more of them as time went by. Nor do they live in a really harsh, semi-arid environment. It includes low-lying coastal flats, stretches of bushland and rocky escarpment, and on the whole it is well supplied with natural resources, including fresh water. On both these points it resembles Bathurst and Melville islands. (See, for example, Hart and Pilling, 1960.)

The Gunwinggu have close ties with their neighbours on the coast and offshore islands, but even closer connections with other mainland peoples farther inland. This means more than having a number of features in common. It raises the issue of boundaries, names, and group affiliations – what people call themselves as a group, what others call them, and how far these names coincide. Separating Tiwi from non-Tiwi is a much simpler matter than isolating Gunwinggu, if only because Bathurst and Melville islands *are* islands, with no territorial overlap on to the mainland such as the Goulburn Islanders have.

Gunwinggu is actually a language name. The Maung name for both the people and their language is Neinggu. Their own name for themselves is Winggu, and they do not call themselves Gunwinggu unless they are speaking English. Otherwise they use the stem *winggu* with person-indicating prefixes. (For instance, the first person singular becomes *ngawinggu*, the second person plural *nguriwinggu*, *nawinggu* means 'a male Winggu person', and so on.) But Gunwinggu has fairly wide currency now as a tribal name, and so for convenience we use it here as if it referred to the people as well as to their language.[1] (The ordinary word *gunbowinggu* means 'fresh water', a point that draws attention to the inland origin of the Gunwinggu.)

The problem of what is sometimes called 'tribal' identification was more relevant traditionally in some areas than in others, but today it is taking on a new kind of relevance for people of Aboriginal descent as their contacts extend farther outside their home regions. Where local people themselves cannot supply an easy answer, it is obviously harder for others to do so except by ignoring or over-riding local opinion.

The Gunwinggu might appear to meet the formal requirements of a tribe (as defined in R. and C.B., 1964: 34-9): that is, recognition of common language, territory, norms and traditions; shared self-identification and identification by others, symbolized in the use of a distinctive name; no rule of exogamy, but a relatively large social unit within which marriage is acceptable and possibly preferred. At this level, taking the label Gunwinggu as referring to a recognized tribal unit has a certain utility. It conforms with local practice and it provides a convenient starting point, a natural unit of study, in the sense that it is a conceptual reality with some basis in empirical reality. At the operational level, however, identification is more complicated and the problem of criteria is more crucial. The question 'Who are the Gunwinggu and how many are there?' is really a composite one, with a number of facets: 'Is Gunwinggu a distinctively different language? What are the

---

1 Also, we use the 'tribal' names Maung, Yiwadja (Jiwadja) and Gunavidji instead of the Gunwinggu names Gunmarung, Yibadja and Gunyibidji because they are fairly well established in the literature. This applies to the mythical Snake man, Yirawadbad, too (see Chapter 6): the Gunwinggu name for him is Yirabadbad.

We worked mainly through Gunwinggu from the Gumadir (R.M.B.) and Gurudjmug (C.H.B.) areas, which were widely agreed to represent 'real Gunwinggu'. We also compiled vocabulary lists for several related 'dialects', especially for the eastern dialect usually called Guru. Capell (1940) made a preliminary survey of Gunwinggu. More recently a phonemic study was prepared by Oates (1964), and a fuller survey of languages and dialects in this region has been in progress under the auspices of the Australian National University; also, a map of Australian Aboriginal languages has been put together by O'Grady, Wurm and Hale (1966).

2

extent and limits of Gunwinggu territory, and what happens at the borders? How can a Gunwinggu person be defined in contrast to others? Does this definition vary through time?' And so on.

Traditional Gunwinggu territory lay on the western and south-western side of what is now the Arnhem Land Reserve. The total population of western Arnhem Land is quite small. Its main centres are the mission stations at Oenpelli (Gunbalanya) on the East Alligator River, at South Goulburn Island, and at Croker Island (until 1968, primarily a settlement for children of part-Aboriginal descent); the government station at Maningrida on the Liverpool River is actually in north-central Arnhem Land. In 1957, the Welfare Branch of the Northern Territory Administration issued a preliminary 'Register of Wards' on the basis of records compiled by the stations.[2] Excluding Croker, in this tentative listing the total figure was more than 400 adults and 300 or so children 15 years old or under. Of these, 155 adults (75 males, 80 females) and 105 children (56 males, 49 females) were classified as Gunwinggu. But today more people who use the label of Gunwinggu live outside Arnhem Land, or at least spend a great deal of their time in other places. Those listed as Gunwinggu in the 1957 'Register' for the Darwin district, which includes the 'buffalo country' or 'buffalo plains' west and south-west of Oenpelli and the area as far south as Pine Creek as well as Croker Island, were 227 adults (113 males, 114 females) and 68 children (29 males, 39 females). Also, half a dozen Gunwinggu were included in the Katherine area, and 14 adults (6 males, 8 females) and 4 children (2 males, 2 females) at East Arm, the Darwin leprosarium which replaced the earlier settlement at Channel Island. For the purpose of this volume these numbers can be taken as a rough guide, because we shall not be

---

2 These lists were tentative, to provide a basis for more detailed checking. Mission records in the past were rather uneven. There is some duplication of names in the 'Register', for example, of people on the Oenpelli mission list who were spending a year or so in the 'buffalo country' (see text) or in Pine Creek. Our own lists, made up from census and genealogies, differ from these in some respects, but conform quite closely in others. The 'Register' labels as 'Gunwinggu' a number of people we would put under other headings, and vice versa, but on the whole the numbers probably balance out. It does give a fair idea of population and regional range, even though these have altered a little since 1957, largely because of an upward swing in the birth rate. For western Arnhem Land and the buffalo country, the 'Gunwinggu' figure is now over 300 adults and over 200 children.

going into the demographic picture.

We begin with a rapid sketch of alien contact in the region where the Gunwinggu live now, excluding Darwin and the townships and settlements farther south. (A fuller account, with source references, is given in R. and C. B., 1954.) Then we look at the Gunwinggu vis-à-vis their neighbours, with enough detail to map out their social and geographical surroundings.

Background to Contact

Western Arnhem Land extends from the East Alligator River to the Liverpool River and almost to Cape Stewart, but the Liverpool-Cape Stewart area is a transition or intermediate zone between the cultures of east and west – or, at least, it is so regarded by people on both sides of it. Some Gunwinggu actually call it Bulgai, or 'middle place'. The eastern part of Arnhem Land, farther from European settlements, had much more intensive contact with Indonesian traders, usually called Macassans or Bugis in the official records, and later with Japanese pearling fleets. The west had some experience of both of these, on the coast and offshore islands. On this western side, too, there were until quite recently old people who claimed to speak and understand trade Malay. The word *balanda* for European can be traced to this contact, both here and on the eastern side of Arnhem Land. And the name 'Macassar' (Manggadjara or Munanga to the western Arnhem Landers) has become a vaguely located point of origin, not only for the early traders, but also for various mythical characters who are said to have come from unidentified islands somewhere to the north-west.

Early in the 19th century, a number of other events anticipated the pressures that later intensified on the western and north-western approaches to Arnhem Land. A small British military post was established near Port Essington from 1827 to 1829, followed by a second attempt at settlement in the same region between 1838 and 1849. Later, until about 1904, a Customs official was stationed in Bowen Strait to collect dues from Macassan praus on their annual visits to the coast. Such places, like the Macassans' temporary shore camps, exerted a drawing power well beyond their immediate environs, but they did not impinge directly on people in the hinterland farther to the south-east.

4

Among the early explorers, such as King, Leichhardt, Lindsay, McKinlay, and Stuart, a few moved farther inland, but they seem to have made little impact there. More far-reaching effects came later, from men with an economic stake in the land and its products or in its coastal waters. On Cobourg Peninsula groups of Chinese were employed in cutting timber, and at least one children's song still commemorates them. Interest in pearlshell was stimulated by growing awareness of the 'Macassar men's' exploits, although in their case trepang was the main attraction. Europeans tried trepang-fishing, too. There was a trepang camp at Port Essington for a few months in 1874, and another on Croker Island in 1877. More important in the long term were water buffaloes, imported from Timor by the first British military settlement on Melville Island in 1824. They ran wild and multiplied throughout the coastal plains almost as far as Darwin on the west, and gradually spread east and south-east toward the Roper River. The Cobourg Cattle Company took up a leasehold for buffalo-hunting in 1876. Other small semi-mobile camps grew up, mostly in the river plains between the East Alligator River and what is now Darwin, and mostly comprising a nucleus of one or two 'white' hunters and a varying number of Aboriginal assistants and domestics and their relatives. They added a westward pull to the enticements already available on the north, and beyond them again lay the townships and settlements along the Alice Springs–Darwin telegraph line—including, from the late 1880s, the Pine Creek–Darwin railroad.

In about 1893, two buffalo-shooters named Cahill and Johnson had a camp at a place called (in a Northern Territory report) 'Alowangeewan', and another at 'Unmooragee', both on the western side of the East Alligator River. Cahill later moved his headquarters to manage the new government station at Oenpelli, on the eastern side of the river. He and his wife played host there to Baldwin Spencer for almost two months during Spencer's 1912 survey of Northern Territory Aborigines. Spencer's material (1913 and 1914) includes much detail on the Kakadu (Kakudju, Gagudju) tribe, or 'Kakadu Nation' as he called the complex of groups he met in that area, and also on the Yiwadja, 'Iwaidja' as he called them, around Port Essington. It seems likely that there were no Gunwinggu at or near Oenpelli in 1912, even under another name. Some of the items Spencer reports do have Gunwinggu counterparts – but not

5

exclusively Gunwinggu, because broad similarities can be traced over a very large area as far south as the Roper River and even beyond it. Other features he describes are distinctively 'non-Gunwinggu', such as the vocabulary and kin terms he lists for the Kakadu. People identifying themselves as Gunwinggu speakers seem to have moved into Oenpelli later, the first of them several years before the government station there was taken over by the Church Missionary Society in 1925.

In 1931, the region from the East Alligator River to the Gulf of Carpentaria and south to the Roper was declared an Aboriginal Reserve and became known as Arnhem Land, a name that formerly applied more widely to the entire upper part of the Northern Territory. During World War II, the whole of the Territory was under military control. Patrols came through part of western Arnhem Land and set up camps in various places, including the Oenpelli area. On the main Darwin–Alice Springs road, from the railhead at Larrimah to a site near Darwin, special Army settlements housed Aboriginal workers and dependents. Aerial surveys really began at about this time, and there was sporadic Japanese activity off the coast.

Later, after civilian authority was restored the westward drift of Aborigines gathered momentum again. Small groups from the Liverpool River–Cape Stewart area headed toward Darwin – coastal people in canoes, others overland on foot. Some of them got no farther than the Goulburn Island Methodist mission station (established in 1916). Others stayed at Oenpelli or in the buffalo country to the west of it. Those we met at Oenpelli and Goulburn Island between 1947 and 1950 claimed that, apart from the attraction of the bright lights of the townships and of Darwin itself, they moved because others were coming behind them and 'pushing' them westward. By that time, Gunwinggu-speakers made up a large part of the quasi-sedentary population at Oenpelli and a smaller proportion of the population at Goulburn Island, and they seemed quite at home in what was for most of them no longer a new environment.

When in 1957 a government settlement was officially started at Maningrida, near the mouth of the Liverpool River, it attracted a number of Gunwinggu, including some who were living in and around Oenpelli when we first visited there in 1947 and 1949-50.

Others are at Croker Island or scattered through the buffalo country, or come and go between these places, and others again now live more or less permanently in Darwin or in smaller centres and settlements farther south. Inevitably, in these circumstances there has been a fair amount of interchange and mixing and, especially, intermarriage – making the problem of tribal identity harder to unravel than it must have been, say, 50 years ago. And at least partial bilingualism is the rule, not the exception.

Gunwinggu in Context

From all accounts, Gunwinggu, like others before them, were drawn to the new settlements by curiosity and a growing desire for the food and goods they could obtain there, including tobacco and, in some places, liquor. They seem to have met no resistance from the local populations, probably because these had been weakened and reduced in numbers, on one hand by the earlier drift to the coast and westward and south-westward to the buffalo plains and the North-South line, and on the other hand by disease. (For example, to quote from the Northern Territory Government Resident's Report for the year 1901, p. 17: 'Mr. Cahill reports of the Alligator River tribe that of about 190 members who composed it seven or eight years ago, only about sixty survive, a large proportion of the deaths having been due to leprosy.') On Goulburn Island, too, immigrant Gunwinggu seemed to be well on the way to a cultural and linguistic 'takeover'. Then, in the late 1950s, renewed missionary enthusiasm for the Maung language stimulated a self-conscious emphasis on Maung identity – although, apart from the language and a few other features, Maung culture has virtually disappeared or survives only in the form of a rather patchy 'memory culture'. (This was so even in 1947, when we first worked with Maung at Goulburn Island.)

At Oenpelli there has also been an enthusiastic spurt of official interest in local language and culture generally, signified by mission sponsorship of Gunwinggu, which local missionaries are encouraged to learn. Well before this development, Gunwinggu was in the process of becoming a *lingua franca* through much of western Arnhem Land. In consequence, it is used quite freely by people who traditionally would probably not have spoken it at all but now are prepared to claim Gunwinggu identification for certain purposes.

7

One example is the so-called Gunwinggu camp on Croker Island. This includes several people who refer to themselves as Gunwinggu only in a very general way and are more likely than not to name some other language, mainly Gunbalang, as a primary basis of identification. Gunwinggu is a well-known name. And because a number of Europeans have heard of it, that makes it more convenient for answering official and other queries than other more obscure or localized language or tribal names.

Gunwinggu have acquired a reputation not only for spatial mobility, but also for cultural vitality, possibly because they give an impression of vigour and independence or, at least, more so than people with a longer heritage of direct contact. Inter-Aboriginal contacts took place not only on ceremonial occasions, but also at buffalo-hunters' camps (and, earlier, the Macassan camps) and on mission and wartime Army and government settlements, as well as in towns. This process has continued. If anything, it has been intensified. But since the scatter appears to be wider and the Aboriginal population is growing, there are always strangers in any gathering – individuals or groups outside the range of people already known or easily identifiable. When such strangers meet, the information they want about each other depends on the context. But the answer to the question 'Who are you?' is rarely a personal name or a kin relationship. If a subsection or some such category is mentioned (see Chapter 4), that is not usually enough by itself – not unless two essentials to identification are already established. These are territory, and language: 'Where do you come from?' and 'What do you speak?'. Answers can be more or less specific, depending on how much information is already available.

In other words, the level of contrast or inclusiveness defines the expected response. The reply 'Gunwinggu is my language' makes sense when Gunwinggu is contrasted with Maung or Gunbalang or Gundangbun or Yiwadja. If the differentiation is within Gunwinggu itself, several replies are possible; but the broader background issue remains – the problem of the 'edges' of one language as against another, especially between neighbours. This should be kept in mind when the more-inclusive language names are mentioned. It is very much like the territorial situation. People do acknowledge the sharing of larger stretches of common territory, especially in connection with the larger language names, but what

8

really counts far more is association with a smaller area containing a number of named sites. Ownership of these smaller areas is patrilineally inherited, within named units called *gunmugugur* and *igurumu* or *ngwoia*. More will be said about these later (Chapter 4), as well as about language choice where there is a difference between father tongue and mother tongue.

The traditional territories of people who claim to be Gunwinggu or accept that identification fairly consistently extend from around the Liverpool River in the east to Tor Rock in the west and well into the rocky Arnhem Land plateau, the escarpment country, on the south. (See Fig. 22.) On the coast to their north they mix with Maung, Wuningag around Cooper's Creek, now almost extinct, and Gunbalang. On their east are Nagara and Gunavidji (Gunwinggu call them Gunyibidji) and, more remotely, Gadjalibi (this is the Gunwinggu name for them) and Djinba. To the north-west are Yiwadja, and to the west a scatter of languages that Gunwinggu call by the collective name Gunbargid. This includes Kakadu, Amurag, Awur, Eri and Wuningag, sometimes Woraidbag (or Woraidbug), and usually Mangeri or Mangerdji, traditional 'owners' of the Oenpelli area. On their south and south-east are Dangbun (speaking Gundangbun, as Gunwinggu call their language), and beyond them Rembarnga. To the south-west are Maiali and, farther on, Djauan.

This is a rough outline. Looked at more closely, still from the dual perspective of language-and-territory, the pattern is more complex. The two main reasons have already been mentioned. One is the presence of small language or dialect units within or between the larger units, and the other is the difficulty of establishing exact referents for certain of these names.

For example, although Yiwadja are most closely associated now with Cape Don and with Croker Island, both of these places were traditionally owned by others: Croker mainly by Margu, some small neighbouring islands by Yilga, and the Cape Don area by Garig, Wurugu and Adawuli – and, of these, only a few Margu survive. Yiwadja and Maung are 'company', 'companion languages', very close in vocabulary. Between them was Mangawulu, a small language unit even closer to Yiwadja: its members now identify with either of these two larger groups and Mangawulu is rarely even mentioned. Maung was spoken on South Goulburn Island and the

9

nearby mainland, Naragani on North Goulburn. Near Woraidbag was Wurilg, described as very similar to it. One of the Gunbargid language group was Waramungguwi – 'like Mangerdji, but with different names for fish and birds'. Others that are said to have 'mixed with' Kakadu were Ngunbudj, and Magabala, sometimes called Gun-garigen from the territory name, Gugari or Gugarigari.

On the eastern side is the marginal case of groups sometimes included under the broad heading of Gunwinggu and sometimes not – those traditionally living around the Margulidjban River and across to the Liverpool and Blyth rivers. From the Oenpelli-Gunwinggu perspective, their local language divisions include Gunwalidja and Gun-gurulg or Guru, which show some vocabulary differences from the Gunwinggu spoken around the Gumadir River. Also, their subsection names (see Chapter 4) link them with eastern Arnhem Land, although in their dealings with Gunwinggu proper they use typical Gunwinggu forms. Again, whether and when they are regarded as Gunwinggu depends on perspective and context and on the kind of contrast that is being emphasized.

The name Maiali (or Gunmaiali) poses a slightly different dilemma. In ordinary speech it means 'understanding' or mind (not physical brain) or sense. But it is also a language label for people who now live mostly at places along or near the North-South road, including Beswick government station, and at scattered settlements between there and Oenpelli. They call themselves this, and so do others. In 1945 we met a number of Maiali in the Mataranka–Katherine–Adelaide River area, most of them on Army settlements. A short vocabulary of Maiali words and some conversational material we recorded then is almost identical with what we learnt later in the Oenpelli region as Gunwinggu. Also, several of the Maiali we talked with in 1945 mentioned close relatives at Oenpelli – who later identified themselves to us as Gunwinggu. Some Maung speakers apply the name Maiali to people from the upper reaches of the Gumadir River, including Gurudjmug, but they more often call themselves Gunwinggu, and when they do acknowledge a Maiali label they usually bracket the two together – for example, in English, 'Gunwinggu, Maiali side'. This suggests that, even if Maiali is not a substitute for Gunwinggu, it is at least as close to 'real Gunwinggu' as the Margulidjban variety is.

The double label points to social as well as to territorial and linguistic interconnections. For instance, 'Gunwinggu, Dangbun side'; 'Gunwinggu, Yiwadja side'; 'Gunwinggu, Maung side' – from a southern Gunwinggu perspective, 'they marry Maung'. Or, for instance, 'Maiali, Djauan side' are believed to have a south-western inland orientation and less contact with, say, Gumadir than more north-easterly Maiali do.

One inclusive definition of Gunwinggu came from a mixed group at Goulburn Island, including two women who were or had been married to Gunwinggu men. The 'big name for the Neinggu', they said, using the Maung form, covered Guru and Margulidjban groups as well as Maiali: this was *'Gunlor ʔ lorgen-they-speak'*. They insisted that this was only a name and had no other meaning. (*Gun-* is an ordinary prefix for a class of 'nouns' that includes language and language names; *lorgen* is in its duplicated form here to show a plural. In other contexts it means 'thoroughly' or 'well'. For instance, it can refer to a child's mastery of vocabulary when he is able to speak properly, or to thrashing someone 'soundly'.) Gunwinggu speakers themselves distinguished different kinds of Gunwinggu, such as 'hard' and 'soft'. One woman with a Dangbun-side father and a Gurudjmug mother put it like this: 'Those who come from Margulidjban, those who talk Guru, soft Gunwinggu is what they speak – but ours is hard, like rock.' She was among those who described Maiali as a 'soft' kind of Gunwinggu, but in fact, although she usually glossed over this, her own kin connections were more obviously with the Maiali side than with Gumadir and the coast.

In other words, recognition of differences is to some extent a relative matter. And, of course, the differences need not be great. Small divergences in vocabulary can be effective symbols of separate identification when other factors reinforce them.

Myth, Language and Territory

The present trend is toward identification in terms of the larger language names. Smaller language and dialect units seem to be more significant in retrospect and among older people. Even in myth, they are not often mentioned. Instead, there are references to the sharing of certain areas by two language units – or, actually, the overlapping of two languages and occasionally more. In Gun-winggu, 'land' in an ordinary sense, not soil or mud, is *gunbolg* (or, in certain circumstances, *gubolg*) – an expanse of country, a place. Another word, *gunred* (or, in certain circumstances, *gured*), has much the same meaning but with a special emphasis: *gunred* is land-in-relation-to-people, or a camp or dwelling place, or a nest. Its stem, *-red*, appears in the usual expression for 'countrymen', people sharing the same territory in contrast to 'strangers'. One way of asking the name of a place is '*Bale ʔgabolg-ngeiu?*', but 'Whose territory?' is '*Nangali nuje gunred?*' In talking about a specific *gunred*, asking its name, the core of the term *gunbolg* is still retained as a land-indicating stem: 'His territory, what is its name?' ('*Gunred nuje, bale ʔgabolg-ngeiu?*'). *Gunred* is territory with human associations; *gunbolg* need not be, although they are usually assumed. In the following pages, unless stated otherwise, we use the term territory specifically in the sense of *gunred*. Apart from transient camps, the focus in both cases is on named sites. These, and not continuous boundary lines, are the main 'markers' demarcating one territory or language unit from another.

Some sites are of special importance because of their religious associations, or because of the prohibitions surrounding them. A number of these, and others too, are prominent in a physical sense. The rocky hills that dot the coastal plain between the East Alligator and the Liverpool, outcrops of the central Arnhem Land plateau, include some distinctive landmarks that can be seen for miles in every direction.

One is Tor Rock, Wuragag – mythically speaking, a very well-known character, and one of the earliest of the First People. He came from Manggadjara ('Macassar'), via Melville Island (Wungug) and Cape Don, with a group of close relatives, all named: in most versions of his story, his mother and father and brother, mother's widowed sister, mother's brother, father's sister, and the mother of his first wife, Waramurungundji (or Wurumurunggoindju). Waramurungundji herself was waiting for him on the mainland, where he parted company with some of the others. All of them are commemorated in rock, but it is Wuragag who dominates the plain. Another high rock formation farther to the east is Nimbuwa. According to the myth, his home was a long way to the south-west, in 'Djauan country, perhaps'. When he was still a young man his father died, and he came north after the full series of mortuary rites had been completed, bringing his widowed mother: 'I can't leave you behind, my own mother – they might kill you!' He looked after her assiduously on the way, and comforted her when they reached the place where her brother was already standing as a high rock. Later on they too (and their dogs) became rocks, but she is a small one, overshadowed by her son.

These two characters have become more famous than most because not only Aborigines but even some Europeans, however much or little they know of the rest of the region, recognize them as landmarks – missionaries, government officials, pilots of small planes, and so on. Western Arnhem Landers' accounts vary, especially in detail, but the main outline is broadly the same as told by men and by women, and in versions we recorded between 1947 and 1968.

An episode in the Nimbuwa series provides one of the rare instances, mythical or otherwise, of quarrelling over territory. Nimbuwa's mother's brother's son, Yiriu, accused him of coming from the east to 'steal my country'. Both were armed, with an assortment of weapons, but Nimbuwa finally yielded to Yiriu's demand and retreated to the east, where he stands now – approximately twenty miles north-east of Oenpelli.

Wuragag was also in trouble. In fact, he was one of the few characters who deliberately transformed their bodies into rock – in most versions, because he was afraid. He took as sweetheart or second wife a Woraidbag girl who had been betrothed to another man, and when a Woraidbag attacking party surrounded his camp, that was how he 'escaped'.

Both Wuragag and Nimbuwa and their relatives, in their stories, originally spoke other languages before they came to where they stand now. For Wuragag, it was first the language or tongue of 'Macassar', then Wungug (Melville Island), and then Yiwadja, and now he is a meeting-place for Yiwadja, Gunwinggu and Maung. Numerous myths use him as a boundary indicator. Nadjarami Wild Bee man and his dog, bringing cycad-palm food from far in the east, changed their language when they reached Cooper's Creek and approached Wuragag, and spoke Maung and Gunwinggu 'because we are in their territory now'. A group of Leech ancestors, too, a man and his three wives, said to one another as they approached this area, 'We'll speak Gunwinggu and Maung now. If we speak Gunbalang, Wuragag might hear us – and Gunwinggu and Maung are his language(s). . . . ' But in most instances the mythical language transition is carried out smoothly, despite this overlapping. It is virtually never resisted or made an occasion for friction. In one rare example, a group of men coming from the north-west and speaking 'Macassar' language changed without difficulty to Yiwadja, but when they came to Maung territory two of them refused to go on farther because 'we don't know that language, we're afraid – we'll stay here'. Another myth makes the same point by implication– not in its content but in what people today say about it. This is a 'sickness' origin myth. Its centre is Wurudja Island beyond Croker, from which one of the First People sent sickness to kill everyone on the mainland as far as Marganala (Murganella) Plain. Northern Gunwinggu who told this story claimed, 'We can't go there, or he might smell our different sweat and hear our different language. Only Yiwadja and Maung can go there, and when they ask the spirit of that First Man they can get turtle eggs and other foods there. . . . '

Most characters are quite ready to drop one language and take up another or use a new language combination. In a number of cases they dig a hole and bury the language they have spoken up to that point, or bury its spirit, and in several such episodes a rock or a tree springs from it to mark the site. Even where that does not happen, the place-name itself in conjunction with the myth is a reminder that the zone is one of some kind of language change. Myth has provided a charter for both narrow and wide-range affiliation, based on the two aspects of language and territory, and, in spite of the innovations and modifications that have been taking place all through the region, it continues to do so.

MAN

Gunwinggu women, Oenpelli, 1950

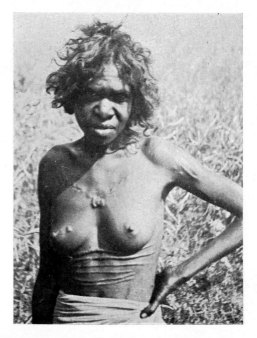

Gunwinggu women, Oenpelli, 1950

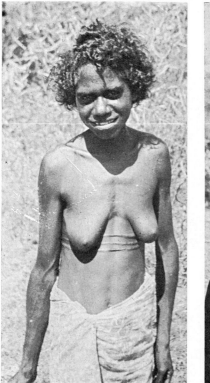

Gunwinggu men, Oenpelli, 1950

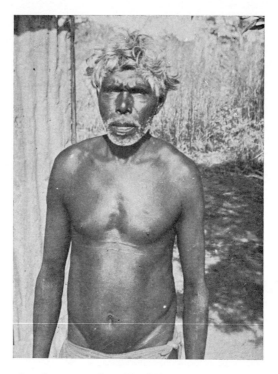

Gunwinggu men, Oenpelli, 1950

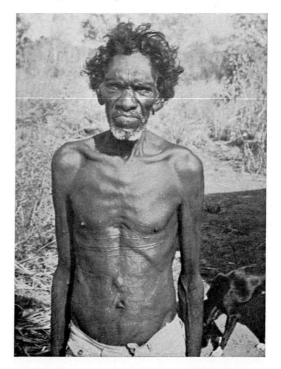

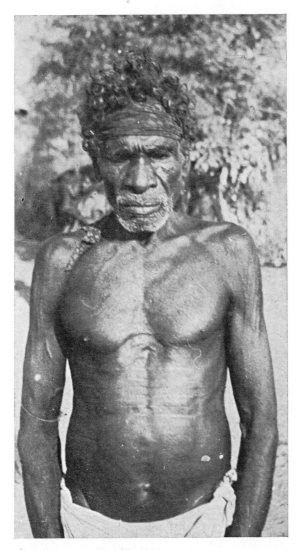

Gunwinggu man, Oenpelli, 1950

Relaxing after collecting rations at Goulburn Island mission, 1964

Yiwadja hut on beach at Croker Island, 1966

Maung and Gunwinggu women. Goulburn Island, 1964

Hot weather shade in the Gunwinggu camp at Croker Island, 1966

A singing group in the main camp at Goulburn Island, 1964

Chapter Two

The First
People

A MORE EXACT title for this chapter would be 'Those Who Were Here First', or 'The First Inhabitants'. When Gunwinggu talk about mythical characters in general, the expressions they use do not mean 'people' in the ordinary sense. The usual word for a person, or people, is *binin*, a *human* being in contrast to others – and these 'others' traditionally included other Aborigines on the edge of the known world and beyond it. More narrowly, *binin* is a male human being in contrast to a female. And a third contrast has been emerging in the contact situation: *binin* as an Aboriginal person, distinct from any other kind of person. Some of the mythical characters were *binin*, at least partly in human shape, even though they were human beings of a special (mythical) kind. But others were not.

These characters, then, are usually referred to by word stems that can be translated as 'early' or 'first' with prefixes to indicate sex or number. The same terms can refer to the land itself as it was at the very beginning, before it acquired the shape and the features it has today. In this sense, the time sequence involved is linear, not cyclical. And when the word for 'people' is used, in this context the 'new people' are those living now or in the recent past, the 'old people' those who lived 'before', 'long ago', in the beginning.

Many characters are unnamed. Some are given general names like Barramundi (fish) or Long-necked Tortoise or Crow. Others have contributed personal names to the pool that is drawn upon by contemporary people. The majority of these are not acknowledged to be translatable unless they can be identified in the speaker's own language. For example, Ngalgoidjeg, the name of one mythical girl, is made up of a stem referring to 'elopement', implying a sweetheart relationship, plus the ordinary feminine prefix *ngal-*: and so it is described as a 'sweetheart name'. Waramurungundji, on the other hand, is not a Gunwinggu name. It was said to be a general Maung term for woman, with the specific mythical meaning of *First* Woman.

Whose Version Is Right?

Inevitably, accounts of major as well as minor characters show some variation, and particularly so in this region of long 'intertribal' contact. Fairly wide agreement on the importance of Waramurungundji is matched by divergence on other points: whether she was ever married to Flying Fox, whether he was actually First Man, whether there were two or more Waramurungundji or only one, whether she left Wuragag, now Tor Rock, in a fit of jealousy because he took a second wife (see also Chapter 6), and whether the honour of being Creative Mother belongs, instead, to the Rainbow. This last, which seems on the surface to be a minority view, is in fact related to the Snake Mother (and Father) symbolism of the *ubar* and *kunapipi* ritual complexes (see Chapter 6).

Gunwinggu explain some variation in myth, if they are asked, by saying that different episodes in the career of a particular character are referred to, or that it is due to elaboration of detail, or that not all the characters associated with a place need be mentioned in speaking about it. Within a certain range, variation is accepted almost without comment. But over and above this is the question of accuracy.

Because people tacitly agree to differ and do not criticize divergent versions, this does not mean they have no views on 'correctness' in myth reporting. In assessing the validity of a given version, Gunwinggu have three major considerations in mind. One is the myth-teller's affiliation with the territory concerned – especially patrilineal affiliation. The second is his or her age. Middle-aged women, for instance, often claimed to be 'like children' in such matters. In the twenty years since we first visited western Arnhem Land, women's knowledge of local mythology has been dwindling.

Many of the older experts have died or become senile. Younger women are deflected by other interests, and their movements are much more limited – they do not know so much of the country at first hand. This leads to the third consideration – sex.

Apart from puberty and birth responsibilities, and some *kunapipi* songs (see Chapter 6), Gunwinggu women have no store of secret-sacred information that they keep secret from men. Sexual dichotomy is built into religious experience. Although they share a great deal in common, men and women conventionally look at myth and ritual from differing angles. Men organize and control the magico-religious rites, all mythically based, and, provided the other two requirements (strong affiliation with the relevant territory, and mature age) are met, they have the final word in any disagreement on the truth of one version as against another. Many 'women's versions' are almost identical with versions told by men, and were said to have been heard from men in the first place. The most obvious differences are at the level of straightforward description or explicit content – concerned with such questions as, What is seen or done, said or heard, and by whom? Other, subtler, differences hinge on symbolic interpretation – What does it mean, and why? It is at this esoteric level that accounts from fully initiated men are most likely to differ from all others.

In the ordinary way, outside the context of ritual, stories of the First People are told informally. The actual telling may come first. Or the story may take the form of an on-the-spot description, while the speaker is touching the main features of a site or pointing to it from some distance away. Men may take their young sons and daughters on guided tours of their own territory, and a husband occasionally takes his wife.

Generally speaking, people know best the stories directly connected with their own territory, or territory that otherwise has some special significance for them. Nevertheless, it is hard to find a character who keeps entirely to one area. A few are truly indigenous in this sense. (One version of a Barramundi site in Gumadir, for instance, holds that Barramundi was 'always there, that was where he began'.) But as a rule, whatever a character's ultimate destination may be, he came to it from somewhere else – near or far, and at almost any point of the compass. His place of origin may be vaguely located as 'far away' or his language as 'unknown to us', and it is only as he approaches familiar ground that the references become more specific.

Myth and Destiny

Most of the mythical characters are not, strictly speaking, ancestral as far as people are concerned, and no attempts are made to link them genealogically with living persons. Some are described as original prototypes or founding ancestors of various natural species, either through a mythical transformation or through some quality inherent in them from the very beginning. No accounts deal with the creation of the earth itself or the sky or the sea. This fundamental setting is assumed to have been already in place, in substantially its present form, when the First People arrived. The mythical era in western Arnhem Land was one of discovery and consolidation. All the main characters helped in one way or another to prepare the land for human habitation. They supplied natural resources, including food (see Chapter 3), and through their actions in life or memorials left after their death they introduced changes in the landscape – in its rocks, watercourses and vegetation, and so on. Above all, they left the spiritual essence which makes the land alive. In this sense they are referred to as *djang*.

To western Arnhem Landers, the land is not inanimate and unresponsive like a thing or an object. Its topographical features are a record of 'who was here, and did what', for anyone who has the verbal keys to it. Especially, the record tells 'who is here *now*'. A *djang* is, by definition, immanent and relevant in the contemporary scene. However mobile they were before, most *djang* eventually became localized, attached to specific places. But their time range was extended, not curtailed. While generations of people come and go, the *djang* live on indefinitely in spirit form. The death of their physical bodies was only a necessary prelude to this crystallizing of their association with a particular territory and the human beings who 'belong' to it. In this respect they differ from human ghosts (*namandi* or *maam*, terms used also for corpses), and also from non-human spirits like the stick-thin *mimi* that live among the rocks and the fat Dadube, Nagidgid the soul-stealer, and *marlwa* and others who are usually hostile to human beings.

Details aside, the wanderings of the First People were not haphazard. The urge that prompted them to set out on their travels in the first place was directed toward a long-range goal: to reach the site where they were to 'put themselves in spirit' – in other words, to become *djang*. As the journey proceeds, that aim is often obscured by other issues; and when they finally meet their fate this is nearly always attributed to a mistake or a wrong action on their own part or on someone else's – they have been side-tracked on their travels or taken the wrong turning or done something silly, or they have been the victims of malice or revenge. And in such a crisis most of them do not put up any resistance although they protest or weep in despair. But even though 'personal responsibility' is emphasized, the theme of inherent destiny persists. A few characters take the initiative themselves and 'turn into' or take on different outward shapes (birds, fish, reptiles, insects), but the usual reason for metamorphosis is that they are trying to evade some other danger. Less often, it is simply and directly that they have at last found the exact place or kind of place (the myths are not explicit on this) they were looking for.

The same theme appears in other circumstances that are defined as being closer in time – the coming of Macassan traders, for instance. Old Mangurug put it plainly in talking about traders she had seen as a child. When she was asked why they came to the coast, her answer was, 'Nobody brought them, they came of their own accord in search of this land. They wanted long yams and meats and, above all, they wanted this land!'

The first People fall into two partly overlapping categories. On one hand are those concerned with the creation of human beings, secret-sacred rites, and rites and practices focusing on initiation, life crises, and so on. The most important of these are not *djang* – at least, not to older men and women; younger people use the term more loosely. On the other hand are the *djang* proper, varying in attributes, but all linked with local sites.

In this chapter we pay more attention to *djang*, without anticipating any further the discussion of myth and ritual in the sphere of religion (Chapter 6). An exception is the Rainbow Snake – an agent of destiny for many of the First People, playing a major part in their metamorphosis or *djang*-ization.

19

In Maung mythology, the Rainbow is predominantly a male symbol. So, in eastern Arnhem Land, is the great Python who swallowed the two Wawalag Sisters. But Gunwinggu are less positive on this.

The reason for their doubt could lie, ultimately, in a linguistic form. One term often used for the Rainbow is *mai*ʾ. In its general sense, this covers a class of living things – animals, reptiles, insects, sometimes birds (although these are usually called *mai*ʾ*mai*) – and its qualifiers show the grammatical gender that includes or subsumes the biologically male (prefix, *na-*). When *mai*ʾ refers obliquely to the Rainbow, however, its qualifiers most often take the form that includes the biologically female (prefix, *ngal-*). Probably this was a convenient way of separating the two referents; there are other examples where different prefixes serve that purpose. Whatever its origin, it does seem to reinforce the Gunwinggu view that the Rainbow is, or may be, female – or, at least, is not always to be regarded as male. The specific names of this Snake, Ngaljod or Ngalmud, like another name that is occasionally used, Ngaldargid (*dargid* means alive, living), point in the same direction. So does the creation myth which credits the Rainbow with having given birth to the first human beings – as the First Mother.

In relation to *djang*, the stress is on the fear-inspiring and punitive aspect of the Rainbow. She (or he) swallows her victims in a great flood (that is, drowns them), carries them about for a time, and then vomits their bones, which turn into stone. When the ending is different, the story has usually come from coastal sites or is told by people with Maung and Yiwadja affiliations. For them, these mythical Rainbows are not invincible, and human beings can fight back. After a swallowing-drowning incident, others hunt her and kill her, and her belly is cut open so that the unconscious victims can be helped out and revived. Even then, however, they have not disposed of the Rainbow once and for all and they have gained only a temporary advantage. The Rainbow is eternal and essentially indestructible, and is not restricted to one time or place or one physical body. She can be in many places simultaneously, ready to punish anyone who breaks a tabu or provokes her in some other way.

To illustrate the kinds of character who appear in these stories, what they did and said, and how and where they became *djang*, here are some specific examples.

The first is more or less typical of narratives in which the Rainbow plays a dominant role in the making of *djang*. Another of the characters is an orphan or motherless child. The combination of Orphan and Rainbow appears throughout the whole region, including the buffalo plains. The focus of this particular story, which is quite widely known, is the Njalaidj dancers. The *njalaidj* ceremony is a non-sacred song and dance complex accompanied by some gift exchange. The central site in this story is in Gurudjmug, in the heart of Gunwinggu territory (see Fig. 2). We have chosen two versions, both from women, to show how the same set of mythical incidents can be approached from different directions. They were told in Gunwinggu. As in all these accounts, we have kept the translation general.

The first version, from a southern perspective, is from Wurgamara, of the Wurig territorial group (see Chapter 4).

'People came from the south, from Dangbun country, to a ceremony in Gurudjmug. A messenger had been sent to tell them exactly where to go. They came through rocky country, and when they reached the creek that goes through Gurudjmug one man climbed a high rock. From there, he heard people calling out: men, women and children were painting themselves, painting their spears and throwers, and beginning to dance and sing. [The Dangbun party went on, and joined them.] But a little orphan, about two or three years old, was crying for cooked *mandaneg* food [see Chapter 3] that had been declared tabu, *mandjamun*; it had been put aside as sacred, as *maraiin*. All morning, all afternoon, and right through to daybreak he kept on crying. Nobody could stop him. And so that Snake came, and ate them. Some of the *njalaidj* dancers climbed to the top of the rocks: they turned into stone there, and their name is Njalaidj *djang*. They brought trouble on themselves – because they first showed him that food and so he kept on thinking about it and crying for it, and so she ate them all. Maidjuni is where some of them stand, on top of the rocks, and Gabari is where the others are, inside the billabong. . . . '

The second version of the story came from Gararu, now dead, of the Ngalngbali territorial group. Her daughter, who helped her to tell it, is Madjawar.

21

'They came from the north, from the sea coast – a group of men, women and children bringing the *njalaidj*. They camped here and there, searching for a place to dance, asking one another, "Where shall we go? Shall we stay here?" They crossed the creek at Balali, and some of them danced while others watched. It was good. "We'll go on," they said, "because you dance so well." They climbed up the rocky hill at Djirggam and looked around, asking one another, "Where do you think we should go?" "Let's go farther on, this way." They went on, camping, and climbing higher, still going through bush country [*manberg*] because there is a large expanse of bush in Gumadir. At last they reached a camp where people were waiting for them, happy to see them, calling out, "Come here! We've made the place ready for you to dance; we've cleared the ground for the ceremony." They all slept. Next morning they got up and began to dance. They danced on and on and on. One girl climbed a pandanus palm and called out as they danced. And a little boy, an orphan, was crying for milk . . . . Nobody thought of saying, "Don't make so much noise, don't upset the whole place or we'll be drowned!" Nobody said that. They just kept on dancing and she kept on calling and the orphan kept on crying . . . and, from underneath, water kept rising upward to where they were dancing and calling and crying. Presently they saw the ground getting soft and wet. They cried out to one another, "Why is this happening? Why is the whole place getting soft and wet, so we can't run away? What can it be?" The orphan and the girl didn't hear their frightened cries because they themselves were making so much noise. Then, after a time, even those two saw water coming rushing toward them. People said, "What's happening? What's eating us here? Oh, we did wrong to make so much noise and to let that orphan go on crying . . . . And now, Ngaljod is coming to eat us!" The water grew wider and deeper as they cried out in fear. She ate them all, those people who were calling out and the orphan who was crying. Water covered them all. They came into spirit form there, calling out the name of the site, "This is Gabari, where we danced and water came up for us and where we made ourselves wrong. It remains tabu ground. Let nobody come close or set foot here, or they will sink beneath the water. Nobody is to come near or touch the place where we stand in spirit . . . " '

(In another version of this story, a man and a woman escaped from the flood by climbing a tall tree. But a mosquito was worrying them. They slapped at it – not hard, just lightly, but Ngaljod heard and swallowed them too. 'Nobody was left.')

Another story centring on Gabari in Gurudjmug tells how two sisters and the elder girl's baby were drowned there. They had left their old father because of his incestuous interest in the younger girl. The Rainbow ate him first and then followed them to Gabari. 'They made that place tabu, and they made that water tabu. Vegetable foods [*manme*], too – women are not to collect them there, in that tabu place. ... People are not to get fish or vegetable foods there, they are not to use fish nets or spear fish or they too may meet with misfortune. And from a distance people can see fire where they are cooking fish – they alone, no people, only themselves in the middle of the water.'

The crying orphan is used as a bad example: because it is hard to deny children something they want, tempting things should be kept away from them. In a Woraidbag story an orphan demanded something that had been declared tabu and sacred – honey from an ochre-painted palm-leaf basket. He had seen men eating it, near him in the camp, and wanted some too. His mother's parents tried to distract him with ordinary honey, then they tried smacking him. People even went out to collect more honey for him, but he wouldn't touch it. In other cases an orphan wants a particular lily root or a yam, or children who are not orphans tease him or he is neglected, not given enough to eat, or he wants something even more unattainable – his dead mother. In a 'bad example' story with a different implication, a homesick young wife kept on weeping for her parents, although her husband warned her not to 'because Ngaljod might get us' – and he was right.

Not all the First People were as insensitive to noise as the Njalaidj dancers. Several moved on to other camping-sites because they were being kept awake – for example, by small water-snails moving near by. One Wurilg-speaking man, lying down after the evening meal, couldn't sleep because his dog went on crunching bones even after he had shouted at it to be quiet. At last he jumped up, crying, 'You're deaf!' and hurled a stick at it, breaking its 'arm'. The dog ran yelping away, and finally became *djang* in country north-east of Oenpelli. In a different story the barking of a Gunwinggu dog, as it cornered a kangaroo among rocks, brought the

Rainbow almost at once to swallow them both.

Another noise disturbing to the Rainbow is the sizzling of a small animal, usually a possum, goanna or bandicoot, that has been left cooking for too long. Or the creature's eye bursts, or, if it is on a flat rock, the rock itself cracks from the heat.

Many characters unwittingly brought the Rainbow in this way – among them two girls who came from the Liverpool River area in search of a good place free from leeches. 'When they reached Gurudjmug creek they told each other, "Now we are in true Gunwinggu country, in Djelama group territory." [See Chapter 4.] They stayed there for a while, eating long yams, *mangindjeg* roots and blue-waterlily roots, and coming back each night to sleep. But they could hear the voice of the *manjalg* wild bee – it was there first. They moved higher up the creek, but centipedes and scorpions almost stung them. They were afraid and moved on again. The place they came to was just right: clean sand, clear water, and no leeches. They made the ground smooth at the water's edge and camped in the shade of a white "apple" tree, asking each other, "What shall we do now?" It was after this that the Rainbow swallowed them, drawn by the sizzling of a goanna they neglected to remove from the coals. They are still there in spirit, sitting under the waterfall at Djurlga [see Fig. 3] – young girls with small breasts, and long hair.' 'We can hear them calling out and splashing in the water.' 'But nobody goes near that pool, except people from that country. Not those whose mothers are from that country, that's different – only their fathers.' 'And nobody is to eat fish from there, especially when new water flows after rain.'

In an account from a different narrator, the two girls were already *djang* when Centipede reached that site – not in human shape, but as a centipede from the very beginning.

'Centipede came from far in the east, looking for a place to live in. She tried one place: it was no good. On she went through the bush to a patch of jungle: no, that was no good. She was following the same road the two Djurlga girls had taken before. Meat ants smelt her and bit her as she came along the edge of the rocks, planting *mangubin* roots near a freshwater spring. She put part of her spirit at Ngarindjobul. Then she went on to Djurlga and lay in the pool beneath the waterfall, but the two girls scolded her. So she went up to a blind corner among the rocks, and saw it was a good place – no creatures, no meat ants to bite her. Scorpion was there already – she had come before with the two girls. Centipede stayed with her. She sat down and became hard, and as she turned into stone she called the name of that place: Djalargaiuwa, "Centipede lies [here]".'

This site is the scene of a different story.

'Two little girls put down their things and cleared the ground. "This is a good place," they said to each other. They made the ground clean, and slept. But centipedes came after them from under the ground. "What's that coming?" they asked each other. "Listen!" Many centipedes were approaching. "This is a good place that we've cleared, so why are they coming here?" "Yes, why?" They struck at the centipedes, but there were too many. "Oh, they are killing us!" "Did we bring trouble on ourselves? Is there a *djang* [*mandjang*] here, killing us because we came to this place?" Centipedes attacked them, biting them, and they lay there and died. The centipedes searched all around in case there might be more people camping there. No, only those two. As they died, the two girls spoke to each other: "What is the name of this place?" "Djalargaiuwa." That's where they died. And the country itself covered them up – tabu country, nobody goes there.'

A shorter story from the same place tells how a man, bitten to death by scorpions, turned to rock there, and it ends, 'Nobody is to hit that rock or climb on to it or get yams there – or scorpions would come up on to us and follow us (so we would die, too).'

These four accounts all come from Gunwinggu narrators, and all of them are quite well known even to people not acquainted with any of the details. Those who belong to a particular area are expected to know more than a bare outline. For others, the main questions are 'What *djang* is there?' and 'What are the implications for human beings now?' Although not all of these versions spell it out, the suggestion is that anyone who tried to camp at Djalargaiuwa would meet the same fate as the two girls did: it is a Centipede place, and to be avoided. The same kind of warning applies to places associated with Leech, or with Louse.

One Louse site is at Yiliburgum, and the story is about a man and his three wives who, in human shape, felt lice beginning to crawl over them – over their hair, legs, arms, bodies. They couldn't get rid of the creatures, although they tried to eat some and 'they tasted good'. The youngest wife was pregnant. Her 'sisters' made all the usual preparations, but instead of a human baby she gave birth to a multitude of lice. Not knowing what else to do, they put the lice in ordinary paperbark baby-carriers, but not long afterward all of them died, the husband first, completely covered in lice. Their bodies turned into stone. 'People are not to collect yams there, or they may die as the Louse people did.'

According to the Gunwinggu narrator, these Louse *djang* people first spoke Gunbalang and then 'Gunwinggu and Maung'. Yiliburgum was described as a Maung name, and the Gunwinggu seem to have no separate label for it. In accounting for that, the narrator said simply, 'They turned their tongue and spoke Maung.' When a place-name is framed in one language but members of another language unit claim it too, this does raise the question of ownership of that territory – much more obviously so than when more than one name is available and the choice depends on the language of the speaker.

Another story connected with Djurlga brings up a different point.

'Two little boys, both *djang*, came from the waterfall at Djurlga, looking for a place to live in. They crossed the water at Mai?yad, climbed the rocks at Muddu and went down to drink water at Garurgen-gani [site of Garurgen Kangaroo woman], still searching for a good place. They crossed the creek at Gwiibindjen, went higher up, and crossed again at Gunbadgoldje ("a Flying Fox name" – "flying foxes are thick in the jungle there"). They came to a crowd of children and went with them into the water to swim, and they saw that the water was good. "We'll stay here," they told each other. Nobody brought misfortune on them. They made themselves, those children – it is a Baby place. Women are not to go there or a child may get them. Only people from that country go there, and see them. The name of the place is Gwiingawara, in Gabari. The children are in paperbark trees and meat ants' nests and in the jungle. If they see people going along, they swim and splash in the water, and if people call out to them they can hear those children calling back. If people light fires, the children cry out in fear and dive into the water. Young girls are not to go near there or they may get children, and, if the ant nests are broken, children will come out in search of women . . . .'

Spirit child centres like this reflect the Gunwinggu belief that human beings are composed of two basic ingredients – material substance, plus something else. That something else is the animating spirit, ideally connected with a person's own father's territory. Roughly the same principle appears in the *djang*, in so far as their spirits live on independently after the death or transformation of their physical bodies. The spirit children at Gwiingawara are *djang* because of their territorial significance, established in mythical terms, but their presence is not marked by any visible sign such as a rock or some other external manifestation. And they have a unique place in human affairs – a specifically defined and highly active role that needs no ritual prompting from human beings.

Myth as Good and *Bad Example*

The explanations provided by myth cover a wide field. The natural environment exists in its present form because of what the mythical characters did to it or what they left behind. Also, the rivers and billabongs, rocks and plains, like paintings on the walls and roofs of rock shelters, are evidence that the stories are 'true'. Some of the efforts of mythical characters were on a grand scale – like the East Alligator River, made by Barramundi-fish (in a western manifestation) as he headed for the sea, or by the Rainbow, rushing to drown two Wild Turkey brothers who had broken a tabu. The stories account for human physical characteristics (in a Kakadu story, women's vaginas are red because that is where two mythical women once hid fire), for the traditional absence of circumcision (see Chapter 6), and for the origin of death. And they supply precedents and warnings in respect of food and territorial and life-crisis tabus.

In myth, a sure way of summoning the Rainbow is to smash a tabu rock – one marking the presence of *djang*, or of a *mar* rock that 'always' had this supernatural quality. In several stories, breaking up such a rock was a deliberate act of revenge and, incidentally, suicide. In others it was accidental but the result was the same. To Gunwinggu, that pattern of cause and effect still holds good. An eastern manifestation of Barramundi, for instance, also in fish shape, was trapped in shallow water and gradually hardened into rock. 'This is a tabu place. Nobody is to touch that rock, except old people with magical power. They clean the grass around

27

it so it won't get hot. If it did, the rock might crack and burst and we would all drown . . . .'

In this sphere of tabus and prohibitions, the injunctions and the believed-in implications are unequivocal. 'Don't touch this!' 'Don't eat that!' 'Don't go near that place!' It is hard to say how far they are actually obeyed, but we are tempted to hazard a guess that breaches are very rare indeed – especially in regard to public actions such as going near a forbidden place, but also in regard to eating forbidden foods. An attempt at privacy or secrecy in eating would be suspect, anyway, suggesting that a person had something to conceal. But in such matters public sanctions are less directly significant than supernatural sanctions. The threat of the Rainbow, in particular, is not taken lightly.

When it comes to the social sphere, the bearing of myth on ordinary life is more difficult to establish. Straight-out reflection of attitudes presents little difficulty: for instance, the readily admitted view that old men prefer adolescent girls, but girls usually prefer young men – expressed in a number of stories, including the Yirawadbad myth (see Chapter 6). In conventional terms, this is a bad example with an ending to suit: the elderly husband kills the young wife who rejected him, and girls are warned not to take her as a model. Other bad examples embody the same sequence of wrong-doing followed by punishment: for instance, stories of an old man who raped his little granddaughter (*mamam*), a boy who committed incest with his sister, and a man with an abnormally large and dangerous penis (*beidbang*) who unintentionally killed a young girl with it. Both teller and audience, children included, linger with interest on the actual 'wrongdoing' scenes, and the laughter and comments suggest that one of their uses is to provide, not merely entertainment, but also erotic stimulation. Such stories seem to have survived more tenaciously than many others – but not, for the most part, officially. They have either gone underground or split into two versions, one for mission consumption and one, unexpurgated, for more restricted circulation.

Nonetheless, illustrations of what *not* to do are nearly as numerous as those that show, explicitly or implicitly, the proper course to take and the proper social setting for it. Ideally, people are born into the right categories and groups, speaking the right languages, as prescribed in myth: and if they maintain this pattern, arranging

28

marriages correctly and generally behaving toward one another in appropriate ways, life proceeds smoothly with a minimum of upset. The myths have a great deal to say on such topics, but their directives are less sharply defined and the sanctions more diffuse than in regard to magico-religious belief and ritual on the one hand, and, on the other, the relationship between people and natural resources, including land.

Chapter Three

Living with
the Land

As HUNTERS AND food-collectors, the Gunwinggu fit easily into the overall Aboriginal picture. Two major features combine to give their particular pattern, or sub-pattern, its distinctive shape. One is to some extent outside their control: the range and quality of natural resources, in a tropical setting that includes sea coast and tidal rivers as well as dry escarpment. The other feature is socio-cultural: the way that the Gunwinggu organize their human resources, their particular cultural heritage – the traditional lenses through which they perceive and define their environment.

On the whole, and compared with many Aborigines farther inland, the Gunwinggu have a territory rich in food and water and raw material for the equipment that is part of their traditional way of life. They know what kinds of terrain suit various foods and what they can expect to find where – and where they are likely to find almost nothing. They can identify the plants they want by obvious signs like growth patterns and foliage ('choosing the right leaves'), and animals, reptiles and birds by their tracks and feeding and nesting habits. This general knowledge is complemented by knowledge of particular areas. Both kinds of information are learnt. The process of learning starts in early childhood, and the basic nucleus that children acquire then is elaborated and augmented in the course of experience.

As well as variation in space, Gunwinggu recognize variation through time. The daily cycle is punctuated by words for daybreak, sunrise, morning, midday, afternoon, late afternoon, sunset, evening, and night ('darkness'). Phases of the moon constitute another cycle. On a larger canvas, the sequence of seasons is linked with the growth of plants and movements of living creatures and, accordingly, with the pattern of hunting and collecting. The point at which one phase passes into another does not depend on a fixed time progression, such as a series of named months, but on the appropriate combination of weather, surface water, and vegetation. Starting approximately in the first half of December, the sequence is:

melenggen, or simply *gudjiog* (rain): First rains of the north-west monsoon 'starting to moisten the ground'; grass beginning to grow; 'old yam' time; some new fruits almost ready.

gudjiog burg (heavy rain): Hot and humid; 'flood time'; grass getting higher; more new fruits and new root foods developing.

banggaren: Cooler weather; rain almost finished; wind from the east bending the long grass; seeds beginning to fall; plenty of new fruits; goose-egg time.

jegge: Cold and dry; lily roots and seeds ready; grass turning brown; burning-grass time.

wurgeng: Beginning of hot, dry weather; eucalypts in full flower, especially stringy-bark; wild honey more plentiful.

gurung: Hot and dry; surface waters recede – even permanent billabongs, as at Oenpelli, may shrink.

Official rainfall data from the three western Arnhem Land settlements at Oenpelli, Croker Island and South Goulburn Island correspond closely to this sequence. Oenpelli has the highest average rainfall (5,199 points). Most rain falls there between November and the end of March, with January the wettest month (average 1,276 points); after April the rainfall drops sharply to August, with an average of two points, then rises sharply to October. For several years Oenpelli recorded no rain at all for the six months May – October. Averages aside, the practical difficulties of prediction are reflected in the range between highest and lowest rainfall figures. At Oenpelli, for instance, the highest January rainfall ever recorded was 3,058 points, the lowest 531; March 2,093 against 188; April 1,629 against nil; November 1,088 against 25; December 2,297 against 217.

Official temperature records are much less complete. Briefly, the mean maximum at Oenpelli is 97.8 °F. in October and November, the mean minimum 62.3 °F. in July; the mean relative humidity at 9 a.m. ranges between 67 per cent (July) and 89 per cent (January), at 3 p.m. between 27 per cent (September) and 64 per cent (January). The differences between Oenpelli, Croker Island, Cape Don, Darwin, and South Goulburn Island are not large, but the Oenpelli mean maximum is a little higher, the mean minimum a little lower, than any of the others.

This is the weather pattern in regions where most Gunwinggu live now, although their traditional territories extended farther inland into the escarpment country – with, probably, a lower average rainfall and higher maximum and lower minimum temperatures. In both cases, it is based on two partly coordinated cycles, with polar extremes of wet or dry, hot or cold. The central feature, the north-west monsoon, affects the inland as well as the coast and brings occasional cyclones, and it is a point of reference for rough reckoning in terms of years – 'last (or next) rainy season', or 'so many rains thrown away' or past. (The Gunwinggu have specific words for the numbers one to four, although instead of four they usually say 'two doubled', or 'three [plus] one'; after that they speak of one hand, two hands, plus one or two feet, and so on, or use items like twigs or pebbles for larger counts that call for something more specific than 'many' or 'much.)

The behaviour of various natural species contributes to the seasonal picture. The *galawan* goanna, people say, stands up on his hind feet during rain because he likes to feel it, but the *bugbug* 'rain pheasant' does more than enjoy it – 'his cry brings more rain'. When the cicada 'talks' a little, new root foods are just starting to grow, but when she talks loudly and strongly they are ready to be dug. A great many creatures, edible and otherwise, and some plants, are the subject of short children's songs that imitate their cries or movements or comment on their distinctive characteristics. Most are not in Gunwinggu and can be translated only in a general way. Some are made up wholly or partly of onomatopoeic sounds representing bird calls, movements of water creatures and so on. Others are half in, say, Maung, and half in Gunwinggu. For a few creatures, such as white cockatoo, dingo and buffalo, there is more than one song.

Like *djang* stories and the myth-ritual complex in general, and like ordinary conversations, these songs reflect the western Arnhem Landers' interest in the totality of their physical environment. Their concern is not limited to things that are edible or in some other way directly useful to themselves. A great deal of what is said does have practical value, like the sayings that where you see chickenhawk, there you find kangaroo, or that the *gigig* bird warns people when a snake is near by, or that the short-necked tortoise likes to eat *mandjimdjim* palm seeds. But interest ranges over a much wider field, such as the behaviour of white cockatoos, magpie larks, flies, seagulls and pelicans ('beaks like fishing nets'), the food they eat and how they set about getting it.

Food Resources and Preparation

Children learn early to read the signs in their natural environment. The songs contain only a fraction of this knowledge. By the time they can run about they should be able to identify ordinary tracks in and around the camps, starting with people, dogs, and small things like ants, beetles and lizards. Whether they go with a foraging group of women or stay at a prearranged spot with elderly people, especially grandmothers, a lot of their time and energy is spent on such matters. Most of their games have some connection with hunting and food-collecting or the tools and equipment that go with it. Boys have miniature bamboo spears and practise on tiny sun-lizards or fish. Later they graduate to slightly heavier spears and throwers. Girls more often practise with real food, collecting with their mothers or other women. Although their baskets are scaled down in size, like their digging sticks, they are worn in the same way, hanging down at the back from a loop slung across the forehead. Some foods must be kept separate, even in cooking. Some can be eaten on the spot, while others need special treatment. Girls have more opportunities for observation in this respect. What boys learn about spear types and handling weapons and hunting procedures comes from a mixture of instruction and hearsay reports, with a minimum of actual observation until they are allowed to accompany adult men and take closer notice of what they do. Kangaroo-hunting calls for greater endurance than women's collecting efforts and for techniques of a different sort. Weapons and implements are important in both, but even more important are the knowledge and skill that come through learning and practice.

Separate words distinguish men's hunting of larger game from women's foraging for smaller things, but there is a considerable overlap. Honey is one food that either men or women collect, depending on circumstances. Five kinds of honey bee are distinguished, including *gubulag*, the only one that 'bites'. Women never hunt buffalo, but until they had access to horses and rifles men rarely did so either – even though one species of coastal tree is singled out as being exceptionally hard, making spear shafts 'strong enough even for buffalo'. (The mythical source of this tree was a Dragonfly ancestor, Maidjaninbir. Not far from Tor Rock, while still in human shape, he pulled out his whiskers and planted them, and 'spear trees' sprang up there.) Nor do women normally hunt kangaroos. But they do not like to forage without at least one dog – 'taking a nose', in the Gunwinggu phrase, although a good dog does more than smell out game.

Gunwinggu have no single term for food or edible things in general. The major division is between plant or vegetable foods (*manme*) and all others. The 'others' come in several categories, with no overall label. One category, *guin*, comprises kangaroos and wallabies. A second, *mai ?*, covers a wide assortment of living mobile creatures from buffaloes, crocodiles and snakes, geese and ducks, to insects. Fish make up another category, separate from shellfish (mainly mussels, limpets and oysters: of minor importance). Wild honey is a further category, and eggs of all kinds another. A general word for flesh (or 'beef') is sometimes applied to fish as well as meat.

Manme, guin, fish, honey, and eggs are edible by definition. *Mai ?* are not. Moreover, some edible *mai ?* are dangerous or risky, *(na)bang*. The same kind of contrast divides 'true' or 'good' or 'sweet' *manme* from 'bitter' (*manbang*) *manme* that is inedible until it has been treated. The distinction between good and bitter has a range of gradations, in the kind of treatment required and in the degree of 'sweetness' finally achieved.

Basic cooking techniques are simple. The flames of a quick fire are used for singeing animal fur, and scorching meat to eat in a hurry. Hot coals and ashes are the most popular medium for small things like goannas and possums, internal organs of larger animals, roots, and lily-seed and other flat cakes. These are grilled, broiled or wrapped in paperbark, but more often they are heaped over

34

with hot coals and perhaps a thick layer of soil or ashes or sand to retain the heat while they cook. For larger creatures, such as kangaroos, an earth-oven hole is dug in the ground. Chunks of termite mound are heated in a fierce fire while the fur is burnt off, and when the flames have died down the wood and termite mound are moved aside and the carcase or flesh is packed around with fresh green grass on a sheet of thick paperbark. Sometimes pieces of hot termite mound are tucked into the abdominal cavity. More thick paperbark is spread on top, then the hot termite mound, and the whole thing is covered with soft earth or sand. Termite mound is preferred to stones because, people say, it holds the heat longer and makes for better cooking. In line with a widespread Aboriginal preference, Gunwinggu like their meat rare. They have a reputation, that now seems to embarrass them, for drinking kangaroo blood. The most some of them do now is to lick their fingers as they cut up the meat, but in their traditional inland environment fresh blood was a convenient source of salt.

Firewood is not normally a problem in this region at any time, but, in general, the supply of natural resources varies according to place and season. Prohibitions based on age, sex, locality, and life-crises or sacred ritual also help to define what foods are 'available'. More broadly, inedible things include very small animals that are 'meat for dogs, not for us', wild beeswax at the bottom of a comb, also eaten by dogs before the leavings are burnt, and the bony little lizards and fish that children hunt in play. Apart from more formal ritual and sex tabus, bitter (*manbang*) foods are denied to children on the realistic grounds that they are too strong.

Among the edible *mai* ? are grubs found in termite mounds, tree larvae (for example, those that have become known to Europeans as witchetty grubs), mangrove worms, rock snails, and, rarely, large and small grasshoppers. Green-ant nests are knocked down, the eggs collected, and the ants crushed in water to make a sour drink – *gunbobang*, bitter liquid, the same word that is used for sea water. There is a saying that, because of a mythical incident, people should not eat fish after eating green ants or 'all the fish might die, frightened of the ants'. Head lice are not defined as food but are eaten casually, although not by everyone. Fish poisons, from bark, sap or leaves, are handled with caution. People avoid drinking from any small pool where one of these has been soaking.

35

Most edible fruits become ripe from about the middle of December onward, depending on the rains. They are particularly welcome because, except for 'bitter' roots, there is usually a short period of scarcity until the new season's long yams and other 'sweet' roots are ready to eat. We counted twenty-three named varieties of fruit from trees, bushes, and creepers that can be eaten straight away. No doubt there are more, but these are probably the most common. Some are sweeter than others – for instance, dark red 'plums' growing near the coast are described as much sweeter than those found farther inland. In one yellow fruit (*mandag* or *mandari*) the skin is rejected but the flesh and the pounded stone are eaten. A bitter plum-like fruit, *manwidu*, lasts into the cold weather but is not much liked. Green 'plums', *mandudjmi*, are preserved by being stored in a dry rocky place for two to three months, then soaked in water and pounded, stone and all, to soften them before eating. Clear or purple tree-gum is softened if necessary by being soaked in water; it is described as sweet.

Other *manme* include fungus, sweet 'honey'-like leaves or petals, pandanus fruit and seeds, various nuts, and cabbage-palm shoots. A soft stone-like white clay is eaten occasionally. Pink and blue water-lily roots and stems are popular; the seeds are crushed, ground, shaped into oval cakes, and cooked. More important even than lilies, and fundamental in Gunwinggu diet, are other root foods that supply much of its bulk.

At the time of our main fieldwork we had no facilities for collection and storage, and so we were not able to have specimens of these plants identified. (The botanical names for a few items were taken from McArthur in Mountford [ed.] 1960: 135.) Nevertheless, a list of the main roots, other than lilies, indicates the variety that is available and how some of them are prepared.

(a) 'Sweet' or non-bitter roots:

garbara long hairy white or purplish sweet yams; very popular. (*Dioscorea sativa* L. var. *elongata* F. M. Bail.)

mangongong small potato-like roots, often eaten raw. (*Curculigo ensifolia* R. Br.)

djarbal, djarbir or *djedbar* long, thin, very hairy root; cooked in coals and eaten straight away, but slightly bitter. (*Curculigo ensifolia* R. Br.)

deidjanbi long, thin root, like *djarbal*.

mangudgeb small sticky potato-like roots.

manidjag small onion-like root; cooked on coals.

mangulaidj small nutty-textured grass roots; can be eaten raw.

modji large nutty-textured grass roots.

ngula, or *baidju* single radish-like stalk.

mangubin inside water, or near freshwater spring; long thin hard hairy roots; tiny, very green leaves; dug up; fibres singed off; dried by 'burning' in quick fire (not oven); broken and kept wrapped in paperbark; lasts for some months; crushed and made into small cakes, mixed with wild honey; can also be mixed with flour.

gugbam 'water peanut'; can be eaten without cooking. (*Triglochin procera* R. Br. var. *dubia* Benth.)

mangoidbang also called 'water peanut' (cf. *gugbam*); in billabongs; must be peeled; bottom part soft, like potato, after cooking; top part nutty textured; cooked for long time; very popular. (Not really 'bitter', despite ending, *-bang*.)

(b) 'Bitter' roots:

manbaram large round or long reddish root, with white flesh; baked with hot termite mound, without peeling (if peeled raw, juices highly irritant to hands); said to be nice but not sweet.

mangodbi large brownish roots, with white flesh; just below surface; some 'sweet'; but some 'truly bitter' if half cooked ('we can hardly bear to taste them'): therefore either cooked in coals and left for a 'long time' until soft, or cooked in oven, from morning until late afternoon or evening, and then eaten straight away. (*Cayratia trifolia* (L.) Domin.)

mandaneg small, rather like pingpong balls, white or yellow, with lot of thin roots; cooked for a long time, and then pounded (for example, with back of axe) to soften.

mangindjeg large round roots, 'bitter' before treatment; cooked, sliced, peeled, then soaked overnight in stream or billabong; very popular. (*Dioscorea sativa* L. var. *rotunda* F.M. Bail.)

gaman large round or oval root; rarely used – 'makes our guts very hot'. 'Echidna woman made it Dreaming because it's very nasty'; 'It is the mother of *jindjinaga*' (below).

jindjinaga small white root, near rocks or salt water; cooked as soon as brought in, left until next day, then cooked again; not cut up, because 'truly *manbang*', and hands should be washed after touching raw roots – 'like poison'; kept well away from children.

gubulurg some round, some long and thin 'like *mimi* [spirits]'; pounded vigorously after cooking.

gerbilg long root, very bitter; rarely eaten; 'bandicoot food'.

mandjingmi large round root; left cooking all night.

mangululudj cooked, then pounded (rarely, soaked in paperbark in water).

mandingu cycad-palm nut; cooked, crushed, shaped into long 'cake' for whole camp; soaked, cooked again; available all year: 'even a little bit swells the belly'. (*Cycas media* R. Br.)

mangugbu round 'nuts' from tree (like small tennis balls); after skin discarded, remainder soaked, crushed with smooth stone, and flattened into damper.

mangulabag tough-skinned root; pounded with stone after cooking.

manbuled water 'yam'; very fibrous.

ngeligen small thin freshwater roots spreading from central stem; cooked in coals, left until following day.

Tools and Equipment

Besides food, the natural environment supplies almost all the traditional requisites for living: tools, utensils, shelter, body covering and adornments, medicaments, and ritual needs.

Some resources can be drawn upon directly with a minimum of modification. The problem is merely where to find them, and which are the most suitable or the most accessible. Fresh green grass is a simple example. Spread thickly on the ground, it is a soft cushion for goose eggs unloaded from a canoe; one variety, when added to honey in a basket, makes the honey easier to carry and to store. For honey-eating, especially by young children, a popular dip-and-suck ladle is a piece of stringybark finely shredded at one end, or a small root or stem from a bamboo-like plant. Echidna quills are used in the same way for eating *mangindjeg* roots. Other kinds of bark, particularly 'cold' inner bark or fibre from a banyan tree, are wrapped around the head to relieve headaches. In some areas, smooth stones for grinding and pounding can be picked up as they are needed, and later abandoned. Kangaroo sinews are ideal for such tasks as mending spears, and kangaroo shoulder bones for knives.

Even in firewood there are preferences. For ordinary use a small tree called *manlargwi* (literally, 'hollow' or 'empty') with very light hard wood and a 'good smell' is liked because it burns easily even in wet weather. For ritual purposes, ironwood is one of the most important woods, especially for warding off ghosts and the Rainbow Snake; *mandudjmi* green 'plum' is another ritually useful wood. Ironwood also makes the best digging sticks, and strong spear-shafts. Paperbark sheets stripped from a tree and cut to the right size and thickness are sleeping mats and baby-carriers, and a few extra folds and twists produce a basket for water or honey or other foods. But again, one variety of paperbark is recognized as more durable, harder to tear. (Loglog Lizard ancestor planted such a tree in the Tor Rock area.) Palm leaves make simple containers or baskets.

Another example of a directly usable resource is a meat-carrying pole – a fresh green stick about three feet long, preferably from a

LAND

Oenpelli Mission Settlement, 1966

Part of the Croker Island Aboriginal settlement, 1966

Part of the Oenpelli Aboriginal settlement, close to Arguluk hill, 1958

Gunbalanya billabong (Oenpelli) and Inyalak hill, where galleries of paintings are located, 1968

Rock shelter on Inyalak hill, 1958

Inside a rock shelter on Inyalak, with repository and paintings, 1958

Edge of the western Arnhem Land escarpment, near Oenpelli, 1958

young stringybark tree, threaded through holes in a meat catch and carried over one shoulder, and finally discarded. A roomy cave with a floor of clean sand is a ready-made shelter, more comfortable and more effective in the wet season than a mosquito hut, and out of reach of normal floods. Red and yellow ochres, like charcoal, call for little extra labour, except as trade commodities.

Fibres and barks are basic ingredients in a variety of artefacts, none of them elaborate, but all exactly appropriate to the purpose their makers had in mind.

The western (for instance, 'Bargid') people used mats and pubic tassels of plaited grass, including *mangulaidj* grass. Apart from paper-bark, Gunwinggu rely more on string or twine, from a number of barks and roots and from animal fur. Women prepare it by rolling and twisting on the thigh, in characteristic Aboriginal fashion. What is done with the finished product depends on its strength and thickness, and these are already defined by reference to its source. Half a dozen named varieties of dilly-bag or long basket, made by a twining technique, are solely for domestic use, some of them designed for specific foods. (For example, long yams are carried separately from bitter roots, and both from 'water peanuts'.) Looseness or tightness of mesh, shape, size of opening and string quality distinguish one variety from another. Other dilly-bags are made for hanging in front of a pregnant woman, enclosing a navel cord, clenching between the teeth in fighting, or holding secret-sacred material; some are decorated with ochres and feathers. Twine and dried roots also make fish traps and nets. In one kind of trap, a large and very wide-meshed basket encloses a 'daughter' basket with two openings, the smaller at the bottom. The commonest fish net is staked out across a stream with three or four posts, and fish are driven into it by men beating the water. Fish poison may be put in or near it as well. (A number of mythical characters, including the two Waralag brothers [see later in this chapter], left relics of such nets, and one especially tough string comes from a grass that Waramurungundji grew by plucking out and planting some of her pubic hair.)

Rafts of light buoyant wood were used in shallow waterways, but canoes of paperbark or of stringybark were wore convenient for transporting people and goods. The canoes were paddled along with hands or flat sticks, or, like a raft, by one man standing, wielding a long pole. Because Gunwinggu were traditionally inland people, although some of them are now at home on the offshore islands as well, they had little use for the large dug-out sea-going canoes of the Maung and their saltwater neighbours.

Other ordinary non-sacred items are stringybark huts, human-hair belts, armbands, necklets of dried grass, goose-wing fans, headbands, mortuary platforms and paperbark effigies, and knife blades of animal bone or stone. Stone axes, and small throwing sticks to bring down geese, have not been a feature of everyday life in this region for a long time. Boomerangs are not common, except in the sphere of ceremony and ritual. Spears and spear-throwers are both hunting and fighting weapons: shovel spears, the shaft sometimes pointed; pronged fish spears; stone-bladed spears, normally obtained in trade from the Djinba but one Gunwinggu man 'always makes his own'; ironwood fighting spears, barbed on one side or on both, were traded across to the Goulburn Islands. Small sharp bamboo spears are mainly for children or for piercing the nasal septum. Sharp, highly polished fighting sticks came from the Yiwadja, and small fighting clubs from Bathurst and Melville islands.

Like other Aborigines, Gunwinggu make careful use of their natural resources and draw the utmost advantage from them in the way of fresh water, food and material furnishings. Their economic organization is nicely calculated to ensure the maximum of comfort and convenience within the limits of those resources and of their overall social framework. Their empirical knowledge is sound, and their application of it is not in the least casual or haphazard. The passing on of that knowledge is dependent entirely on oral transmission, a process that seems to have been highly successful. But the items comprising it are not self-contained or separate. They are presented as part of a larger complex in which the non-empirical is at least equally important.

The First People's Practical Guide to Natural Resources

In this non-literate society, accounts of the First People are not only a storehouse of comments on social and linguistic arrangements, and on the mystic link between man and his natural environment. More prosaically, but just as importantly, they include material of direct practical relevance to everyday life in that environment.

The stories centring on a cluster of sites or a strip of territory are like a loosely organized collection of guide books, where basic information is embedded in quasi-factual accounts of local history. Without giving a complete picture, they indicate what visitors can expect to find there: what kinds of terrain, vegetation and food, what difficulties or dangers, whether insects are troublesome, what surface waters will last through the dry season or whether water must be dug for, and so on. Geared to the demands of semi-nomadic living, the stories are a convenient medium for transmitting a series of 'hints to travellers'.

The material may have a direct bearing on the main theme or plot or none at all. It can be elaborated or cut short or even omitted altogether, depending on the speaker, the listeners and the situation. Most of it is non-controversial and taken for granted – statements on regional 'geography', nature lore, and the tools, techniques and resources of a hunting and gathering economy in this particular environment.

Many stories are verbal route maps, a record of places through or near which their characters moved. Some lists are extensive, and some accounts include a fair amount of detail, especially on areas that are in some way out of the ordinary.

One is the rough escarpment country, where travellers are likely to find their way blocked by rocks and steep gorges. A mythical character who got lost there was Nabiridauda, an old Honey *djang* man from the Dangbun side who was trying to reach the coast; he was laden with baskets, full of flowers to eat on the journey, bees, honey, and dry seeds for planting. Another old man, Nawulabeg, coming from Balbanara in the far east, met two Dangbun girls and decided to go back with them to Dangbun territory. They approached the escarpment from the north, and for a long time saw no bushland at all. Every way they turned, they were confronted by barriers of rock. Their search for an opening to the south always brought them back to the same spot, until at last they decided to go westward instead. Later the two girls separated from Nawulabeg after a quarrel and turned south again, and again got caught among rocks and great caves and were forced to turn back. Other stories tell of dogs or kangaroos trapped for ever among high rocks – except in a couple of cases where the dog had special powers, so that every time he barked a section of the rock-face tumbled down to clear

41

a path for him (or, in another story, a mass of trees parted and drew back as he ran, making a long bare plain). Episodes of this kind warn people to take care if they must cross the worst parts of the escarpment – unless they have been used to such country from childhood, as the Dangbun are supposed to have been.

Myth-reports link other places with crocodiles or snakes. In some overnight camps, characters sleep on tree-platforms because the mosquitoes are not so thick at that height, but these need not be special Mosquito sites. One Mosquito *djang* is a rocky point on Argulug hill overlooking Oenpelli. The hill itself appears in other stories, too, but this small part of it belongs to Mosquito. He arrived here as a man, from Woraidbag and Amurag country where the Rainbow Snake had swallowed all his relatives and he alone had escaped by hiding in mosquito shape. Looking westward from the top of Argulug he saw his own country, far away across the plain beyond the East Alligator River. To the north and north-east he saw Wuragag, Yiriu, Nimbuwa and Gunmaiinburg, already metamorphosed as rocky hills. 'What shall I do with myself, now she has eaten my mother and father? I'll turn into stone, too.' He made a great crowd of mosquito 'eggs' and then 'put himself *djang*'. 'Nobody goes near that point. Even people belonging to that country don't touch that rock – or she [the Rainbow] may kill us too!'

Techniques associated with the food complex are not tied so directly to particular localities, except where they are suggested by objects the First People left behind – like a pair of food-grinding stones that belonged to Garurgen Kangaroo woman or metamorphosed bark containers or fishing nets or axes. One fundamental technique is fire-making. In a Gunwinggu story, fire was an import from overseas.

One section of the Wuragag myth tells how he first brought fire to the Australian mainland. In this version the origin of his action was self-interest because he and his companions, living in 'Macassar', did not like raw meat. The narrative outlines the process, step by step: choosing two lengths of dry root from a bush, finding a mangrove shell to cut a hole in the horizontal ('large' or 'mother') stick, and twirling the upright root in the hole until sparks appeared. As they enjoyed a cooked meal they decided that the people of western Arnhem Land should share this new benefit, and they therefore set off at once for the Australian mainland, to the place where Wuragag himself was later to become Tor Rock. This version includes a short piece on visiting etiquette. Arriving at their destination, the strangers do not hurry brashly into the camp but sit quietly at a distance, children playing near by report their presence, and eventually several local men come out to identify them (first question, 'Where do you come from?') and then to make them welcome.

In most stories fire is simply a basic 'given'. But nearly all contain some reference to foods – to making or planting, catching or collecting, preparing, and, finally, eating them. So, too, people talking about their own experiences at various places frequently mention the foods they recall in connection with them: 'We were at such and such a place then, eating fish and red plums and lily roots . . . . ' 'They were at so and so, eating honey and long yams . . . . ' The story characters usually prefer to mix their foods – they do not like a monotonous diet of, say, only goose eggs, or only meats, or only vegetable foods. They eat small snacks of fruit or lily stalks or animal organs, and so on, in the course of a day, keeping some to take home. And they watch the sun to be certain of making or reaching camp before dusk. They camp at a site for a night ('sleep') or two – in the conventional phrase, 'three' – or for an indefinite period, moving on 'when their nights there were finished'.

When supplies are plentiful they linger, making the site their base or returning to it in the late afternoon for a month or so. They leave their main possessions there – baskets and bags hanging in trees, with things like ochres and 'knives' inside. They build a stringybark hut or find a comfortable cave, and old people and children stay at home waiting for what the others bring back. In one story, a small family group (two sisters, their joint husband, their parents, and the elder wife's child) stayed on in an area that was rich in food instead of joining in an *ubar* rite (see Chapter 6) some distance away. After a time, the husband went to tell the *ubar* participants, 'I left the others back there. We can't come yet, there's so much meat and honey and *manme*. When we've exhausted it, we'll come. So stretch out the *ubar* rites, make them last longer . . . . '

Much of the background in *djang* and other stories is the one familiar to the narrators themselves, from personal experience or the reports of others – for example, the use of ordinary cooking procedures. If a couple of men travelling together spear a kangaroo,

43

they wait until they find a suitable place and then collect termite mound and firewood and prepare an oven. They singe off the animal's hair and remove its entrails through a cut in the throat, and put aside the 'small things' (heart, liver, kidneys) and fat from it to cook on the coals and eat while they wait for the rest of it or before taking the rest home. When an animal is cooked, people leave it to cool a little in case their fingers get burnt, and only after that do they cut it up and share it around (for instance: 'cut down the back, cut off the legs, and distribute it'). For their early morning meal, after 'spitting time', they eat 'old' food left from the day before. If they are tired, they 'hunt for two days and rest in camp for two days', or lay in a supply to last for a little longer. They are fairly careful with material objects as long as these are useful, but easily abandon them afterward. One character, Aidjilad, made a bark canoe when she came to a tidal creek at Mulwar (see later), loaded her belongings into it, sat down inside, and paddled upstream to fresh water. There she took out her things, turned the canoe upside down out of reach of the tide, tied it securely with string and cooked the sea-foods she had brought with her before continuing upstream on foot. (The canoe is still there, changed into a kind of 'soft stone'.)

Mythical behaviour reflects the assumption that people travelling in company should share their food and should not eat alone.

Greediness is deplorable and wrong, but it can also be funny. When they were men, Frilled Lizard turned on Long-necked Tortoise because he gobbled up all the fat from everything they caught. Alternatively, Long-necked Tortoise and Echidna were women, and this time it was Echidna's babies that Tortoise gobbled up one by one instead of minding them when it was her turn to stay in camp. The humour in both of these stories lies in the way they are told, and especially in the graphic descriptions of the surreptitious gulping-down of the fat or the babies, the angry accusations, and the final dramatic fight.

In a more serious story, one man in a group travelling south near Nimbuwa killed a small rock wallaby and ate it secretly by himself, but its sizzling attracted the Rainbow, who swallowed him and his companions as well. (As the water covered them, they cried out, 'What is eating us? This is tabu ground. What is the name? Mandju-ngorbi is the name. Let nobody come near here; this ground remains soft for ever!' Mandju-ngorbi is the site of other *djang*, too, including

44

two Gunwinggu boys who cooked a possum beside the deep billa-bong among the rocks and were eaten by the Rainbow. Their story concludes: 'Nobody, male or female, is to go near there or they may drown. If rock wallabies go there, they drown. And there are no fish in that deep water . . . . ')

Aidjilad was killed by a huge wild Dog, Mulwar by name, that died shortly after eating her because its belly was distended with fat and 'fat oozed from its nostrils'. The Dog's fate reflects a warning that, aside from any question of sharing, it is unhealthy to over-eat or to over-indulge in delicacies like fat. Two Yiwadja brothers who caught and cooked a large fish found it had 'too much fat, it made their hearts bad', and so they threw most of the fat away uneaten. Another warning concerns the practice of putting a religious tabu on food. By implication, abuse of this is like stealing. Lumaluma the Whale (see Chapter 6) was responsible for bringing many important rituals, but one reason for his death was that everywhere he went he commandeered all the best food by placing a religious tabu on it; after that, ordinary people could not eat it: 'They were afraid it would make them and their children sick.' (When they heard his *maraiin* clapping sticks they would call to one another, 'Quick, hide the food!') Also, people who collaborate in any enter-prise should divide the proceeds. Djuddjud 'Fish Eagle' man was in a group netting fish in a saltwater creek at Croker Island, but the others would not give him any of the catch: – 'He was just beating the water for them, for nothing.' Hurrying to the mainland he asked the Rainbow, his *wulubulu* (mother's mother's mother), to kill them, and after that he changed from a man to a bird.

Some stories indicate inedible creatures and plants only by implication, but others provide explicit comment. In a north-western Gunwinggu version of the Loglog Lizard story that gives him a Yiwadja origin, he dug white clay and painted himself, trying to take on his lizard shape, and as he did so he declared, 'Men don't eat me, and I eat only flies.' Every variety of native food encountered in local experience is found in myth. Changes resulting from outside contact have done away with many traditional techniques that are perpetuated in myth as routine behaviour. Other techniques, and tools, have continuing relevance. But even more relevant is the record of 'what foods are most likely to be found where'. Part of the record tells 'who put them there', or found them there, in a narrative sequence that brings the information together in a coherent frame.

Some individual stories suggest that certain foods belong to a specific character or group of characters, but the wider picture does not bear that out.

Old Nawulabeg, already mentioned for his unsuccessful attempt to reach Dangbun country, began his story as a *mangulaidj* (grass-root) 'nut' man. He brought with him several baskets full, for eating on the way after his main course of meat and for planting in any patch of water where he thought they might take root and grow. He gave names to many places as he did so. Another old man from the east, Djinba-speaking, with white hair hanging to his waist, had special charge of *mangoidbang* ('water peanuts'). He carried four long baskets, slung at front and back over each shoulder. After passing Nimbuwa, already stone, he planted white 'apples' and left deposits of white clay and his stone axe, but these were only sidelines. In a different myth, the central character is an old man living in the sky, responsible for the practice of pounding and crushing *mangoidbang* and shaping them into flat cakes. A third *mangoidbang* story also concerns an old man – one who actually turned into a *mangoidbang* root. He stood, shoulder deep, in a billabong until little fibrous hairs sprouted all over him and he no longer bore any resemblance to a human being.

Another case in point is the 'bitter' *mangindjeg* root. On one hand it is associated with two separate women, and on the other it is traced to a single act of punishment or rage.

One of the women, Ngalmoban, came from Balawuru creek, high in the rocky country south-west of Oenpelli – where Gunwing-gu, Maiali side, meet Gundjeibmi and some Djauan. She carried a long basket of banyan fibre. As she went along, she would slice *mangindjeg* roots with a large mussel shell she always carried, leave them in water overnight, and eat them next morning; and some she threw out from her bag at various places to which she gave names. She 'put herself Dreaming' as a red-ochre painting on a rock at Mori, two or three days' walk south of Oenpelli, near a large creek that comes down to the Landing on the East Alligator River. In the painting, she leans forward holding the shell as a warning: 'She first showed people that children are not to eat *mangindjeg* and new-season's long yams – if they do, that shell will cut their backs.'

In contrast, the second woman's association with *mangindjeg* was inherent in her from the very beginning, but it does not appear at the climax of the story from which she takes her name – Cicada woman, Ngalgindjeg-ngalgindjeg. She first 'made herself' beneath the earth as a true *mangindjeg djang*, in Gunwinggu country at Nabainnyungur near Nimbuwa, in Madjawar local group territory, but after she emerged above ground she took the shape of an old woman. *Mangindjeg* roots were her only food, and the story tells how she prepared them: slicing them with the sharp shoulder blade of a kangaroo, cooking them in hot ashes, peeling them and then soaking some in a paperbark basket in a nest of fresh grass in a small sluggish creek and some in a long basket hidden in a large billabong. The action is shaped around her struggle to prevent a hostile *maam* spirit, first from eating each new batch of prepared *mangindjeg* and then from killing her, and it culminates in her last-minute escape into the sky as a cicada. Her baskets and digging stick are rocks now, at Girilibal, to which she first gave the name.

Two other stories account for the poisonous nature of *mangindjeg* before treatment. In one, allocated to Woraidbag country, Garurgen Kangaroo woman was slicing these roots one day when her husband, Gulubar, ordered her to delouse his hair immediately or he would urinate on them: and when she refused, he did so. This made them too bitter to eat even after washing: 'Oh, what am I to do?' she cried. 'Go and soak them in water,' he told her. 'By tomorrow they will be sweet and we'll eat them.' In the second version, two girls were cooking long yams in a cave when their brother asked for some. He urinated on the yams after the elder girl refused to let the younger bring him any – ' . . . because you're her full brother, and it's not good for you to eat her!' (This story was told immediately after another from the same person that dealt explicitly with brother-sister incest.)

Over and above the distinction between sour and sweet, several stories claim that there is a contrast in taste between coastal and inland foods. Three from Mangurug, a north-western Gunwinggu with Yiwadja ties (see Fig. 14, Chapter 5), directly reflect her own personal preference. In one, two girls from far in the west approach the mouth of a tidal river in 'Mangerdji and Gunwinggu' territory and see saltwater creatures and fish for the first time. They express surprise at the sight of a crab ('This thing with hands, whatever *is* it?'), tease it with a digging stick, and then drag it from its hole, seize its 'hands' and twist them off: 'Shall we try to eat it, sister?' They make a fire, cook it, and taste it: 'It's good! Let's stay by the sea and eat these nice sea-foods!' In Mangurug's second story, two young sisters come from North Goulburn Island to the mainland, to Gunwinggu country, where the elder girl cautiously tastes some bush food. 'She was used to saltwater creatures, but she tried and it was all right – she didn't vomit.' In the third story, Vulva woman from the east ate only coastal things until she reached Gunbalang and Maung country. Then she killed a bush creature and 'tried to taste it, but it wasn't salty and so she threw it away, onto the fire'. (It sizzled as it burnt, attracting the Rainbow, who swallowed her – but not before she had named the site to commemorate herself.) Another story, this time from an inland Gunwinggu perspective, from Wurgamara, tells how Aidjilad (already mentioned) also came westward following the coast, camping wherever she saw plenty of crabs and naming various places as she came. She would not eat bush foods at first because 'she was afraid of them', but after turning inland she tried some and found that they 'tasted good' – 'It would be wrong for me *not* to eat these nice foods.'

The contrast between coast and inland is not confined to food. Mangurug also gave a version of the two Waralag brothers' story. They came south-eastward from Yiwadja country on the coast, and once they were inland in 'Wuningag and Gunwinggu' country they would not camp in any place where they heard creatures talking (animals, birds, insects – anything). In their case, it was not that the noise kept them awake, but they were afraid of being attacked 'because they came from the coast'. Until they were adjusted to the inland environment, therefore, they travelled all night without sleep, 'hurting their feet on the rocks in the darkness'. (A side warning: 'It's not good to travel in rocky country at night.')

This glimpse of the First People's practical guide gives some idea of its coverage, from the predominantly local to more widely relevant advice on living off the land. But the land provides more than material subsistence – it includes the dimension of the spiritual or non-empirical. The guide caters for this, too.

48

At one level the *djang* stories, *in toto*, reflect quite faithfully the round of domestic life and its territorial setting, but to document this would involve much fuller treatment of all the available accounts and the people responsible for them. At another level the stories are explanatory statements reporting how things came to be as they are now, and these lead directly to 'ought' statements, including flat prohibitions that leave no room for questioning. Food tabus belong in this category. Some concern particular life-stages or life crises: for example, certain foods are tabu to menstruating women, and, traditionally, before the birth of their first child women should not eat goannas. Others are associated with religious rites (see Chapter 6). Others again are tied to specific localities; decreeing, for example, that only local land-holders should eat fish there, or that only they or only old people should eat new fish following the rainy season, or that only men should eat new fish and new goose eggs while women must wait until burning-grass time.

A different version of the Djurlga girls' story (see Chapter 2) from a Gurudjmug perspective ends with this statement: 'One thing they don't like is *mangindjeg* roots being soaked in the water there. Rain might come for us if we do that, because the string might come off the bundle or it might sink down to where they are, and they don't like that. They would get Ngaljod to eat us. And children are not to go there to spear fish. Only old men with white hair can spear fish when the grass is dry, just before burning-off time. But first they must call out to those girls, asking them "Would you please listen to us and give us fish? Send fish for us?" Old men and women eat that fish, but not children. And so they take the fish a long way to cook it, hiding it from children – or those children might see it and cry for it, and then their mothers and fathers would feel sorry and give them some, and then a great flood would come and drown them all. It is tabu, at first [at that time]. Dogs, too, are not to be given the bones of that fish: and so those people break up the bones, and burn the skin too. Later on, when all the grass has been burnt, they can give fish [from that place] to children and mothers and young men ... they give it to us all. Even then, they don't cook fish near the water. And they are not to spear fish in the middle pool – only in the bottom pool, close to where they make their camp, not in the top pool by the waterfall. They are not to eat fish there, it is tabu for ever. And it is not until the new rains come that those two girls allow women and children to approach that place where they "made themselves" first. . . . '

Some myth-based prohibitions have obvious practical merit. Bitter foods, for instance, are not only dangerous before treatment – they are also unpalatable; and this might not seem to need any mythical underlining, at least for adults. But even in the ordinary way, aside from the special rules governing ritual occasions, myth draws attention to circumstances where special caution is needed. A mythical prohibition on going near a certain stretch of river may be followed by the comment, 'The water is always rough just there,' or 'It is dangerous, with many crocodiles.' Deep pools with steep sides are risky places to visit, and after heavy rains the low-lying coastal plains and narrow gorges are subject to rapid flooding. Here is a plausible basis for warnings about the Rainbow. In many stories in which the sizzling of a small animal brings the Rainbow the reason is that it is being cooked on sand or on a flat rock near the water's edge. (This sequence was mentioned so often that on a couple of occasions one of us attempted a joke when people were talking about successful catches: 'Hope you didn't cook them in a sandy place!' But in each case the response was serious: 'No, we took them to high ground and cooked them there.')

In discussing what is characteristic or significant about a particular site, one major issue is whether it is open or closed and, if so, to what categories of people. Comments of this kind are very numerous indeed, both in myth and in ordinary conversations. As a repository of practical information, the stories are kept up-to-date through contemporary experience. They are a source of guidance and precept, but much of their content is subject to testing and checking – and so, indirectly, this part of it supports and validates the more portentous events and decrees that are not traditionally open to query.

The Gunwinggu picture of their environment is cross-cut by a number of contrasts: between fresh and salt water, inland and coast, bush foods and sea foods, low ground and high ground, fertile soil and bare rocks. Sometimes, overall, the contrast is presented as a threefold one: two potentially uncomfortable or dangerous extremes – swamps, plains, gulleys and watercourses subject to flooding; and dry, barren heaps of rock – and a middle zone of habitable land or 'bush', *manberg*, reasonably safe and dry but not arid. (*Manberg* is, also, the 'mainland' as distinct from the coastal islands.) In fact, this is just what the region looks like from the air during the wet season. The dryish scrub with its duller foliage is easily singled out from the bright-green patches of grass and jungle and lily leaves and wide expanses of water in low-lying areas, and from the jagged grey and red sandstone escarpment with its patchy or sparse vegetation. Where rainfall and surface waters are concerned, Gunwinggu face the possibility of having too much at some times and some places, too little at others. Without rain, the main root foods and fruits cannot develop properly. With too much, people are overwhelmed and cannot take advantage of the resources in the richer but more easily flooded lowlands. Their myths and rites reflect their interest in maintaining a reasonable balance, also, between these two undesirable opposites.

On a much smaller scale are the contrasts between raw and cooked, edible and inedible, harmless and dangerous (*manbang* or *nabang*). Danger in a different sense attaches to the concept of *djamun*, 'set apart' or 'tabu', as against ordinary or mundane or secular. (In the contact situation, *djamun* is the Gunwinggu word for 'policeman'.) The concept of *djamun* is especially significant in the sphere of religion. So are two further contrasts that receive a lot of attention – between young and old, and between male and female. Another contrast is between human and non-human, but for practical purposes this presents few problems. The definition of people, *binin*, was traditionally restricted to members of those groups that intermarried and shared in the same complex of myth, ritual and trade. They did not necessarily speak the same language or have the same kind of social organization: but, generally speaking, the greater the degree of common understanding, the more clearly they were recognized as being human. The notion of humanity was (is) spatially quite limited, and groups that are known only by name and nothing else usually do not qualify. Within the local region, there is no confusion between human beings and *djang*, nor between human beings and ghosts, although ghosts were originally human and still are, in a way, whereas spirits like *mimi* and Nagidgid never were.

51

We have been looking at people in relation to their natural environment, which in one sense is also their supernatural environment. One point that stands out quite sharply is their virtual self-sufficiency, the fact that their traditional needs and wants can be met almost entirely from their own resources and through their own labour. The commodities that change hands in intertribal trade are mainly extra refinements, not basic necessities. Such exchanges are important, first, in widening and sustaining social relationships and, second, in diversifying material goods, enhancing local standards of living but not underpinning them. Everything else can be obtained and replenished locally, with relatively little effort or cost. But remember that we are not concerned here with individual persons acting alone. Groups of people are innolved, complicating as well as simplifying the use and handling of vatural resources.

It is not only in collecting or harvesting their food and other resources that people form different combinations based on such divisions as age, sex, and 'household' membership. The actual consumption of food also emphasizes cleavages and contrasts as well as commonalty and likeness. Differences in social and ritual status are symbolized in various food tabus on the basis of age, sex, territorial affiliations or ritual considerations. Social separateness is underlined by separateness in eating – as regards either the time and place of eating or the foods allowed. People so separated out may (a) share in the same meat catch or the same catch of food as others do, but eat this in a different place or at a different time; or (b) be restricted to different kinds of food or food collected separately, eaten either separately or in company. (See Chapter 6.) In this as in other respects the social dimension is not additional to the economic dimension. The two are so closely connected that a thorough examination of the one must automatically involve an examination of the other.

Chapter Four

The Patterning of Social Relations (1)

BASIC UNITS AND DESCENT

THE BASIC STRUCTURE of Gunwinggu society can be looked at from two points of view. One emphasizes social units – the ways in which persons are grouped or classified together, primarily on the basis of birth and descent, either patrilineal or matrilineal. The other emphasizes person-to-person relationships: these are most highly conventionalized or systematized in the sphere of kinship – which recognizes both matrilineal and patrilineal descent.

In this chapter we concentrate on the main structural units in this society, the framework the Gunwinggu use in identifying one another and their immediate neighbours in western Arnhem Land. Because the last chapter dealt with people in relation to land, we begin with the same topic, this time from the angle of social relationships. The Gunwinggu conform with 'typical Aboriginal' practice here: for them, territorial rights are predominantly patrilineal. But in other types of social unit they stress matrilineal descent.

All normal Gunwinggu adults are quite articulate on all the points outlined in this chapter. The difference is that they learn them first through concrete examples, through actual people, and it is only later on that they see them in terms of a generalized system. For anyone living in the situation, that is the ideal way to go about it, but it is also a lengthy process. Here it is simpler to take the framework first, before looking at it in relation to people.

The bond between a person and his own country is also a bond between father and child. Wherever he was born, a person's 'own territory' is, almost by definition, the same as his father's. The whole region is divided among people whose claims to it rest on patrilineal descent. Other associations are recognized, too: for instance, with a person's mother's country (which is also her father's) and with *her* mother's country. These have a bearing on kinship and, indirectly, on marriage. But real belonging and full rights in a country come directly from the father – ideally, from the actual physical father, the genitor.

As part of the myth-ritual complex, the main emphasis is on specific localized sites within the larger territory: for example, Gabari in Gurudjmug. (See Fig. 2.) The more inclusive name is the 'large name' of the country, *gubolg-ngebaidjan*; the site name is the 'small name', *gubolg-ngejau*. *Baidjan* means 'big', or 'great', but not in the ordinary sense of physical size. In the context of kinship, for example, it is the stem of the ordinary reference term for mother and mother's brother; and *jau* (yau) is the paired contrast in this relationship. Perhaps for that reason, and because women tend to stress matrilineal descent more than men do, women who spoke some English translated the two expressions above as 'mother country' and 'daughter country' (although *jau* can also mean 'son').

In fact, the territorial tie is the main structural indicator of patriliny. Each territory is associated with a named unit of patrilineal descent, the *gunmugugur*. (The Maung word is *namanamaidj*: – see Elkin, Berndt and Berndt, 1951: 294-8.) In turn, each of these is linked with another name that is much less widely known. This is the *igurumu* or *ngwoia* (eastern Gunwinggu), a stylized exclamation that is used also in ritual invocations and is therefore sometimes said to be bigger, more important, than the *gunmugugur* name. Most *gunmugugur* and *igurumu* are conventionally described as belonging exclusively to one language or another. Actually, in a large number of cases they do not. One reason is the changing pattern of linguistic identification already mentioned. Another is that some *gunmugugur* are split into two or more groupings connected with quite separate areas. There is no indication of how this came about.

Ideally, all personal names except nicknames come through the *gunmugugur* as personal gifts from immediate paternal relatives in the parents' or grandparents' generations, either their own names or others remembered from a generation or so back, and they belong to the local territory. In practice, more people seem to be evading the rule. This means that names are becoming less useful as clues to *gunmugugur*, and territorial, identification.

When a *gunmugugur* name (for example Madjawar) is referred to by itself, it sometimes takes the *gun-* prefix, but it need not (for example, *gunmadjawar*). In reference to a person, it usually takes the male or female prefix (for example, *namadjawar, ngalmadjawar*). The principal Gunwinggu names of the various *gunmugugur* and a number of others are listed in Appendix 1.

Most people know a wide range of *gunmugugur* names, outside as well as within their own interactory spheres. Pronunciation of some of them varies, and some are possibly duplicated in different areas. They are not translatable. On the eastern side, toward and around the Liverpool River, they are divided between the two patrilineal moieties, *dua* and *jiridja* (yiridja) (see Fig. 4), and the practice is spreading farther west. Some *gunmugugur* are 'bigger' than others and can subsume smaller names in the same large territory. For instance, Djelama is a 'big' *gunmugugur* and Nguluminj is a minor one. *Gunmugugur* that overlap in reference to certain sites (such as Barbin and Maiirgulidj at Djurlga) are 'company', in the sense that they have one stretch of country in common although for other purposes they are separate. The word usually translated as 'company', *-gaidjuren*, means 'follow each other', or 'mix together', and is applied in other circumstances too. It need not imply a formal association.

Gunmugugur names run into hundreds, with some clearly identifiable as Yiwadja, others as Maung, others as Nagara-Gunavidji, and so on. This raises the question of size and scale, especially in relation to the rough estimate of 'Gunwinggu' population in Chapter 1. In fact, most of them are very small. Nguluminj and Yi(gi)lugidj are almost extinct, and many others have less than half a dozen living members. Quite possibly, numerical size is a major criterion of largeness or importance. Patrilineal descent is the conventional basis of *gunmugugur* membership, but *social* paternity can affect it. For example, a child may adopt the *gunmugugur* affiliation of a step-

(to page 57)

55

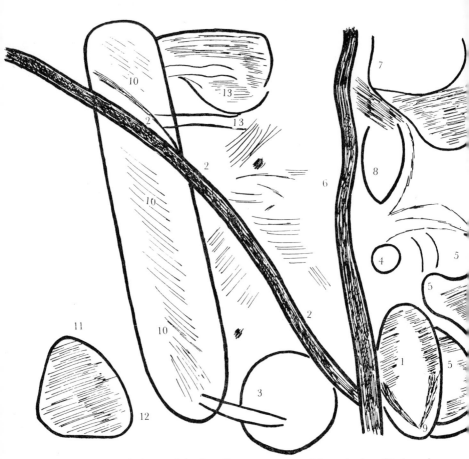

Fig. 2. Aboriginal map of the Gurudjmug area: some of the main sites. (Redrawn)

Notes:

1. Gabari waterhole, near head of Cooper's Creek.
2. Gabari creek.
3. Gunyiguyimi waterhole.
4. A *njalaidj* ceremony was held, close to 1; here, at 4, people were dancing.
5. People who came from the north for a *njalaidj* ceremony at Gabari now stand here as rocks. (See Chapter 2.) In the version associated with this Figure, a little orphan boy cried day and night for food: his elder brother came back, heard the child crying and was angry: he struck a tabu rock, and the Rainbow came with a great flood and drowned them all.
6. Namalaid, Orphan, was here.
7. The Orphan's elder brother went up to here and turned into rock.
8. Fishing net and pandanus strips used by the saltwater (coastal) men who came for the *njalaidj* dancing.
9. The elder brother's dog, Djanbugan, that he used for hunting goanna.
10. Nabamuli billabong.
11. Gurudjmug Hill. *Galawan* Goanna *djang* is at the top of this hill (12).
13. Paperbark trees, now *djang*, left by the drowned people. (Among those drowned here were people who brought the *wurbu* dancing from the salt water – from Port Essington.)

All this area is Djelama *gunmugugur* and Magaliraga *igurumu*. The country or people associated with it are known in general as bani? Gabari or bani? Gurudjmug. (An alternative way of referring to people who come from or belong to a certain country is to use the stem *-gang*, which usually means 'carried' or 'took'; for instance, . . . *birigang* Gurudjmug, 'they were Gurudjmug people'.)

father who rears him, especially if he was very young when his own father died, or he may later claim dual affiliation from 'both his fathers'.

The cases mentioned in Chapter 5 (Figs 13 and 14) and Chapter 7 (for example, Fig. 20) include *gunmugugur* labels for the main participants. In addition, the Aboriginal maps (Figs 2, 3 and 4) illustrate territorial divisions from a different perspective. They were prepared by three men to show something of their own and adjacent territories: the first man is Djelama, the second Maiirgulidj, and the third Born. They are simplified versions that do not include all the major sites or alternative names or meanings, and they have been redrawn for reproduction.

Gunmugugur names can apply to regions as well as to social units (for example, *gubolg-danig*, Danig country; *gubolg-djelama*, Djelama country).

This brings us to the first Gunwinggu marriage rule: *gunmugugur* are, ideally, exogamous – people of the same *gunmugugur* should not marry. However, Gunwinggu recognize that some of their neighbours do not share this rule. Also, they acknowledge that a few *gunmugugur* with the same name are actually separate units, attached to different territories. For them, the important thing is that a child should not have the same *gunmugugur* as both its parents – that there should be a balance or contrast between patriline and matriline.

Because the main local sites have ritual significance, relations between a man and his father's patriline are important in the sphere of religion. Traditionally, Gunwinggu had no separate names for formalized ritual groupings based on this kind of linkage but extending beyond the *gunmugugur*, but they have adopted from eastern Arnhem Land the twofold (moiety) patrilineal division into *dua* and *jiridja* (yiɹidja). Until a few years ago, these patrilineal moiety names had very little bearing on everyday life. They were used mainly in ritual activities, but, probably because of the connection between patrilineal descent, religious ritual and territory, they were also applied to stretches of country, especially on the eastern side (for instance, *gubolg-dua, dua* country). This picture

(to page 60)

57

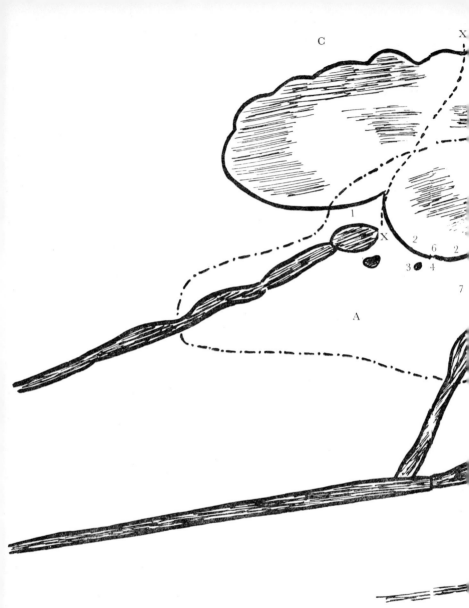

Fig. 3. Aboriginal map of Gumadir: some of the main

Notes:
x - - - x Aboriginal tracks.
1. Gubudji waterhole. An old Fish-poism *djang* man lieved here.
2. Edge or fringe of hill.
3. Marelyi.
4. Djalargaiuwa – Centipede place.
5. Guguraidja caves.
6. Also Centipede *djang*.
7. Manyalg-gabodju?mi – Bee and Honey name.
8. Nabulg-gabandaid.
9. Djurlga.

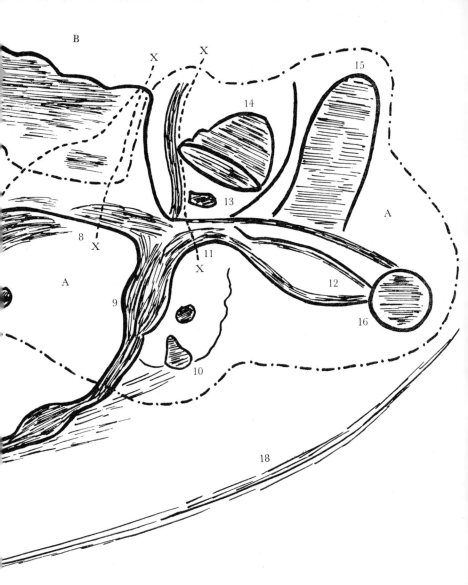

10. Nabalagaid, a *jarijaning* (yariyaning; see later in this chapter) *djang* man, now rock. (In a different version he was an orphan, a younger brother, and Djelama *gunmugugur*; his elder brother's name was Nagundjagu.)
11. Mibanar, river and short track.
12. Gundinug hole – water running down.
13. Gwingura hill.
14. Big hill, with metamorphosed *ubar* at top (Wurubig).
15. Long hill, Demid. A group of mythical people drowned here; hill 14 sank down and they went to 15, but were drowned.
16. Galardjang. According to Manggudja (see Fig. 14, Chapter 5), who drew this, his paternal grandparents and patrilineal ancestors lived here; during the wet season they made bark houses.
17. Deleted from map.
18. Gumadir River.

Two girls from the east, both *jarigarngurg* (yarigarngurg; see later in this chapter), came to 11, looking for water. (See Chapter 2 for another version.)

They heard a noise and went on to 6, then went farther on to 7, where they found honey, and heard bees at 8. Going on to 9, they dug a well: water came up. They sat in it, washing themselves and drinking, until the water rose and drowned them.

All this country, from 1 to 16, is Maiirgulidj *gunmugugur*, Nagurulg *igurumu*. This area is marked A on the map, and its boundary is indicated by a dot-and-dash line. In the area indicated as B is Barbin *gunmugugur*, Nabambidmag *igurumu*. In the area indicated as C is Ngalngbali *gunmugugur*, Namalinggunja *igurumu*. The country and people in general are known as bani?Gumadir for A, B, and C, who, even with different *gunmugugur*, are regarded as 'one family'. However, B and C can be called bani?Gudjegbin.

is changing, although rather slowly, and today the names are becoming more generally accepted farther west.

Aside from the *gunmugugur*, other social units focus on matrilineal descent. In this, the Gunwinggu resemble their northern neighbours the Maung and differ from the north-eastern Arnhem Landers who have influenced them in a number of other respects – mainly indirectly, through the medium of Gunwinggu groups around Margulidjban.

Matrilineal Descent

Every Gunwinggu, full or otherwise, belongs to three kinds of unit based on matrilineal descent. All of them cover the total population, but they slice it at different levels of inclusiveness – the first into two, the second into four, and the third into eight. These are moieties, semi-moieties, and subsections.

Moieties

The basis of the system is a simple division into two named halves, or moieties, *madgu* and *ngaraidgu*. (Maung use the same basic names.) Every Gunwinggu person is born into either one or the other. That is determined in advance, because it must be the same as his mother's – which is the same as *her* mother's, and so on, back through the line of matrilineal descent. These names are inflected: they vary according to sex and number, sometimes according to person. (For example, *ngamadgu*, 'I [am] *madgu*'.) In general they are often in masculine singular form, *namadgu* and *nangaraidgu*. (For a female, the prefix *ngal-* replaces *na-*. And the plural is most often shown by duplication: *madgu?madgu*, or *ngarangaraidgu*, people of the *madgu*, or of the *ngaraidgu*, moiety.)

The two labels are used in a number of ways. One is in marriage arrangements, for instance. The second Gunwinggu marriage rule is that the matrilineal moieties are exogamous: a husband and wife should not belong to the same moiety. This ideal has not been seriously challenged. In actuality, there have been a few instances of intra-moiety marriage in recent years. They are conventionally regarded as wrong, but in practice they are tolerated or excused, usually on the grounds that some outside influence is responsible. For example, 'This is a Yiwadja custom,' or 'The missionaries have interfered with our rules.'

Personal names are usually avoided in conversation, and names of the dead are tabu for a year or so, if not longer. Various substitutes are available. One is nicknames or joking names, but the tendency is to avoid these, too. Otherwise, moiety names are a 'first line' of identification in singling out individuals from a larger group, but, because the moiety division embraces everyone, this is useful only so far. In reference, it is sometimes used in describing the actions of people who are already identified, without bringing in personal names. (For example, in talking about a camp fight, 'That *namadgu* hit *nangaraidgu* on the head, then that other *nangaraidgu* came running and hit *namadgu*.' This kind of account can become rather involved, even with only three or four persons under discussion. It relies partly on audience participation to straighten out ambiguities. For instance, 'Which *namadgu* did that, elder brother or younger?') In address, if someone calls out one of the moiety labels near a group of people, this alerts all of them who belong to that particular moiety so that they listen for the next, more specific call.

Semi-moieties

The narrowing-down process brings in a second set of categories. Each moiety includes two named subdivisions that are also directly matrilineal in descent: a person belongs to exactly the same subdivision as his mother, mother's mother, and so on. For reasons we need not go into here, in first writing about this area we called these phratries; but since only four are 'truly Gunwinggu', the term semi-moiety is more appropriate. The third Gunwinggu marriage rule is that these semi-moieties are exogamous: husband and wife must have different semi-moiety labels. In conjunction with the second rule, this means that a person marries someone of another

(to page 64)

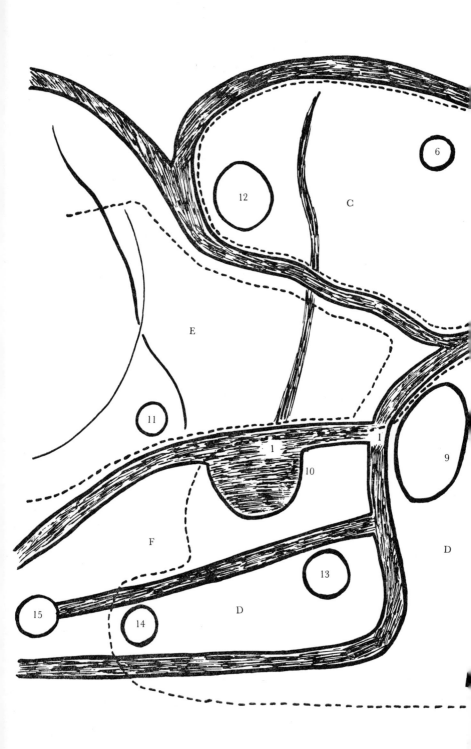

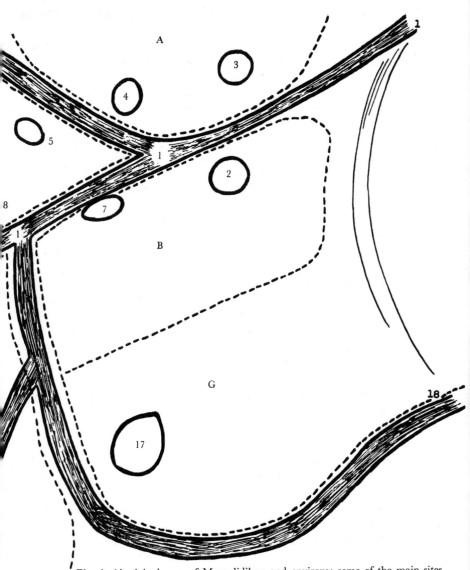

Fig. 4. Aboriginal map of Margulidjban and environs: some of the main sites. (Redrawn)

Notes:

1. Liverpool River, Margulidjban.
2. Manawugan (and Manidjanggarira, now called Maningrida).
3. Nirgala waterhole.

4. Nabiwo-gadjangdi waterhole – Wild Bee *djang*.
5. Gabulrudmi waterhole.
6. Monggari waterhole.
7. Gulbalyara – Emu *djang*.
8. Guridja waterhole.
9. Bulgul – Namargun, Thunder and Lightning *djang*.
10. Gunraʔgani waterhole.
11. Mandaidgaidjan waterhole – Long-necked Tortoise *djang*; also Echidna and Carpet Snake.
12. Mumenger waterhole.
13. Gagodbeboldi waterhole – Paperbark Tree name. Aidjilad (see Chapter 3) was killed here by a giant Dog.
14. Mugamuga waterhole.
15. Yirolg – Worm or Maggot *djang*.
16. Magarabulu waterhole.
17. Mamaidba waterhole.

Note that the *dua* and *jiridja* patrilineal moieties fall symmetrically on each side of the main course of the Liverpool River (marked by 1). Broken lines indicate *gunmugugur* boundaries.

Dua moiety:
Territory A, sites 3 and 4: Malbari or Madbadji *gunmugugur*, Mararumbu *igurumu*.
Territory C, sites 5, 6, 8 and 12: Born *gunmugugur*, Nagolgborn *igurumu*; country of Dubungu (see Chapter 7, first betrothal case), who drew this.
Territory E, site 11: Wurig *gunmugugur*, Guwadu *igurumu*.

Jiridja moiety:
Territory B, sites 2 and 7: Maningererbi *gunmugugur*, Mangigi *igurumu*.
Territory D, sites 9, 10, 13, 14 and 16: Marin *gunmugugur*, Gumbaldja *igurumu*.
Territory F, site 15: Barbin *gunmugugur*, Nabambidmag *igurumu*.
Territory G, site 17: Bobereri *gunmugugur*, Mararidj *igurumu*; including all country to 18.

---

semi-moiety in the opposite moiety. And if moiety exogamy is important to Gunwinggu, semi-moiety exogamy is far more so: it is a 'last-ditch' rule. However, there is no extra rule specifying which semi-moieties are preferred as intermarrying pairs.

These units are not aligned with specific territories in the way that the *gunmugugur* are. Some women do identify various sites by semi-moiety names, but this may be a secondary association following from the fact that the mythical characters associated with them also bear semi-moiety labels.

The conventional semi-moiety names are fixed forms, not inflected for person or number. In informal discussion and conversations, the ordinary words for the principal symbols that go with them are often used instead: they are shown here. The labels are arranged under moiety headings. (Note: 'j' in these names is pronounced as 'y'.)

TABLE 1

SEMI-MOIETIES AND
PRINCIPAL ASSOCIATED SYMBOLS

Moiety	Semi-moiety	Symbol
ngaraidgu	*a.* jarijaning	*gundung* (sun)
	b. jariburig	*gunag* (fire)
madgu	*c.* jariwurga	*gugu* (fresh water), or *manbelg* (pandanus palm)
	d. jarigarngurg	*gunwade* (stone or rock)

These are the 'true Gunwinggu' names. Others are used, too. For instance, under *ngaraidgu* come *geralg, nabiwo* or *nawulgain* (wild bee), and *donggol* (fire-stick); under *madgu* come *jaribulgidj* (or *jigarabulgidj*, equivalent to *jariwurga*, water) and *djoned* (march fly). But these are clues to *non*-Gunwinggu or only partly Gunwinggu affiliation. *Geralg* and *nabiwo* are classed as Djauan, *nawulgain, donggol* and *jaribulgidj* as Djauan or Dangbun, and *djoned* as Kakadu or Amurag.

It is not only the human world that is divided up into these compartments. They apply to the natural world as well, or at least to the greater part of it:

jarijaning, sun: saltwater crocodile (sometimes wrongly called alligator) and freshwater (long-nosed) crocodile; barramundi fish; two varieties of turtle; spotted cat; leech; echidna (in one version); three varieties of goanna, including *galawan*; one variety of wallaby; a round but otherwise scorpion-like creature; several kinds of bird, coastal as well as inland, including pelican; falling star; *mangoidbang* 'water peanut'; *djedbar* and *deidjanbi* roots.

jariburig, fire: shark; small turtle; dugong; dingo; buffalo; bullock; horse; several kinds of bird, including kingfisher and brolga, the *djuri* parakeet whose coloured feathers are used in sacred *maraiin* string, and (in several versions) the *bugbug* pheasant; two varieties of land snake; cicada; *gadderi* wild bee.

jariwurga, fresh water, or pandanus palm: green ant; white cockatoo; 'black' kangaroo; possum; bandicoot; wild turkey; blue-tongue lizard; several varieties of fish, mainly from salt water; two kinds of wild bee, *lorlban* and *gubulag*; frog; long-necked tortoise (in some versions).

jarigarngurg, stone or rock: several varieties of bird, including djabiru, goose, emu, and two kinds of pigeon, a small pandanus bird, and (in some versions) *bugbug* pheasant; three varieties of water snake, and one land snake; long-necked tortoise; echidna (in some versions); stone axe; tobacco; sea water; several varieties of fish, including mudfish and catfish; *manjalg* wild bee.

When we first worked in this region, up to 1950, virtually every adult could give the semi-moiety affiliation of almost any animal or natural feature – with a few exceptions, mostly things like small insects or grasses that were regarded as unimportant. Now, many of them cannot. This could be a consequence of the decline in mythical knowledge, at least as regards details.

On the face of it, the rationale for grouping certain features together and separating others is not at all clear. Gunwinggu themselves have no explanation except the mythical one that these connections were established 'in the beginning', in the creative era. 'Conception totemism' seems to be irrelevant in this connection, and the various items under each heading are not explicitly sorted out on the basis of any further social groups or categories. Also, there is no tabu on a person's eating or killing or handling any creature or plant or thing just because it is classified in the same semi-moiety as himself. A closer examination must take into account all the ritual ramifications – for example, which creatures or foods appear in various rituals and how their presence there is interpreted. It is at this level that explanation should be sought – in the complex of myth–*djang*–territory–sacred rites, with its patrilineal implications. Several clues point in this direction; but the pattern is obscured by a number of contradictions, and we are still in the process of exploring it. However, a glance at the examples set out here shows plainly that it is not a matter of simple contrast and similarity as far as the semi-moieties are concerned – for instance, between fresh and salt water, between land creatures and water creatures, between larger and smaller, fierce and timid, and so on. Both contrasts and similarities are more subtle, and Gunwinggu 'home-made models' of their own social organization do not articulate them.

Subsections

The third matrilineal category seems to have come into western Arnhem Land later than the others, although it is quite well integrated there. This is the subsection system, that is found over a large part of the north and centre of the continent. In fact, it has been spreading fairly rapidly even in areas that have had a fair amount of outside contact. (See R. and C.B., 1964: 47-60.) It consists of eight named divisions, usually called subsections: four in each matrilineal moiety. And it distinguishes between generations, as the other two matrilineal categories do not. Also in contrast to the other two categories, descent in this system is *indirectly* matrilineal; we call it this because, although a person's subsection depends on his mother's, it must by definition differ from hers. Like the other categories, it can be approached in two ways. One is to look at it impersonally, *as* a system. The second is to see it from the vantage point of someone actually involved in it. This means using it as a kind of social map in classifying other people, individually or in groups, especially in terms of kinship. It is a system that is put to work, not an intellectual game. Its popularity rests on two features: (a) its flexibility in relation to the grouping of kin, and (b), at the same time, its preciseness of categorization, as an easily remembered set of behavioural indicators, classifying all kin and non-kin into segments of the social interactory compass.

Another important feature of the subsection system is its dual descent or double descent organization – through males as well as through females. In actual practice, descent through the matri-line is always emphasized – both generally, wherever the subsection system is found, and specifically among Gunwinggu. However, the system does take into account patrilineal descent, and it includes patrilineal moieties that traditionally were unnamed. The ordinary Gunwinggu subsection labels are very close to the Maung, Gunbalang and Yiwadja terms, but the Margulidjban conform with the eastern Arnhem Land style.

Subsection patterning is organized around two interrelated topics: descent, and marriage. A child's subsection follows almost automatically from his mother's, and his father's is usually said to have no bearing on it. This is not entirely the case, as we shall see, but its influence is mainly indirect.

The basic 'descent model' is simple and fixed, and so it is a convenient starting point for understanding the system itself.

If we take only feminine forms (prefix, *ngal-*), and show descent from mother through daughter and daughter's daughter, the pattern forms two separate cycles, one in each moiety. The four terms in each case represent four generation levels, and a woman's children must be of the subsection (and generation) succeeding her own in that particular cycle (Fig. 5).

The daughter of a *ngalngaridj* woman is always *ngalgamarang*, her daughter is always *ngalbulan*, and so on. Only females appear in the cycles, in this schematic diagram, because it is females and not males who transmit subsection affiliation. For example, the son of a *ngalngaridj* woman is *nagamarang* (masculine prefix, *na-*), but his children's subsection depends on his wife's and not on his own.

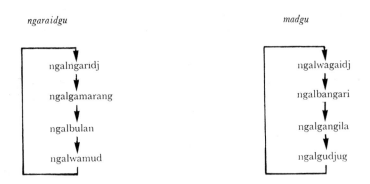

Fig. 5. Subsections: matrilineal descent cycles.

The fourth Gunwinggu marriage rule is based on subsection relationships. As far as subsections are concerned, the formally correct pattern of marriage preferences can be set out as in Table 2. This shows male as well as female terms, and the sign = indicates a potential marriage link. (Thus, the formally correct spouse for a *nangaridj* man is a *ngalwagaidj* woman, and for a *nawagaidj* man a *ngalngaridj* woman.)

TABLE 2

FIRST-PREFERENCE SUBSECTION
MARRIAGE PATTERN

	ngaraidgu		*madgu*	
A1	nangaridj ngalngaridj	=	nawagaidj ngalwagaidj	B1
A2	nabulan ngalbulan	=	nagangila ngalgangila	B2
C1	nawamud ngalwamud	=	nagudjug ngalgudjug	D1
C2	nagamarang ngalgamarang	=	nabangari ngalbangari	D2

For some purposes these eight sets of terms are treated as four sets of pairs – that is, as a four-section system. The pairs are *nangaridj* and *nabulan, nawamud* and *nagamarang, nawagaidj* and *nagangila, nagudjug* and *nabangari*, and their feminine counterparts. The second-preference or preferred-alternative subsection marriage pattern, therefore, looks as in Table 3.

TABLE 3

SECOND-PREFERENCE SUBSECTION
MARRIAGE PATTERN

	ngaraidgu		*madgu*	
A1	nangaridj ngalngaridj	=	nagangila ngalgangila	B2
A2	nabulan ngalbulan	=	nawagaidj ngalwagaidj	B1
C1	nawamud ngalwamud	=	nabangari ngalbangari	D2
C2	nagamarang ngalgamarang	=	nagudjug ngalgudjug	D1

Schematically, without the Gunwinggu terms, the system can be set out as in Fig. 6.

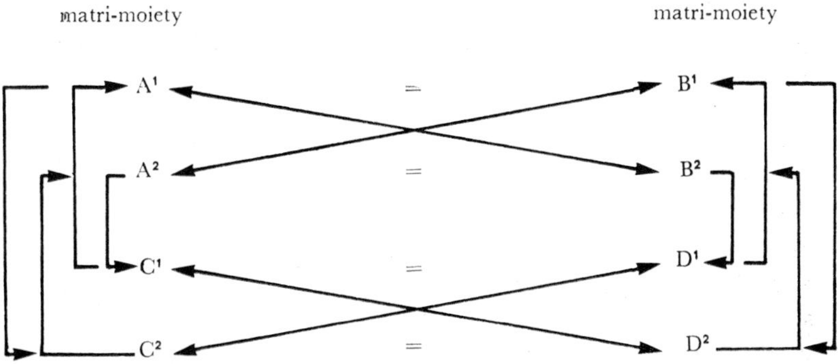

matri-moiety   matri-moiety

Fig. 6. Subsections: marriage and descent pattern *(a)*. Diagonal double-headed arrows indicate alternative marriage choices and vertical arrows point to offspring.

According to the fourth marriage rule a woman marries, preferentially, a man in the opposite subsection in the opposite moiety and of her own generation level or, alternatively, the generation of her grandparents. If he were in her parents' or children's generation levels, however, this would not be seriously 'wrong'. Regardless of her spouse's subsection, provided he is of the opposite moiety, her offspring's subsection remains constant, dependent on the matrilineal descent cycle. Even intra-moiety marriage would not affect it.

69

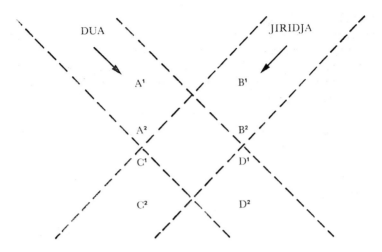

Fig. 7. Subsections and patrilineal moieties.

Nevertheless, patrilineal moieties are built into the subsection system. The division looks as in Fig. 7, in which are used the same symbols (A^1, etc.) to indicate subsections, and the introduced patrilineal moiety names from eastern Arnhem Land.

To recapitulate, then. Intermarrying pairs of subsections are arranged according to generation levels, but not in the same sequence as in the basic descent model. In the marriage-plus-descent model the first pair represents a person's own level; the second, immediately below it, his (or her) grandparents' level; the third, his parents'; and the fourth, his children's. For ritual purposes, a man's son should be of the same patri-moiety and in the correct generation level, or, if that is not possible, in the man's parents' generation level. Preferential and preferred-alternative marriages ensure this.

Supposing, however, a woman marries outside the preferential and preferred-alternative range of subsections, although still keeping to the rule of matri-moiety exogamy. Because of the matri-descent cycle, this would put her husband and her son in opposite patri-moieties. Ritually, this would be disastrous; but we know of very few cases of it, and none of them among men deeply involved in traditional religious affairs.

In actual fact, then, the patri-moieties, traditionally unnamed but now named, do impose a limitation on who a woman's husband should be – although not so much on who her child should be, as far as subsections are concerned. Yet, who a man's son is, or would be if he himself married a particular woman, is important. It is therefore essential, ritually speaking, for him to marry a woman who will bear sons belonging to his own patri-moiety. This linkage is reinforced by *gunmugugur* affiliation.

The convention we have adopted, in setting out the subsection labels diagrammatically, owes its origin to Radcliffe-Brown and Elkin and has been widely used by Australianists. The rationale for the use of the symbols A^1, A^2, etc., has been discussed elsewhere (R. B., n.d. [1]. The practice of using particular symbols to stand for the various subsection labels is quite arbitrary, except that the symbols we select must be consistent and must reflect some internal quality of the indigenous system. For example, because the capital letters A, B, C and D each represent two parts of a single section, the division is shown by attaching to each letter the numbers 1 and 2. This signifies the structural similarity between A^1 and A^2 and, further, it implies that the relationship between members of these two subsections is very close – that for some purposes they may be virtually identified. However, this internal quality could well be shown in another way. Also, there is no reason why, for example, *nangaridj* should be A^1 and *nabangari* D^2. Any such symbol can be substituted for a subsection term as long as internal consistency is maintained, and as long as the arrangement of the symbols themselves does not distort the empirical facts – a very real possibility (see R.B., *ibid.*). But, contrary to Barnes's comment (1967: 125-7), 'the order of intermarrying pairs is' *not* 'arbitrary', even though (as noted) 'it is possible to give two' or more different representations 'of a single system by altering the tabular order'. For example, see Fig 8. In this figure double-headed arrows represent alternative marriages, which 'short-cut' each descent cycle but do not infringe the alternate generation principle.

Or, again, see Fig 9, in which the same principle is involved.

If the symbols used here are taken to stand for the Gunwinggu subsection terms, then intermarrying pairs are not arbitrarily ordered or arranged but conform with preferential and alternative marriage forms. In other words, excluding the question of 'wrong' marriages, intermarrying couples can be shown in only two basic ways, in their preferential or their alternative marriage patterning,

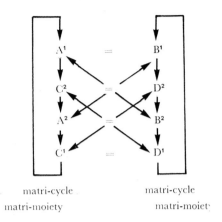

Fig. 8. Subsections: marriage and matrilineal descent cycles.

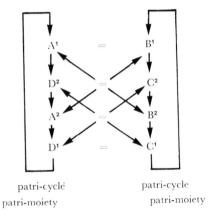

Fig. 9. Subsections: marriage and patrilineal descent cycles.

if the primary rule of the subsection system is to be adhered to – namely, that descent is indirectly matrilineal. (Structurally it is directly matrilineal; in regard to specific labels it is indirectly so.)

The second point to be made here concerns different devices for presenting section and subsection systems. There is much to be said for shedding the alphabetical symbols. W. H. Douglas (1964: 126) arranges Western Desert sections as segments of concentric circles, with double-headed arrows to indicate marriage and ordinary arrows to indicate offspring. Hiatt (1965: 49) also prefers concentric

72

circles, in this case for the subsection system, but with boxes instead of segments; like Douglas, he includes no alphabetical labels for the subsections themselves. Lévi-Strauss (1962: 109) contributes concentric circles for the Aranda, and Barnes (1967: 126-27) experiments with the same kind of framework: both use symbols in place of the Aboriginal subsection labels. And there are other examples which we need not note here. The real question is whether the circle or concentric circle technique of representing subsections and other social units provides more flexibility and clarity than the other, first, technique. Does it add anything in terms of explanation? And does it facilitate cross-cultural comparison?

The accompanying diagram (Fig. 10) contains the *same* material as do the more conventional presentations (Figs 5, 6 and 7 and Tables 2 and 3), but here it is arranged in concentric circles and ovoids. In constructing this we have retained our usual symbols for convenience, but we could have used instead the letters A to H, or the numbers 1 to 8, provided we supplied a key to the original subsection terms. Comparison of this diagram with the earlier tables and diagrams shows that, in fact, it *says no more and no less*. One conclusion we can draw from this is that the choice between a table and a diagram, or between diagrams, as a means of presenting the subsection system, depends to a large extent on aesthetic considerations – although the empirical situation is necessarily a limiting factor.

Moiety and semi-moiety affiliation is fixed before birth and cannot be changed. Conventionally, this applies to subsection affiliation too, but in actual practice it is more flexible.

Subsection labels are often used directly to identify individual people in a gathering, without calling moiety or semi-moiety names, particularly if some extra clue is added – for instance, a term that can be translated as 'youngest'. (If someone calls out, '*Ngalgangila mabid!*' – 'Youngest *ngalgangila!*' – this attracts the attention of any *ngalgangila* woman or girl who thinks of herself as the youngest of several close sisters.) In general, apart from this, subsections are mostly supplements and not substitutes. Where there are other more specific ways of reckoning relationships, these take precedence – for example, where close kinship is genealogically traceable or implied, or close territorial links are acknowledged (as in membership of the same *gunmugugur*). But outside a certain range these specific pointers

(to page 75)

73

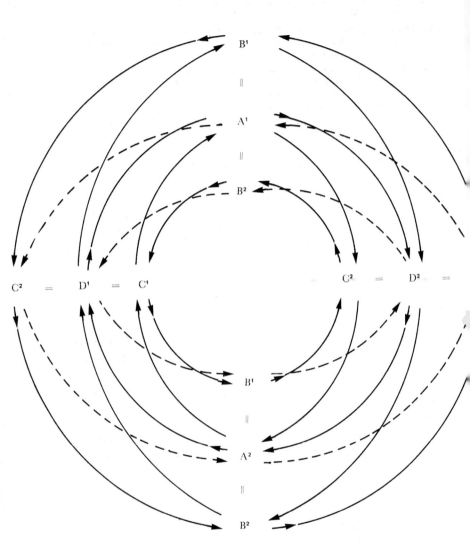

Fig. 10. Subsections: marriage and descent pattern *(b)*.

Key:

Arrows forming concentric circles link father and son. Each full circle represents
a patrilineal cycle and moiety: the outer circle is *jiridja*, the middle circle
dua, and the inner *jiridja*, alternating.

Alternating generation levels run horizontally and vertically across and down
the diagram. That is, C2, D1, C1 and C2, D2, C1 (shown horizontally)
alternate with B1, A1, B2 and B1, A2, B2, (shown vertically).

= sign represents marriage arising from regular and first-choice marriage, as well as those that are regarded as alternative.

Unbroken-line arrows forming ovoids link mother and child, and each full ovoid represents a matrilineal cycle and moiety; the outer ovoid is *madgu,* the inner ovoid *ngaraidu.*

Broken-line arrows forming ovoids also link mother and child, and again each full ovoid represents a matrilineal cycle and moiety; the outer ovoid is *ngaraidgu,* the inner ovoid *madgu.*

The two sets of ovoids formed by broken- and unbroken- line arrows are identical, since matrilineal descent is constant, but both are included to take into account alternative marriage forms.

---

become less relevant. One major advantage of the subsections, in such cases, is their wide regional spread. They simplify communication and adjustment at the edges of the local situation and to some extent beyond it. For Gunwinggu moving outside their home area, the subsection system is something they have in common with people of other 'tribes' whose social programming of behaviour and attitudes is otherwise very different. Conversely, outsiders can be accommodated in local Gunwinggu perspective, at least in a nominal way.

Gunwinggu have only one word, *gunmud,* for all three matrilineal units – moieties, semi-moieties, and subsections. This means that the only way of obtaining information on any one of them, in regard to particular cases, is to spell out examples of the kind of *gunmud* concerned. Thus: 'He's *namadgu,* maybe?' Or, 'Is he *jariburig,* or what?' Outside this context, *gunmud* in general means the fur or hair of an animal – kangaroo, possum, and so on, not human hair. But the stem -*mud* has other meanings, too. Ngalmud is one name for the Rainbow Snake. And in reference to *djang* (see Chapter 2), the same stem is translated by English-speaking Gunwinggu as 'Dreaming', pointing to a timeless spiritual quality that all *djang* share with the Rainbow. It has a different meaning in *namud,* a circle of people related by ties of kinship – but not only by matrilineal ties.

Chapter Five

The Patterning of Social Relations (2)

KINSHIP AND DESCENT

A PERSON's *namud* is not the total range of people he calls by kinship terms, but the narrower circle of more immediate kin that he can, ideally, depend on for help and support. It is not a group, but rather a potential or quasi-group. The assumption is that at least some of its members are likely to be within easy reach of one another even if they are not actually living together. One way of putting it can be translated as 'those various kin', implying that its composition is not fixed. The relatives most likely to be included are consanguineal, and closely so: own parents and siblings, parents' own siblings and their children, own grandparents, grandparents' siblings and their children, and grandchildren. When full relatives in these categories are lacking, others take their place, as a person's kin perspective shifts slightly to bring them nearer.

Terms

The Gunwinggu system of kinship reckoning is like other Aboriginal Australian systems in one general respect: a relatively small number of terms is applied to a large number of people, and most inter-personal relationships are framed in the idiom of kinship. Subsection patterning provides an extra range of alternatives. Beyond a certain point, the reference to actual or implied genealogy peters out and the terms used become simply category terms, based on nominal or courtesy kinship. The terminology is based on a genealogical

76

model, but the relationships expressed through it need not be. Characteristically, when missionaries and anthropologists and other 'outsiders' are nominally accepted into the local situation this is often done in terms of subsections. Allocating a subsection label is the first step, and the second is its extension into the field of kinship: 'You are such-and-such [subsection label], I am such-and-such – and therefore I call you so-and-so [kin term]!'

For Gunwinggu, the system appears to work quite smoothly. The population is small enough for most people to have at least a rough idea of one another's affiliations and relationships, within the range of ordinary interaction. They use their own particular *namud* circle as a basis, and fit others into it or around it. What makes the system more difficult for non-Gunwinggu is the fact that they have more than one set of kin terms and use these in slightly different ways. They are:

(a) Ordinary terms of address, or vocatives. These are the easiest and the most straightforward. Usually they take the form of reciprocal pairs (for example, father–son, mother's brother–sister's son, and so on). (See below.)

(b) Ordinary third person reference terms (for example, my father, your mother, his elder brother, and so on). Some of these are directly translatable, some not. (See Appendix 2.)

(c) The special vocabulary used between mother-in-law and son-in-law. This has its own terms for certain relatives, but divides them into fewer categories.

(d) A set of more polite or more indirect reference terms, called *gundebi*. This is a little more complicated than the others – which is partly why it has been losing ground. Young people use it rarely, if ever; and older people now use it even less than older people did a few years ago and in a more limited way, not drawing on the full set of available terms. The terms themselves are quite simple, and some of them are basically the same as ordinary forms of address and reference. They are also conceptualized as if they were reciprocal pairs (for example, father–son, etc.). But *gundebi* is more precise than the other three sets of terms. For example, when two persons are talking about a third, the term they use for him (or her) can alter according to the relationship between the two speakers themselves. The overall patterning of *gundebi* terms is not the same as the overall patterning of ordinary address and reference terms, even

77

though they coincide in some points. Also, *gundebi* draws attention to relationships that might otherwise be glossed over. For instance, when a woman uses ordinary affinal ('in-law') terms in speaking to or about her husband's parents, these are the same for everyone, because they depend on that particular *structural* relationship (between any wife and her husband's parents). However, if her marriage did not conform with the ideal, if she did not stand to him and to them in the right kin relationship, this shows up in the *gundebi* terms. That could be another reason for its decline in popularity.

Each set of terms is straightforward, even in the *gundebi* case. Gunwinggu themselves can list them (apart from *gundebi*) and discuss them without hesitation. But most Gunwinggu are not so articulate when it comes to looking at each set in relation to the others, coordinating the terms within as well as between the various groupings, and explaining the circumstances in which one term is used rather than another.

This outline covers some of the main points of the Gunwinggu kinship system, without elaborating on it. (A fuller account, including a schematic table, is set out in R.B. 1966: 1-57.)

The following list (Table 4) includes all the ordinary terms of address and their meanings from the standpoint of a male speaker; where a term has a different meaning when a female is speaking or if a term is used only by females, the letters *f.s.* appear after the meaning. These are the principal kin terms that Gunwinggu (a) use in direct address and (b) give consistently in response to such questions as, 'What do you call so-and-so?' – questions we asked in genealogy-taking and in conversations. Nevertheless, not all of them are actually used as direct vocatives. A brother and sister should never address each other in such a direct way; nor should a son-in-law and mother-in-law. The rule applies to distant as well as to close relationships. Most direct-address terms can also be used in reference, but as a rule only if 'my' is spoken or understood. In this list, the reciprocal of each term is shown by the final number tatached to it. (For example, for term 1, *garang*, 'mother', the reciprocal is 8, *djedje*, 'child' or 'offspring'.)

TABLE 4

TERMS OF ADDRESS

Key to abbreviations: r. = reciprocal; *f.s.* = female speaking; *m.s.* = male speaking;
E = elder; Y = younger; F = father; M = mother; Z = sister; B = brother;
C = child; S = son; D = daughter; H = husband; W = wife.

1.	garang	M (r. 8)
2.	mula	MYZ (r. 8)
3.	ngaba (ngabad)	F (r. 7)
4.	gogog	EB (r. 5); B, *f.s.* (r. 6)
5.	dada	Y same-sex sibling (r. 4, *m.s.*; r. 6, *f.s.*)
6.	jabog (yabog)	Z (r. 4); EZ, *f.s.* (r. 5)
7.	gulun	C (r. 3); BC, *f.s.* (r. 10)
8.	djedje	C, *f.s.* (r. 1)
9.	ngadjadj	MB, 'uncle' (r. 16)
10.	belu	FZ, 'aunt' (r. 7)
11.	gagag	MM, MMB; DC, *f.s.*; ZDC (self-r.)
12.	mamam	MF, MFZ; DC; BDC, *f.s.* (self-r.)
13.	mawa	FF, FFZ; SC, *m.s.*; BSC, *f.s.* (self-r.)
14.	maga	FM, FMB; ZSC SC, *f.s.* (self-r.)
15.	wulubulu	MMM, MMMB (self-r., *f.s.*, or r. 8); DDC, *f.s.*; ZDC (self-r., or r. 8)
16.	ganggin	ZC (r. 9)
17.	ganjulg	Second-choice spouse, when opposite sex: MBC; FZC (self-r.)
18.	gagali	Most eligible spouse, when opposite sex: MFZDC, FMBSC, MMMBC, MMFZC, MMBDC, etc. (self-r.)
19a.	nagurng	'S-in-law', DH, *f.s.*: MMBS, FZDC, etc. (r. 19a or *b*)
19b.	ngalgurng	'M-in-law', WM: MMBD, FZDD, etc. (r. 19a or *b*) Both 19a and 19b are in the third person form, suggesting constraint and partial avoidance.
20.	bindoi	Special relationship between, for example, 9 and 16 (self-r.)
21a.	ngalmuni, ngalbinmuni	SW; HM, *f.s.*
21b.	nabinmuni	HF, *f.s.*
22.	meiameia or maiamaia	MFF (self-r.) – Maung term.

In Chapter 4, we said that relations between people in various subsections were treated as kin relations, conventionally patterned. This pattern is most consistent when no other factors (for example, close genealogical kinship) intervene. Excluding such complications, the correlation of kin terms with subsection categories is as shown in Table 5, from the point of view of a man or a woman.

TABLE 5

SUBSECTIONS AND KINSHIP TERMS

gogog, dada, jabog	A1	=	B1	gagali, ganjulg
gagag, mawa	A2	=	B2	mamam, maga
garang, mula, ngadjadj	C1	=	D1	ngaba, belu, ngalgurng, nagurng
wulubulu, djedje, ganggin, meiameia	C2	=	D2	gulun

The schematic Gunwinggu kinship diagram (Fig. 11) is included so that the terms can be seen more easily in relation to one another. It is based on the assumption that a man's ideal wife is a MMBDD (a *gagali*), but additional possibilities are available – for example, a *ganjulg* cross-cousin (see hereunder), along with some in the grandchildren's generation. As far as this last is concerned, there is the convention of 'junior' marriage brought about through a man's partial identification with his *gagag* (MMB), and this is reflected in the presence of junior and senior kin terms at both the grandparents' and grandchildren's generation levels.

While cross-cousin (*ganjulg*) marriage is structurally consistent with *gagali* marriage, these two forms are clearly demarcated, but in the extension of junior marriages the *ganjulg* marriage as a permissible marriage is underlined.

When we speak of kinship terms, we usually have in mind a more or less formalized set of labels that apply only to people recognized as kin. A complete coverage goes further, and includes not only these specific labels but also substitutes for them: for instance, ordinary items of vocabulary that are put to this special use but may not be volunteered by people giving kinship terms in the narrower sense.

As an example, we can look at a sister from the viewpoint of a brother. In ordinary Gunwinggu speech *dalug*, 'woman', never takes the feminine prefix *ngal-* because the female reference is an intrinsic part of it. When that prefix is added, making it *ngaldalug*, the meaning changes: it becomes a distinct term with an impersonal flavour, and this is the proper way of speaking to any male person, however young, about anyone who stands to him in a 'sister' relationship. In direct speech it means 'your sister'; in third-person reference, 'his sister'. It is used *to* a brother about a sister, not *by* him. The expressions he himself uses (meaning 'my sister') are not kin-specifics – a point that is significant in understanding the relationship. Even at their face value, they suggest distance or separateness. The commonest of them are ordinary words for 'thing', 'old woman', 'white-haired person', 'corpse', 'malignant spirit'. This is a Maung practice, too. So is another practice that emphasizes a different and more personal side of the relationship. Conventionally, a girl's nickname or joking name is chosen in the first place by any of her close brothers – but not vice versa. (Boys and men normally get theirs from members of their own sex, such as their *gagali* or cross-cousins.)

In most cases, the terms that specify any kin relationship supply some clues to the attitudes and behaviour associated with it. One kind of clue lies in their form. Not only brother–sister but also son-in-law–mother-in-law terms suggest avoidance of direct face-to-face contact, in the impersonal prefix that does not appear in corresponding forms for other relationships. Another clue is the semantic aspect in a narrower sense – the meaning ascribed to the content of a term. In the brother–sister example, other terms that cover mixed-sex as well as same-sex siblings connote solidarity: for example, they 'stand' with one another. (See Appendix 2; also R.M.B., 1966.) A third kind of clue rests on the question of whether and how far different persons use the same terms in speaking to or about someone else. More than one term is available for every relationship, and even when one is held in common the others need not be. The nearest approach to a completely shared kinship perspective is the case of full brothers on one hand, full sisters on the other. But the overlap is never complete, or almost never, because a man and his full brothers do not have exactly the same life experiences, including marriage. Nor do a woman and her full sisters. The difference in perspective is greater between siblings of opposite sex – between a man and his sister, but there is common ground here too. In particular, they share the same reference terms

(to page 84)

Capital letters indicate males and lower-case letters females.
= sign indicates a marriage link.

Inverted commas round certain kin terms indicate: in the grandparents' and grandchildren's generation levels, preference for 'junior marriage' (that is, the system reflects a general preference for young women as wives); in a person's own generation, second-choice partners, but not actual GANJULG/*ganjulg*, or in the case of a GANJULG/*ganjulg* not an actual MBC or FZC; in a man's children's generation, an alternative partner for his S.

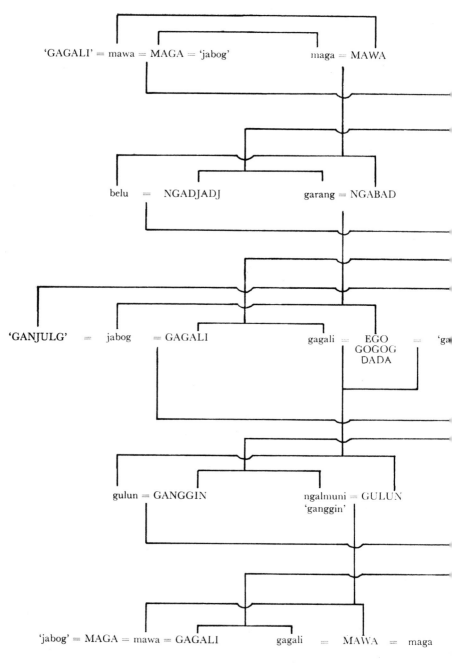

Fig. 11. Schematic representation

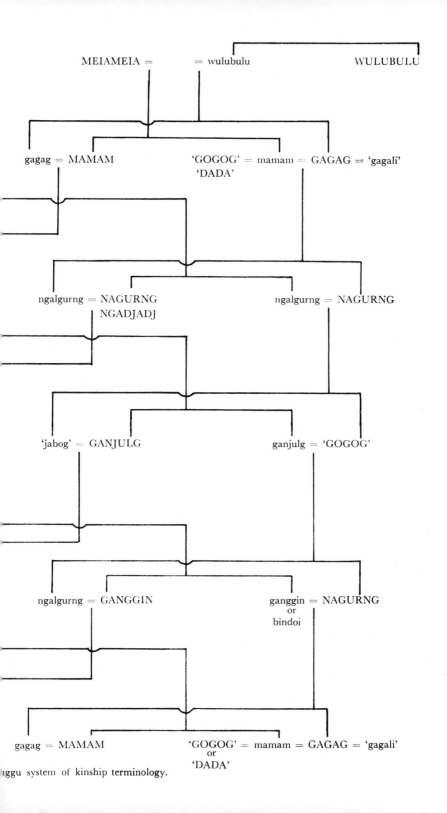

…nggu system of kinship terminology.

for each other's children – which are not the terms used by their spouses. A man's sister's children are his *jau* (yau; *ngaljau* for a girl). and also hers; he is their *baidjan*, she is their *ngalbaidjan*. His own children are his *bewud* (*ngalbewud* for a girl), and hers too; he is their *gongomu*, she is their *ngalgongomu*. In relations *between* a brother and sister, the highlight or the most vocal emphasis is on contrast, even though other aspects are just as important. In relations between both of them together as a sibling pair, and the generations immediately above and below them, the highlight is on their shared perspective as siblings. We can look at it schematically like this (Fig. 12), omitting sex-indicating prefixes, and using the symbol ←✕→ to summarize the ideal state of affairs between any brother and sister – a state of constraint-plus-cooperation.

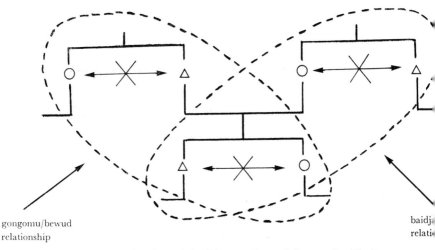

gongomu/bewud
relationship

baidj
relati

Fig. 12. Brother-sister relationship: extension to their respective offspring.

Key:

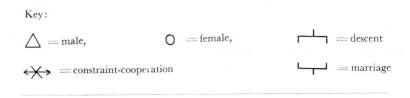

△ = male, ○ = female, ⌐‾⌐ = descent

←✕→ = constraint-cooperation ⌐_⌐ = marriage

Fig. 12 shows what could be called a combined-sibling, divided-spouse orientation, in their roles, first as offspring (in their 'family of orientation') and then as parents (in their 'family of procreation'). Gunwinggu have no single term for both parents together. Nor do they have a single vocative term for daughter or son from the viewpoint of father and mother together. In third-person reference the ordinary word for child, *wud*, is sometimes used, either alone or in the form of *wudjau*. This last can indicate a shared parental perspective, whereas *bewud* implies specifically the perspective of a father and father's sister, just as *jau* (yau) does for a mother and mother's brother.

Or, to take another term, *gagali*: this connotes 'eligible spouse'. Its stem, *gali*, is central to a number of expressions pertaining to marriage or sexual union. (This at once calls to mind the north-eastern Arnhem Land term *galei*, a potential or actual wife, but in that area it refers to a maternal cross-cousin, a mother's brother's daughter. The resemblance is not haphazard. Several other terms are even closer to eastern Arnhem Land forms, particularly in the special son-in-law–mother-in-law vocabulary.) Also, one reference term for *gagali* is *-gobeng*. This is actually the ordinary word for spouse, an inflected form that takes various prefixes and sometimes incorporates the word *binin*, 'man' or 'person'. (For example, *nagobeng* or *nabiningobeng*, 'husband'; *ngalgobeng* or *ngalbiningobeng*, 'wife'; *ngagobeng* is the first person singular form.) Another *gagali* reference term is *ganjulg*. This is the usual term for cross-cousin, suggesting that in some circumstances the two are identified, and in fact a cross-cousin is a second-choice spouse.

Then there are the reference terms for father and (feminine forms) father's sister .One of them, *gongomu*, refers to the way a small child is carried on its father's shoulders, astride his neck. But another should be used only for a person's own or very close father (and father's sister), because it suggests a personal relationship that is not extended to other 'fathers' – the belief that a man sees the spirit of his own child before its birth. (See Chapter 7.) The term is inflected and varies for person and number (for example, *nganbonang*, 'my father'; see Appendix 2).

Of course, kinship terms are merely pointers, for Gunwinggu themselves as well as for us. They take us part of the way, but beyond that we need information about both content and context. For example, the reference terms for mother and mother's brother show that there is partial identification between them, and because these terms can be translated as 'big' or 'great' this hints at their importance; but what the terms do not reveal is the assumption that a mother should be helpful and indulgent, whereas a mother's brother should be helpful but firm and authoritative. For example, a man has jurisdiction over his sister's son in two important spheres, religious ritual and marriage arrangements. His concern for his sister's welfare and good name is directly linked with his interest in the children she is expected to bear – children of the same moiety and semi-moiety as himself. In the same way, kin terms alone do not indicate the partial constraint or partial formality that is conventional between child and father and is extended to father's sister. In all such cases, the terms make sense in relation to the rules and in relation to actual behaviour. But before turning to the subject of behaviour, we must look at the question of how closeness in kin relationships is interpreted: What happens when each person has so many 'mothers', 'mothers' brothers', 'fathers', and so on?

Every kin position has more than a single occupant, and some of the terms make this explicit, but the blueprint focuses on paired type relationships, between, for instance, a mother and son, a brother and sister, and so on. The rules that specify the right behaviour in each case allow for adjustment according to degree of closeness, especially genealogical closeness. The bond between actual parent and child is recognized as uniquely personal and, in that sense, irreplaceable. This applies particularly to a child's exclusive relationship with its mother during pregnancy, and its less obvious but equally 'real' pre-natal spirit contacts with its father. A motherless child or orphan acquires that label even if its mother's close sisters are still living. Several women talking about their past experiences recalled how emotionally upset they had felt on the death of their own mothers, even though other close relatives had been around at the time.

The distinction between close and more distant kin comes out also in the *gundebi* system of reference. In this system, actual relatives like own *mawa* and *maga* and their close siblings are called simply that – *mawa* and *maga*. The special terms for other persons classified as *mawa* and *maga* apply only outside that range.

Otherwise, generally speaking, the degree of closeness in any

86

Ubar postulant astride the ubar *drum: he represents the* namalawul *snake which is classified with* Yirawadbad. *Behind him is a row of novices. Oenpelli, 1950*

Two ubar postulants representing Balngbalng *night birds (*djurul, *owl) on a nest: they wear cane necklets symbolizing* balmadbara *tree snakes. Behind is a row of novices. Oenpelli, 1950*

In the final ubar
sequence, a row of
squatting Kangaroo men
wait to enter the ubar
ground where they will
destroy the wangaridja
shade. Oenpelli, 1950

On the ubar ground. Men representing Gulubar kangaroos surround the wangaridja
shade in which Galgbeid (red wallaby) hide. Oenpelli, 1950

Women at the edge of the main camp await the men's return from the ubar ground. Oenpelli, 1950

Women dance forward to meet ubar novices returning from the billabong where they have been ritually immersed. Immediately behind them are two women standing on a forked stick. Oenpelli, 1950

Two women stand on a forked stick in the concluding ubar sequence. Each is of a different matrilineal moiety; they swing the lida *rattles, as men return with the novices after their immersion. Oenpelli, 1950*

relationship does not depend on hard and fast cut-off lines in genealogical reckoning. It is assessed subjectively according to circumstances – that is, according to the number and range of appropriate persons available.

For example, take the son–father relationship. If a man's own father (A), his acknowledged genitor, is living, then A is his own true father in contrast to other fathers, even though the contrast between A and any of A's surviving full brothers is slight. But should A die, his brothers, if any, will be regarded as 'own father', although this may be qualified by adding 'big' or 'small' (older or younger) to the father term. If none of A's full brothers is living, the closest 'own father' will be A's eldest brother with one parent in common, then the next oldest, and so on. Recognition of closeness extends outward along these lines, taking into account the number of actual grandparents in common, then the number of actual great-grand-parents, or close great-grandparents. Even beyond that range a man can be acknowledged as a close father if nobody else is nearer, genealogically or otherwise. Nevertheless, even though genealogical proximity is significant in this kind of reckoning, outside the immediate sphere of primary relationships (actual genitor, actual grandparents and their close siblings, etc.) it can be offset by other factors. One is territorial affiliation. Two men from the same or adjacent small territories or cluster of named sites are 'brothers' even if no genealogical links can be traced. Each is 'close father' to the other's sons, and may be acknowledged as 'closest father' if no 'father' from a common grandparent is living. Ideally, the territorial bond is indicated and symbolized in the sharing of the same *gunmugugur* and *igurumu*, or, at the next level of closeness, in being 'company', 'mixing together' in one large territory or adjoining small ones. The fact of being neighbours is important in itself, but mythical and ritual connections are even more so.

Sharing the same territory implies not only a common language but also a common dialect. However, a man and his close father may differ on this score if he chooses his mother's language or dialect in preference to his father's. This is offset, in practice, by the fact that it is hard to find an adult who cannot speak or understand another language or at least another dialect, however imperfectly.

Another factor that affects both terminology and behaviour is a marriage link. A distant father, or a person previously called by some other kin term, can become a fairly close father if he marries a man's own mother or her close sister. (There are no separate Gunwinggu terms for step-parents or step-siblings.) In such an event a strong personal tie can develop between the two men. Physical proximity enters here, just as it does in other kinship and quasi-kinship reckoning. It can mean a difference between, say, 'closest acknowledged father' and 'closest effective father'.

In other words, closeness in kin relationships depends for practical purposes primarily on who is available, and availability includes accessibility.

Actual genealogies vary enormously in span and in the number of close kin with clearly traceable connections that they include. Among middle-aged to older people, the number in their own and ascendant (parents', grandparents') generation levels ranged from over a hundred to half a dozen or so. An interesting example was Midjara, a Dangbun-side woman, now dead. In 1949-50 she was about 50, with seven grandchildren. (One of these died in March 1950, and two others had died earlier.) She had a widely branching genealogy that spread territorially from traditional Dangbun country to townships on the North-South road and through the buffalo plains. She was interested in other people's relationships, too, except on the northern and north-eastern coast. Nevertheless, although she reported that her own mother's mother had had only one sibling, a boy, she knew nothing at all about him: whether he had survived beyond childhood, or, if he were still living, in what direction she might look for him. (Her *gunmugugur* was Durmangga, and her husband was Nawundurba; see Fig. 13.)

Given her interests, this ignorance was unusual, especially as there seemed to be no reason for it apart from simply having lost touch. But most genealogies are very shallow. Notwithstanding the *wulubulu* (MMM, MMMB) provision, it is difficult to go beyond the grandparents' generation. At that point siblings tend to merge, and this can affect the reckoning of paternity and maternity on a specifically individual basis. Differing versions of their genealogies came from several people who were middle-aged and older in 1949-50 and had one or both parents in common. This happened even when personal names were specified. (We did not ask for personal names of the dead, but recorded them if they were volunteered.) In many instances a woman did not know the territorial unit (*gunmugugur*) of her *wulubulu* or even of her father's mother, and in a few the same applied to mother's mother. This was usually because she could not remember them as individual people, identified from first-hand experience or from other people's reminiscences. ('I never saw her', 'I was a small child when she died' – and so on.)

Behaviour

To say of a person 'I don't know what to call him' implies that he is right outside the system. If he is only on the fringe, subsections are a bridge to the appropriate kin term. Such terms are more than labels, they are keys to the attitudes and actions conventionally expected between persons who use them, and each one evokes a cluster of meanings for speaker and listener. The pattern is only approximate, because the range from consanguineal to nominal kinship is so wide. Beyond the nucleus of close kin, expectations as well as sentiment grow progressively weaker unless other considerations reinforce them. Expectations associated with close kin are more diffuse, too. In a situation like this where so much of behaviour, both mundane and religious, is geared to kinship rules, one way of organizing it is to see that those rules are fairly specific – as they are here. Details of what to do and what not to do are part of the content of every relationship, and children begin to learn them through precept and example almost as soon as they can talk. Teaching about attitudes and sentiments is mixed almost inseparably with teaching about practical details. This applies even to immediately personal ties, such as the tie between own parent and child, but with a difference. The difference is that particularized rules map out only small areas of this relationship and do not define its totality: expectation of mutual help and support in all circumstances sets the tone for action, even though the content of the action varies.

Gunwinggu accounts of the rules governing kin behaviour are highly consistent, from adults of both sexes and all ages. Statements we recorded at intervals over a period of twenty-odd years show very few discrepancies. The expected content of kin behaviour does not seem to have changed greatly in that time. What possibly has been changing is the proportion of marriages and sweetheart liaisons conventionally regarded as wrong – but we do not know

89

enough about the rate in the purely traditional (pre-contact) situation to be sure of this. Even so, except in a few blatant cases efforts are still made to observe the proprieties. The usual procedure is to juggle with subsection affiliation, the most loosely anchored feature of the descent-cum-territory complex. Normally, genealogical kinship takes precedence over the kinship patterning that goes with subsection relationships, but in a conventionally wrong relationship an attempt may be made to look at it the other way round. For instance, a young man wanting a surreptitious affair with someone who is not 'straight' for him adjusts his own subsection label, so that according to subsection rules he now calls her *gagali*, 'eligible spouse'. This does not resolve the difficulty, particularly if her husband or some other interested person learns what is going on; but until then, or until the young man and woman tire of each other, it makes for an enjoyable combination – a sweetheart, the spice of the conventionally forbidden in a new style of joking relationship, and a show of following the rules while actually going contrary to them. The range of potential sweethearts available on this basis is very much wider than the range of approved marriage partners. One custom that was coming into vogue among young men and women in 1950 was the *djuruwari*, a sweetheart relationship between people calling each other *gagag*. Because they belong to the same matrilineal moiety (though to opposite patrilineal moieties) this is formally wrong, and manipulating subsection affiliations is wrong too. Consequently, it is something 'other people' do, or at least not something to boast about too freely or too seriously. If it is handled lightly – and provided the others immediately concerned (husband, wife, etc.) make no fuss – then it can be *publicly* regarded as an escapade-in-words instead of an actuality, like the accusations and threats that are a part of the content of joking relationships. It is impossible to say how often this kind of thing happened, or how often it happens now. A few relationships of the sort emerge into the open, mainly because some effort is made to stabilize them or obtain public sanction for them – that is, to make them more than sweetheart liaisons. Others remain at the level of semi-public gossip. But the point here is the attitude toward the rules, the fact that even young people endeavour to keep the formal system more or less intact. They may manipulate it informally for personal and mostly short-range ends, but they do not try to throw out the system itself.

For many purposes, social positioning is kinship positioning: how a person is related to the central figures in given circumstances – such as a birth, a betrothal, an initiation rite, a marriage, an illness, a quarrel, a death.

Obligations, rights and duties are dependent to a very large extent on kinship positioning, both in the domestic sphere and as a basic substructure in religious affairs. Kinship rules permeate the division of food and labour resources, and the coordination of activities in almost all enterprises.

A death, for instance, highlights the way kin are mobilized for tasks traditionally associated with a particular happening. Mortuary rituals range from a semi-private affair for a very young child (where the mother is helped by her own mothers or grandmothers, sisters, or co-wives) to the conventional full-scale sequence – though this sequence could apply to small children too.

Apart from individual mourning, mortuary arrangements for adults and older children are handled by men. The dead person is the focus of attention, first in the obvious and direct sense and secondly as the key to the organizing of action at such a time. His (her) age, sex and status and the circumstances of the death all have a bearing on the course of events. But most of those events take place in the wider framework of kinship obligations and commitments. A person legitimately expects to rely for his last rites on people who stand to him in certain specified kin relationships, and when he dies there is no need for a leader to allocate duties or select personnel. The traditional pattern defines not only what should be done, but also who should do it. Children learn through watching and listening how people should behave on the death of a brother, sister, father, and so on – with the usual provisions regarding closeness of relationship, and who is available in the various kinship categories (and, in a situation where some quite strenuous work is involved, who has the ability to cope with the necessary tasks). Some of the traditional tasks, and (in parentheses) the people conventionally responsible for them are:

(a) Carrying news of the death to other close relatives. (The death-messenger can be, for example, a cross-cousin, *ganjulg*, of the dead person, or a sister's son, *ganggin*, but never a brother for a dead sister.)

91

(b) Building a rough mortuary platform. (This may be done by, for example, a not-too-close father.) The dead were occasionally buried, but Gunwinggu say that exposing the corpse on a platform in the bush was preferred.

(c) Making a small *djuandjuan* 'stick' figure of paperbark or twine to stand by the platform, its short arm pointing to the corpse and its long arm pointing in the direction of the new camp-site, because people always move camp after a death. (A not-too-close father and a full *ganjulg* may be responsible for this; or a mother's brother, provided he and the dead person's mother did not come from the same mother – it does not matter if they shared the same father.)

(d) Carrying the corpse to the platform. (Done by the same men, or others in the same categories.)

(e) Holding up a sheet of bark or a blanket to screen the corpse, to guard against an outburst of emotion that could lead to fighting; wrapping it in paperbark, binding it firmly to the platform, face downward, and covering it entirely with cane and hard grass, then making a fire beneath it with chunks of termite mound to retain the heat. (Done by, for instance, two or three not-too-close *nagurng*, even for a woman, but a *gagag* who is an actual mother's mother's brother from the same mother should not even look at the corpse except from a distance, and men who call a dead woman close *gagali* should not look at her corpse at all 'in case they go blind'.)

(f) If a new widow is the target of more than ordinarily heated accusations, she may be hidden at first 'in case she is speared'. If a *maneiag* peace-making rite is held (see Chapter 7), some man substitutes for her as the 'accused' to run the gauntlet of her husband's relatives. (This man may be, for example, a not-too-close father; or a close *nagurng*, but not her own son-in-law.) Following that, she may be attacked by one of her close, but not full, brothers; his spears are 'pulled away' from him but he is allowed to strike her on the head with his spear-thrower.

The number of more or less active participants is greatest in the group ceremonies and rites that punctuate a mortuary sequence, culminating in the *lorgun* (see Chapter 6). But one sort of participation is enjoined on all adults regardless of their relationship to the dead person. Conventional sounds and gestures of mourning are expected of everyone in the camp where the death has occurred and in any other camp that is formally advised of it by a death-messenger. The expectation rests most heavily on those with the closest kin and personal ties. Weeping, wailing and self-inflicted injury are the customary signs: for women, mostly head-gashing; for men, spearing in the thigh, especially for a parent, son, or daughter. The more prolonged they are and the more blood flows, the stronger is the inference of real grief. In one Gunwinggu expression, it covers the mourner's chest and back; in another, it is like the scene when a buffalo is slaughtered. Conversely, when the signs of mourning are perfunctory or absent, other people are quick to notice and comment. Reproaches of 'lack of proper feeling' shade into accusations of responsibility. A mourner who fails to mourn, and particularly a widow or widower, is a ready-made suspect – not necessarily as having carried out sorcery, but at least as having connived at it or left the way open for it.

Over and above these specialized gestures, mourning entails other acts that underline separateness or avoidance. Close mourners abstain from certain foods, and from group participation in certain events. For example, a dead girl's parents should not be present during the first corpse-disposal rites; her father can share in the first mourning and ritual washing (cleansing) feast but he should eat separately; her mother should not share in it at all, and in any case she is not supposed to feel hungry. ('She can't eat much: she keeps thinking of her daughter.')

The division of labour is flexible enough to allow relatives in certain categories to substitute for others – but not for all others, nor in all respects, and avoidances and prohibitions remain fairly firm. And this same 'limited scale of preferences' operates in many other task-centred situations.

For Gunwinggu, kinship is not only a set of signposts for orienting behaviour on the basis of the past. It is also concerned with perpetuating the system in the future, continuing the same relationships with new personnel. Traditionally, marriage takes place within this system and not outside it, and so does the production of children.

Marriage Preferences

The fifth Gunwinggu marriage rule is actually the most important. It is focused on kinship. On this account it cuts across the other four rules, which imply kin relationships, but it goes beyond them in specifying *which* kin relationships should be involved in a marriage. It involves one basic premise, and stipulates certain conditions. The premise is that in any marriage arrangement the prospective husband and wife are already related in terms of kinship, preferably consanguineal kinship, and stemming from this is the subsidiary premise that the persons arranging the marriage should also be kin, and preferably close kin.

In an ideally correct marriage, all of the four units or categories already mentioned are in order: husband and wife are of different *gunmugugur*, moieties, and semi-moieties, and of appropriate subsections; and, preferably, they speak the same dialect of the same language – not just Gunwinggu in a general sense, but the same kind of Gunwinggu. However, although these points are regarded as quite important, they are not predominantly so. By far the greatest weighting is attached to kinship. It is sometimes implied that, if kinship arrangements are right, these other requirements follow automatically. Exceptions are catered for by defining rightness rather flexibly where actual cases are concerned. The exact point at which right becomes wrong is not clear. What is clear is that there are two extremes: the ideal, with which people *should* conform; and the indisputably wrong, which traditionally, as far as we can tell, would not be tolerated. In between are degrees of rightness and wrongness, in other words, degrees of acceptability. We call this a *preferential* marriage system. We are not justified in speaking of 'prescription', if by that we mean obligation to marry a person in a specified category, with sanctions enforcing conformity to the rule.

The ideal spouse (see list of Terms of Address, Table 4) is a *gagali*, and the ideal mother-in-law from a man's point of view is a *ngalgurng*. Relatives a man calls by the term *gagali* include MMBDD, FFZSD, FZDDD, and MBDDD – and conversely for a woman, since the term is self-reciprocal. A correct marriage is more than a union between two eligible partners. Bound up with it is the assumption that the pair do not take the initiative themselves and that their kin are active, not only in arranging it, but also in sustaining it. Ideally, such arrangements are made some years before the actual marriage. In fact, at this ideal level the arrangement is built into the system, and all that people need do is act in accordance with their allotted roles. The *nagurng-ngalgurng* relationship is crucial: a man conventionally looks to his close *ngalgurng* to provide him with a wife. In construct accounts (that is, people's general statements about what happens in such cases) and in myths, the problem of choice is hardly mentioned. In actual cases several considerations impinge on it, over and above genealogical ones.

(a) Everyone who is physically normal is expected to marry – a girl at puberty, if not before, and a man by the time he is thirty to thirty-five. Traditionally, there are no middle-aged Gunwinggu bachelors. (b) A man may have two or more wives simultaneously, but not vice versa – however, he rarely has more than three at one time. (c) Full sisters should not share the same husband. (d) In an eligible family, the oldest eligible brother or sister has prior betrothal claims. (e) A man should be older than his wife, especially at her first marriage, and the assumption is that he is usually at least as old as her mother. (f) Conforming with the ideal of reciprocity in social relationships, there should be a 'balance' in marriage arrangements, preferably through an exchange of persons, and especially of eligible females, although this is not explicitly structured. (g) A girl's father has some rights in deciding on her future husband, but her mother and her mother's brothers conventionally have a major say. And (h) the distance a young wife has to move from her parents should not be so great that they cannot easily keep in touch with her.

In sum, all of these considerations extend the possibility of choice even for close *nagurng* and *ngalgurng*. Women seem to emphasize the matrilineal 'side' more than men do. In general, we found that they were most likely to cite as an ideal union one in which a woman gives her first daughter to her actual mother's mother's eldest brother's eldest son, as most eligible *nagurng*. This trend appeared in ordinary conversations and in comments on actual cases and on myths, and in responses to the question, 'Who is your/their true *nagurng*?' Or, in reference to children not yet betrothed, 'Who is your/their mother's true *nagurng*? Where will they look for a wife/ husband?' The chosen *nagurng*, then, waits for his *ngalgurng* to bear her first daughter and supplies her with gifts of food in anticipation, and when the birth is imminent he should be on the spot, ready. If that child is a boy, he waits for the next. If she bears no daughters at all, he may look elsewhere for a wife; he may do so anyway, while he is waiting. But, supposing it is a girl, the betrothal should be confirmed almost at the moment of her birth, with the first afterbirth blood. Hence the term for betrothed wife, extended to any betrothed wife: *gulbagen* (*gulba* = 'blood').

The behaviour between a man and his *ngalgurng* is governed by the assumption that she is a potential, even if not yet an actual, mother-in-law; that she will, or may at some time, give him a wife, and that in return she expects from him both tangible gifts and general support in trouble. One statement sums this up concisely.

A woman is told: 'On this matter of finding a husband for your daughter, you can't just choose around the country among other people: this is something between *nagurng* and *ngalgurng*. Give your full *nagurng* your first daughter, with the first blood. You are not to give her to someone who doesn't speak *gungurng* language with you. . . . ' A man is told: 'You are to give [things] to your *ngalgurng*, you are to work for her and find food for her. If that girl is small, you can't refuse her anything you have, even large things. You are not to eat and fill yourself with food. Work for her and for her mother and father. If there is quarrelling, you are to stand by your *ngalgurng*.' The statement continues, outlining more impersonally the proper behaviour for a son-in-law: 'Nobody is to strike her before his eyes – he can't look at her blood; if they spear her, he may fly into a rage and break them in pieces . . . . If he gets honey, he is not to give it to others, only to her father and mother, because they gave him their little daughter. Others too, the girl's *gagag* and *belu*, *maga* and *mamam*, they share the food and meat that he brings. If he spears a fat kangaroo, he is not to give any to his own father and mother. They say, "Don't give it to us, take it to your *ngalgurng*, who gave you your betrothed wife." His *ngalgurng* doesn't cut that meat with a knife. If she were to cut it roughly, then next time he went looking for honey he would find all of the bees dead. And she doesn't break the bone, using an axe, but her husband cuts the meat into small pieces for her. . . . ' And so on.

This statement and others like it imply that a man does not move too far from his betrothed wife and her immediate relatives. The warning is sometimes made explicit, that he *should* not stay away from her in case she becomes too friendly with a boy nearer her own age: he should make sure she becomes used to him, 'taking food from his hand' without shyness, so that later on she will make no fuss about accepting him as a husband.

The food-giving aspect of the transaction is viewed as entirely appropriate between full or close *nagurng* and *ngalgurng* – in fact, as an intrinsic part of the relationship. But, because of the room for choice in any particular case, it is potentially more than that. The issue of gifts and services could tip the balance in favour of one *nagurng* rather than another, although it seems to be much less significant here than in eastern Arnhem Land. How far it actually influences decisions in making the initial selection is hard to assess, because so little is said about it in that connection. The matter is raised more often in relation to betrothals that have already been arranged, or are already being contemplated because they seem desirable on other grounds (such as kinship and propinquity). Threats of withdrawal – of the girl on one hand, the goods and services on the other – are nothing out of the ordinary in quarrels. They represent an explicit acknowledgment of the bargaining potential inherent in the exchange.

In one case where this issue came up in preliminary betrothal discussions, it was combined with several others – spatial proximity, regional differences, and a daughter's duty to care for her parents in return for what they had done for her. The girl was an only child. Her mother and mother's brothers from Djalbangur (Wadjag *gunmugugur*) and mother's 'mothers' from Gurudjmug (Djelama *gunmugugur*) wanted to marry her to a Gurudjmug man, a close *nagurng* of her mother. Her father (and his brothers), from Gumadir (Maiirgulidj *gunmugugur*), opposed them because, the father said, 'She wasn't born in the south, where you come from, but here in the north among us. We don't want her to go to another country where she can't give meat and such things to her fathers . . . . ' The argument went on for several years. The girl herself was in the Oenpelli mission dormitory, and so the matter was not viewed as urgent. By 1949-50, when she was about ten years old, the discussions were becoming more heated, especially since her father considered she was old enough to marry while her mother disagreed and was obviously reluctant to be separated from her. The girl herself knew about the dispute. Apart from what she heard at first hand, betrothal and marriage were talked about freely among girls of her age and younger. But she played a passive part and would not express an opinion – even to her mother (so her mother reported). About four years later she was married to her father's choice (see

(to page 99)

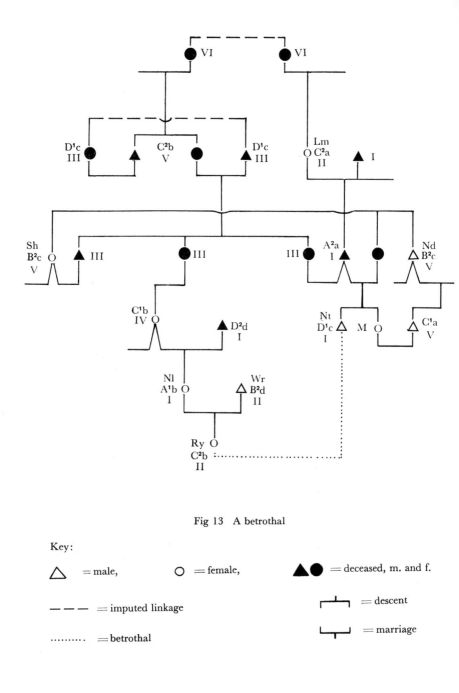

Fig 13 A betrothal

Key:

△ = male,   ○ = female,   ▲● = deceased, m. and f.

- - - = imputed linkage   ⌐⌐ = descent

.... = betrothal   ⌐⌐ = marriage

A1, A2, B1, etc. = subsections (see Tables 2 and 3).
a, b, c and *d* = semi-moieties (see Table 1).
I, II, etc. = *gunmugugur* affiliations. That is: I = Wadjag, II = Maiirgulidj,
    III = Wurig, IV = Djelama, V = Ngalngbali, VI = Madjawar.
Lm, M, etc. = abbreviations of personal names. That is:

Lm	= Mandjalima	Nl	= Ngalgindali	Sh	= Gararu
M	= Medeg	Nt	= Nalbret	Wr	= Wurungungu
Nd	= Nawundurba	Ry	= Guluwirid		

Notes on Fig. 13:

(a) Nalbret is also married to Mandjuraidj, who is Danig; her mother was Wadjag, Ngalgindali's FBD. His first, 'true' betrothed wife was the daughter of one of Mandjuraidj's mother's sisters by her first husband, Rul *gunmugugur*. She was also C2b; she died young. Mandjuraidj's first husband was Madjawar, the son of Gararu by her second husband.

(b) Mandjalima's second and third husbands were Durmangga, half-brothers (D2c and D1d), and her two daughters from them married Nalbret; but the mother of Medeg's husband was Madalg. Mandjalima has a close brother from a common *wulubulu* (MMM) at Goulburn Island, who identifies himself as Gunwinggu; his wife, a close sister of Wurungungu from a common *wulubulu*, identifies herself as Maung.

(c) Ngalgindali's father's mother was Maiirgulidj, her MFM was Durmangga, her MFFM Buru, and her MMFM Gamurgban.

(d) Ngalgindali calls Nalbret and his sister *nagurng* and *ngalgurng*; Mandjalima she called *djedje* (reciprocal *garang*, 'mother'); Gararu she called *mamam*, as the wife of a *gagag*, but Nawundurba was *nabiningobeng*, 'husband', because she was once betrothed to him. Neither he nor her first betrothed husband (his half-brother, also Ngalngbali, from a Wadjag mother) ratified their claims to her. She first called Wurungungu *ganjulg*, 'cross-cousin', and then *ngaba*, 'father'.

(e) Well before 1966, Mandjalima, Nawundurba, Gararu, and Nalbret's mother were all dead. One of Nawundurba's sons by one of Mandjalima's daughters (Durmangga) was married to the daughter of Ngalgindali's half-brother (same father). One of Nawundurba's daughters from the same mother had as second husband Marwana (now dead), the Madjawar son of Gararu (see Fig. 20, Chapter 7; her third husband was Balada, in that figure); her daughter from him, born in 1954, was betrothed to Wurungungu but not expected to marry him.

Fig. 13). This was a not-so-close *gagali*, in a genealogically traceable connection, with the added advantage that he belonged to the same *gunmugugur* as her mother (Wadjag) and that he lived in the same area as her parents. (By 1968 she had five children, four boys and a girl, and both her parents appeared to be very much bound up with them emotionally.)

In first-choice unions, then, husband and wife are genealogically related as *gagali*. In second-choice unions they are genealogically related as *ganjulg*, cross-cousins; once they marry they call each other *gagali*, too, but only as a courtesy term – they are 'not real *gagali*'. If two *gagali* are sweethearts even for a short time, and never marry, they may go on referring to each other as -*gobeng*, 'spouse'. Conversely, if this term 'spouse' comes up in response to the question 'What do you call him (or her)?', it at once suggests such a relationship, in the past if not in the present.

In cross-cousin marriages, the timing of betrothal is particularly crucial. If such a betrothal is confirmed quite early in a girl's life by relatives, above all by her mother and mother's brother, and preferably at the time of her birth, that in itself legitimizes it for practical purposes – but not to the extent of identifying it with the ideally correct type of marriage. However, if that opportunity lapses and no betrothal is arranged between them, the cross-cousin relationship may change as far as terms are concerned so that the two call each other by the terms for 'father' (*ngaba*) and 'daughter' (*gulun*). (The change of term seems to take place usually before the girl reaches puberty.) From that point on, marriage between them is regarded as wrong, but not outrageously so. We recorded a scattering of instances in early marital histories of people who were elderly in 1947, as well as in current unions. Their formal shortcomings were frankly admitted to the extent of labelling them 'wrong', but without the aura of shame and defensiveness that still surrounds 'really wrong' (for example, intra-moiety) unions. Because the *nagurng-ngalgurng* relationship is identified so closely with the mother-in-law – son-in-law relationship, in practice the terms are often used in this second (affinal-category) sense even when there is no appropriate genealogical link.

De facto gagali and *nagurng-ngalgurng* are expected to behave substantially as if their bonds were 'real'—that is, as if they were based on genealogical ties. A man has the usual obligations toward his actual mother-in-law, his wife's mother, including partial avoidance, but what is uncertain is how far he and she are obliged or entitled to use the special *gungurng* vocabulary in speaking together. It is the only proper medium of conversation in this affinal relationship, but ideally it is restricted to 'real' *nagurng-ngalgurng*, where the genealogical connection is traceable or implied. The solution in the past was possibly some kind of compromise, but today the trend is toward dropping the *gungurng* vocabulary in any circumstances, these included.

Otherwise, minor departures from the ideal marriage type do not attract much notice in the ordinary way. They are most likely to come to the surface in arguments and quarrels. A husband and wife in such circumstances have a ready-made grievance that either of them can use, even after years of marriage. They can accuse each other of being only *ganjulg* and not real *gagali*, adding (for instance), 'Those [named] are my *gagali* – I should be married to them, not to you!' 'My mother didn't give me to you [or vice versa]; you're not the right husband [or wife] for me!' Accusations of the same kind are exchanged between son-in-law and mother-in-law too, but mostly indirectly in monologues, or statements addressed to the camp in general without mentioning names.

An example of two formally correct unions in which the second balanced or 'paid for' the first is outlined in Fig. 14.

Close kin on both sides are most active in trying to keep a marriage intact and prevent breaches when it is a formally correct union for which they themselves were responsible. They take steps to break up extra-marital relationships that seem to threaten it, and to discourage marriage with partners they define as unsuitable. A man's close relatives, especially his mother and mother's brother, like to keep an eye on his wife in case she betrays him with someone else, and her close relatives do the same to him. Kinship and marriage interpenetrate, not only in initial arrangements but, even more importantly, in the perpetuating of the union and in the further ramifications deriving from it. A man does not compete for wives with his father. The rule against marriage with two full sisters simultaneously (breaches are rare) lessens the possibility of competition between brothers, and traditional wife-lending arrangements in one respect reduce it still further, but in another exacerbate it – for example, if the wife wants to remain with her temporary spouse while her husband wants her back. This is connected with recognition of primary and secondary spouses, but to discuss that would mean bringing in too much detail for this short overview.

Residence Patterns

Although we speak of residence (more appropriate than 'domicile' with its connotation of settled housing), the Gunwinggu pattern of living was traditionally semi-nomadic – 'semi-' because the region

(to page 104)

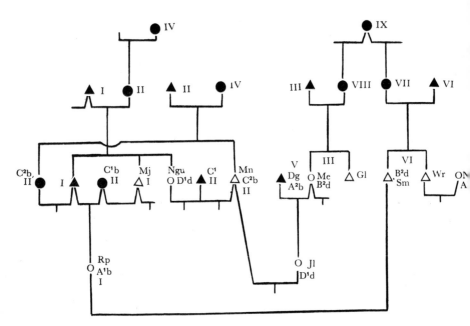

Fig. 14. A marriage exchange.

RITUAL MARAIIN

Painting a maraiin novice with crocodile tongue and red kangaroo designs. Oenpelli, 1950

Emerging from the dua *moiety sacred shade: Goanna men writhe along the ground; men bend over them; the first holds the short-nosed crocodile* maraïin, *and the second, the mosquito. Oenpelli, 1950*

Having emerged from the jiridja *moiety shade, two men posture with diving bird* (galabaibai) *maraiin; behind, and between the singing man (back to picture) and two ritual leaders (clapping hands), is a row of men pulling out the spotted stingray* (mandjir) *maraiin. Oenpelli, 1950*

A row of Gulubar kangaroo men, with the short-nosed crocodile maraiin in the foreground. Singing men and leaders to the right. Oenpelli, 1950

From left to right: *crocodile maraiin; sacred dilly bag held in mouth of posturing man with long mullet (gulbadbad) maraiin; row of Kangaroo men; song men and ritual leaders. Oenpelli, 1950*

General note: The first of the two unions depicted above was that between Gurindjulul and Manggudja, the second that between Yildimbu and Mikinmikin.

Additional notes on Fig. 14:

(a) Other cross-linkages took place in this constellation of persons and units, before and after this particular exchange, but it was this that people singled out for comment. For example, in 1949-50 it was the subject of a current gossip song. As usual, the song included no personal names, but the songman himself supplied them in annotating it. The gist of the song was Yildimbu's complaint that Mikinmikin would not stay with her: 'I've been with him for a long time. He gave my uncle, *ngadjadj* [Manggudja], a girl [Gurindjulul], and my uncles [Manggudja, Namaragalgal, Wurungungu] paid him back with myself. And now he leaves me and goes after other women. They say he has no pay [exchange-commodity, *jurmi*], but he has – he has me!'

(b) Mikinmikin's full sister had one daughter, who married first a Maung-side Gunwinggu (Maninggali) and then a Yiwadja (Gamurgban) man; her daughter (same name as Mareiiga) also married a Maung man (Djelama). Mangurug's brother Midjaumidjau also has a Yiwadja wife. Mareiiga, Namaragalgal, Manggudja, and Wurungungu have close relatives at Goulburn Island, Maung and Gunbalang as well as Gunwinggu.

(c) Mangurug's eldest daughter, Burundi (from her first husband), and the youngest, Nama (from her second husband), were married quite young, Nama for a very short period, to the Gadbam man whose death at Goulburn Island is mentioned in Chapter 7. Burundi's last husband was Yiwadja-Margu, a close MBS of Mangurug. Her second husband (Mandjulngoin) was the father of Balada (see Fig. 20, Chapter 7; Balada's mother was Danig). Balada's second and fourth wives were daughters of Gurindjulul and Manggudja (see Chapter 7, elopement case). Burundi's son (Mandjulngoin) married another daughter of Gurindjulul and Manggudja, and one of the daughters of this union is promised to Yildimbu's and Mikinmikin's younger son. Burundi's daughter (Mandjulngoin) married a Djelama man, and one of the daughters of this union later married one of Namaragalgal's sons. (The boy's mother, who died before 1947, was a sister of Gurweg's son's wife – see Fig. 20.) Nama's second husband was a full brother of another of Namaragalgal's wives (Durmangga; her mother was the MMZ of Mandjuraidj, mentioned in Fig. 13), from whom he had a daughter who married one of Yildimbu's full brothers. Nama's daughter from her current, 'wrong side', husband is betrothed to a son of Gurindjulul and Manggudja (see Chapter 7). Yildimbu's and Mikinmikin's elder son made a sweetheart match with a Margulidjban (Gurulg) girl; this took the form of an official mission-style marriage at Oenpelli, and therefore is seen as blocking his betrothal arrangement with the daughter of Balada and his dead wife (the eldest daughter of Gurindjulul and Manggudja); the girl is still unmarried, but has borne a son whose *gunmugugur* is claimed to be Maninggali.

These are a few of the cross-linkages which could be shown. To include others would mean bringing in further names, and more detailed genealogical diagrams to show the main connections; the actual picture is much more complex. But this should give some idea of the 'density' of social relationships, and the way in which new linkages are built up on the basis of those already there.

(d) Yildimbu and her third child, Gurindjulul's and Manggudja's eldest daughter, and Burundi's daughter were dead by 1958 and both Mangurug and Mareiiga were showing signs of senility, although Mareiiga was still alive in 1968. By 1966, Namaragalgal's third wife was dead too, and by 1968 Burundi's husband.

in which they moved about was usually circumscribed. In this they resembled other Australian Aborigines, with the difference that they did not need to travel so far or move camp so frequently as those in more arid areas.

Changes in life-style following alien contact probably crystallized first and most conspicuously in this sphere of spatial mobility, and they were cumulative. Movement away from the traditional home territories was sporadic and small-scale, and undoubtedly not intended to be permanent. The long-term effect, however, has been almost that. It did not happen all at once. There was some coming and going, and even now a small minority still remains outside the framework of almost total involvement in settlement-centred ways. On mission and government settlements and in timber or buffalo camps, close kin are more often than not together. The tradition of hunting and food-collecting has been maintained, though normally as a part-time adjunct to other activities and as a means of supplementing other foods, and excursions are limited to a day or so's walking distance of the main settlements. The most dramatic change is not so much in this as in overall residence patterns. It is a fundamental change in social relations and in the social environment generally.

Studying the limited movements of small parties today can yield useful information on a number of points – food-collecting and preparation, for instance. What it cannot do is recapture the *social* dimension, the context of relations between groups and between persons. This does not apply only to western Arnhem Land. It is just as relevant to regions like the Western Desert, drained over many years by the pull of the settlements on its fringes. The effect of loss of independent control, and reduced ability to hold full-scale ritual performances, is slower to make itself felt among small residual groups that are trying to retain a semi-nomadic way of life. What *is* noticeable is the skewing of the population and the role-status system by the number and range of 'missing persons'. The shift of population toward settlement-centred residence was apparently accelerated in western Arnhem Land by the establishment of Oenpelli, and World War II and subsequently intensified welfare and mission programmes have virtually consolidated it.

In 1947 and 1949-50, Maningrida had not been started and the Oenpelli staff was still small. Little groups of people were still on the move outside the settlements, but many of them were oriented toward Darwin or the buffalo camps, or made periodical visits to one centre or another even when they did not settle there. To see what the earlier situation might have been like, we fell back on retrospective accounts – the only source of information on that topic, since mission and other records say virtually nothing on it. Our enquiry had two parts to it. One was concentrated on the territorial dimension – the location of various events or gatherings, where people were living on different occasions, and the range of territory over which a given person usually moved. The second was concentrated on the social dimension – who was present during those events or gatherings, and who was living with whom.

In the first, one sort of evidence came from statements like, 'Before, this [cluster of named sites] was where my fathers used to live.' Such statements are still made, fairly consistently. More specifically, in case-history material a series of places can be pinpointed: where a person was born, went through different growth stages, was betrothed, married, participated in this or that ceremony or rite, had (bore) each child, where a spouse or a child or some other close relative died – and so on. Because place of birth or the place where a woman first realized she was pregnant is not critical in religious affairs, as it is in some areas, this consideration does not affect group movements to any extent: a pregnant wife need not be rushed to her husband's country when the birth is imminent. Data on the territorial aspect were quite easy to obtain, especially in 1949-50, from middle-aged and elderly people recalling their past life before they became more or less sedentary. The second aspect, the social, was more elusive. Clearly, case-histories did not mention everyone who was present in the same place at the same time, and we did not explore this avenue systematically for the total population to provide a comprehensive large-scale record. Nevertheless, information on both aspects, social and territorial, is substantial enough to suggest the kind of pattern that may have existed, during a period extending from a little before World War I to the early 1930s.

The characteristic pattern in Aboriginal Australia was one of small dispersed foraging groups that coalesced from time to time into larger units, especially for ceremonial and ritual purposes. These smaller groups tended to be patrilineal and patrilocal in emphasis:

that is, to have a core of agnatic kin and to keep near enough to the patrilineally defined territory, if not actually in it, for adult male members to meet there and perform the rites connected with it. This seems to have been the case among Gunwinggu too, with some modification in detail.

In western Arnhem Land, the population in and around the larger or most popular sites ranged from a single nuclear family to constellations of fifty or so, and more on special occasions. Quite often a combined camp was made up of one or two polygynous families plus parents of any or all of the spouses and other relatives temporarily attached to them. When the husbands were not close brothers or when fathers and adult sons were not in the same camping complex at a given time, at least a few such men (brothers, fathers, sons) were likely to be somewhere in that vicinity.

The major seasonal movements hinged on the wet-dry cycle. As the rains became heavier and low-lying country began to flood, people moved up to higher ground, camping in bark wet-season huts or in 'cave huts'. When the waters retreated and the rains eased they moved down again.

In every territory, and according to season, certain sites were favoured camping-places – with mythical precedent underlining their advantages. A person who wanted to get in touch with others had thus two sources of information for finding out where they were. One was direct evidence, including the assortment of space-and-time clues they had left behind in the physical environment. Some of these were casual, such as footprints, abandoned fires or shelters, branches that had been lopped for cutting out honeycombs, or trees stripped of bark for canoes or huts. Gauging the freshness of the prints, the coolness of the ashes, or dryness of the foliage or wood, provided answers to the question 'How long ago were they here?' Other clues were deliberate, like the long arm of the paper-bark mortuary figure, or a long footmark scraped on the ground to show which way the makers of it had gone. In addition, the searcher might climb to high ground and look for the smoke of fires, and listen for the echo of distant sounds, especially children's voices or the barking of dogs or the chopping of a tree. All of these indicated the presence of people, but not *which* people. For that he might be able to draw on verbal evidence: statements of intention from the people concerned, or probability statements from others.

('Why don't you try such-and-such? They went that way.')

These routine procedures were part of the ordinary course of observation, whether or not a person was specifically in search of anyone. The framework that integrated them was the set of territorial charts or maps built up from mythical and more personalized accounts, and made more 'real' through first-hand experience. In broad terms, these suggested the territorial range outside which people were expected to move less freely. People from around Tor Rock would not ordinarily be found in the Margulidjban area, or vice versa. Gurudjmug people might come to coastal Gumadir, and recognition of sharing a common source of fresh water was paralleled in the sharing of myths and rites, but in certain respects they faced in opposite directions: Gurudjmug had Maiali and Dangbun links and an inland orientation; Gumadir looked to Maung and Gunbalang links, toward the coastal plains and river-estuaries rather than toward the escarpment.

Gunmugugur and genealogical ties broke up this wider picture, supplying cross-linkages and extending or narrowing the usual round of camping or visiting in each case, but the regional perspective has not appreciably altered. For instance, Oenpelli is a meeting-place for Gunwinggu from various regions as well as for members of other 'tribes'. However, Gunwinggu now living at Goulburn Island and Croker Island have a predominantly coastal background, whereas the usual orbit of Maiali-side Gunwinggu lies south and south-west of Oenpelli, toward inland centres outside the Arnhem Land reserve. Thus, although the *gunmugugur* indicate primarily patrilineal descent and territorial affiliation, they are also rough pointers to actual regional distribution. In present circumstances they can be no more than approximate. Nevertheless, for many adult Gunwinggu men in Arnhem Land itself the paternal territory symbolized by the *gunmugugur* still has some significance, and until recently it was a focus in mundane as well as in religious affairs.

Men did not keep only to their *gunmugugur* territory, but from our accounts they showed a preference for spending much of their time there and in immediately adjoining areas – as a few of them still do. And it was in such a territorial constellation that other people would expect to find them. Within that range, they would normally know all the main features: all the *djang* and sacred sites, tabu and otherwise, terrain and vegetation, and distribution of water and foods. The verbal mapping that made this possible was not confined to the spatial dimension. Information on spatial arrangements, answering the question, 'Where ... ?', was not enough. The question of 'When ... ?' was equally important. In other words, time was a necessary ingredient. Two kinds of time were relevant here – in a sense, two *levels* of time. In Gunwinggu thought, they are basically one: the level of the environment-as-given. The first concerns myth and ritual, with its distinctive time perspective. It might be described as a part of the man-made environment, but for Gunwinggu it is not man-made: it rests on a series of 'god-given' events and decrees that are irreversible and unalterable; all that contemporary man can do is recapitulate and sustain them through ritual. The second kind of time, natural or seasonal time, could be described as a part of the physical or natural environment; for Gunwinggu, however, this is directly linked with the sphere of myth and ritual – but it is something that contemporary man can influence, if not actually control. It takes the form of seasonal fluctuations (in rainfall, wind, temperature, and ground conditions) and the associated movements and growth of natural species and growth of plants. It was, traditionally, more immediate in its impact on everyday living because it virtually determined where, within a given range of territory and on ordinary occasions, people were most likely to be. Even the timing of ritual occasions was dependent, for practical as well as for conceptual reasons, on this elemental consideration of seasonal time. At both levels, the emphasis was on bounded change – change within limits. In the purely human sphere, the spatial distribution of people was perceived in the same way, as involving movement and change on more or less predictable lines.

Detailed information and inference were the basic ingredients in this pattern, where residence – discontinuous settlement – was as important as mobility, and where people did not need to live together to have an approximate idea of one another's whereabouts. The usual practice, it seems, was for a number of people to settle at and around a given site when conditions there were suitable, using it as a base. As in myths, they would leave their main belongings and young children in the care of old people, and scatter through the surrounding area for a day or several days at a time. In these small collecting and hunting parties, men and women sometimes went separately and sometimes not, depending on what kind of food they were after. For example, men might spear fish in a billabong while women dived for lily roots not far away. Or a man and his wife and children might move through different parts of the same area and meet at a prearranged place, either spending the night there or returning to the main camp together. The most popular base-camp sites seem to have been, naturally enough, those richest in food resources, whether or not they were close to *djang* or sacred ritual grounds. They were rather like road or railway junctions or well-known halting places – places where a traveller would look first, in searching for people connected with that region through birth or marriage.

Patrilineal, and paternal, associations were indisputably important in this respect. But the normative assumption of patrilocality was not inflexible. For one thing, although women do not hand on their patrilineal associations directly, they have a direct interest in them. It is not only men who express attachment to their paternal territory. And, in references to ownership of a given area, women's names are mentioned along with men's. Because *gunmugugur* are exogamous according to Gunwinggu rules, husband and wife normally come from different territories. If they come from the same or adjacent large countries, the pull in opposite directions was not likely, traditionally, to be much of a problem, and in addition there would be more cross-linkages between them. But another factor is the influence of matriliny, not merely in a lineal sense (that is, in relation to the *gagag* descent line) but also in personal relationships: the personal bond between mother and daughter, and daughter's daughter, and the strong position of a close mother's brother, especially in respect of his sister's son. Traditionally, it was not unusual for a woman to be in the same camping-group as her daughter and daughter's husband for quite long periods. The time factor does not come out at all clearly in retrospect, but the visits seem to have varied from short ones to almost permanent association in the case of widows.

Women are not economically dependent on men for subsistence – on the contrary. The foods collected by women are the most dependable and substantial part of Gunwinggu diet. Although women do not spear kangaroo or catch larger fish, with the help of dogs they can catch small animals like bandicoots and possums as well as goannas, in addition to finding the usual vegetable foods. But it was not, and is not, the practice for women to travel alone or even in pairs over long distances or for more than a day or two at a time. The mythical precedent (many of the First People were lone women, or pairs of adolescent girls) has no counterpart here. Husbands, and betrothed husbands, like to minimize their wives' opportunities for extra-marital affairs. Even if they are not jealous, their prestige is at stake. If a man setting out on a journey without his wife does not ask a close brother to look after her (implying a sexual relationship), he expects older women in the same camp to see that she remains faithful to him. By the time a widow is too old to be re-allocated, she is also too old to do much active wandering about by herself. In addition, Gunwinggu women seem more reluctant to camp alone for long, without a man's company, than some of the eastern Arnhem Landers are. (Until quite recently, on the north-eastern side of Arnhem Land, small groups of women would spend several days together away from their husbands, collecting specific foods like seagull eggs – but only if they were middle-aged and older in local reckoning. In a large polygynous family, a man liked to keep his young wives under his eye but allowed the others much more latitude.)

Men, however, frequently move about alone or in pairs. And outside the circumstances of religious ritual, in any small camping-group, ordinary decisions on 'where to go next' appear to have rested with a husband or his father. A woman joins in discussions, puts her point of view, and perhaps argues or quarrels, but in any real clash of opinion she is usually the one to give way. Personality factors influence her response and the way the decision is arrived at, and older women have more say than younger ones, but claims of male authority are not merely a convenient fiction. Men have, or had, more sanctions at their disposal. Also, because men control the major religious rites they are able to organize easily on a group basis – whereas women did not, traditionally, unite to form an active front vis-à-vis men.

Interpersonal relations between husband and wife, and the wider field of relations between men and women, are not directly affected by the factor of descent. Nevertheless, descent is not only the main ordering principle in kinship and marriage arrangements, and in membership of various units. A more diffuse influence can be ascribed to it, too.

Patrilineal descent is significant, above all, in respect of two features: land, and the complex of sacred belief and ritual. Both of these are fundamental goods, tangible and visible pointers to the dimension of the non-empirical or transcendental. They are the pre-eminent symbols of continuity, retrospectively and also in regard to the future. In the various categories based on matrilineal descent, however, the emphasis is on social relations as such – in themselves, and not as reflecting important realities outside them or as keys to group involvement of the same order. Similarly, the *gunmugugur* of a person's mother, and of his paternal and maternal grand-mothers, have a bearing not only on intermarriage but also on choice of 'tribal' or socio-linguistic affiliation. Where the matrilineal moieties and semi-moieties are important ritually, this is in the context of patriliny, or organized within that framework. Men use matrilineal descent for certain purposes, in relation to the foci of patrilineal descent: land-holding, sacred ritual, and the production of children to maintain these in a patrilineal sequence. Women use it in reference to bearing children (stressing the mother–daughter link), and arranging suitable marriages for their daughters so that this matrilineal continuity is ensured in what they regard as the proper way.

It is not so much that men and women are brought up to see things differently, although to some extent that is certainly true. In spite of *indirect* continuities (for example, linking father and daughter, mother and son), patrilineal and matrilineal descent as such are both acknowledged as significant. The question of which is more important is rarely raised. When it is, the answers vary according to circumstance and speaker. Their spheres of reference are distinct enough, and their interdependence is strong enough, to minimize serious strain between them – even in the simplified way they are usually conceptualized, as lines of descent through females or through males, in both cases highlighting a brother–sister pair in each generation.

Chapter Six

The Sacred and the Secret

THE GUNWINGGU SHARE with all other Australian Aborigines a traditional focus on belief and activity that can be described as magico-religious. Within this sphere are to be found not only basic cultural values, but explanation – in non-empirical terms – of the earth and the universe around them as they know it, and as they experience its semblance of continuity within the context of predictable change. In other words, in this dimension reasons for life-as-it-is are sought, and found. The reasons are mythic, and purport to explain or justify virtually all aspects of social and cultural life: religion is relevant to all aspects of living. Myth is the explanatory counterpart of real life, and in its ritual manifestation it is part of real life.

Traditionally, religion was *the* major integrating force. It was not so much that Gunwinggu were intensely religious or preoccupied with religion. Religion was built into their way of life, taken for granted. At certain periods and in relation to specific cults it was highlighted and religious feeling and action were more intense. Also, the structure of religious action was stratified, in terms of leaders and adherents, initiates and novices, men and women, and so on. But religion as such was accepted by everyone, at least at the level of conformity-in-action, which was all that was asked of them, and everyone – men, women and children – participated in varying degrees.

The Gunwinggu and their neighbours shared a closeness with nature and a direct dependence on it – a preoccupation that is reflected not only in their mythology, but also in ritual activity. They saw themselves as an integral part of their physical environment, not set apart from all the other living things within it but having an intimate relationship with them. This relationship and the kind of spiritual identification it involves have been called totemic, but the term has some disadvantages.

To put it briefly, all human and other beings are believed to share a common life-essence, derived from the major creative spirits – the original creators. The primary factor distinguishing mythical beings from contemporary men and the creatures around them on which they depend was their shape-changing propensity. In the creative era they were either man or other natural species as the context demanded. They could change their shape – but not their character. In many instances, they turned into something else when their tasks (of creation or of establishing some custom or practice) were completed, or because their predestined period of life in one particular form had come to an end. (See Chapter 2.) While they set a pattern of living for the oncoming generations, they did not sever their connection with those 'new generations'. A binding *social* relationship was established and maintained, in supra-kin terms, with each person, mainly through *gunmugugur* territorial group membership. Through this channel in particular, man kept the same sacred essence held by the major beings and also by the *djang*.

Patrilineal descent is of predominant significance in all sacred ritual. Matrilineal descent in broader social terms is also relevant in religious matters. Through these links, the sacred past lives on in the present. But its contemporary manifestations do not live on only through human beings, and in one sense they are believed to be independent of man. The First People died or changed shape or became rocks, but in essence they were indestructible: and their outward shape, although relevant in everyday terms, was in fact irrelevant in religious terms. A rock site, a tangible manifestation of a particular spirit being, was evidence of its existence, its eternal presence in that country and its awareness of the needs of man.

A *djang* which turned into an animal or bird or some other creature left in *every* representative of that particular species a living, observable example of its original form, and of its character and its spirit; the Rainbow is the *original* Ngaljod snake, and with the same relevance to man as she always had.

Gunwinggu religious expression is directly related to the country and what it contains. The great ritual cycles are concerned with this, with fertility, and with the coming and going of the seasons. The main spirit beings symbolize in our terms, activate in Aboriginal terms, the cyclical progression of life – growth and depletion and, then, through ritual intervention, renewal. It is in this respect that they are inseparable from, yet independent of, man. It is not that coercion on man's part is necessary to achieve continuity. These beings are not unpredictable, any more than are the coming and going of the wet and dry seasons, the growing of grass and its drying and burning off, insemination and birth and death, and revivification in one form or another. The seasons in general are predictable, just as the spirit beings are – their characters, their purposes, were defined in the creative era and are in themselves changeless. It is, rather, that man has a part to play, a part that they established. They themselves in the mythical era carried out ritual to sustain the condition of life that they created, and man continues that tradition. They instituted ritual, not only for themselves but also for man.

This theme recurs in the sacred myths and songs. The sacred beings are of man and yet independent of him. Man uses ritual to re-establish or maintain contact with them, and in doing so ensures the continuity of life which all, man and sacred beings, hold in common.

The usual word for what men do on the sacred ground in general terms, *-jimeran* (-yimeran), is sometimes translated as 'making [themselves]'. (The basic stem, *-jime* or *-jimi*, means 'say', 'make' or 'do', and this is what could be called a reflexive form.) It is also one way of describing the final transition of the First People: *birijimeran djang*, 'they became *djang*'. The idea of transformation is inherent in it: 'becoming' something else – in this context, becoming 'set apart', sacred.

Ritual represents, symbolically, the actions of the sacred beings. It re-creates the state of affairs they first formalized, and the songs that are sung during ritual performances are believed to reproduce, or recount, the events in which they were involved. Each rite is primarily a religious experience and part of a predestined scheme, but it is also instructional and revelatory. Knowledge must be handed on, and it is within this context of secret-sacred ritual that novices are taught.

The Social Dimension

Gunwinggu initiation does not include a physical operation or test as it does in many other cultural regions in Aboriginal Australia. Circumcision and subincision have not been adopted to any extent, except on the fringes. The major trials of novices consist of learning at varying levels the significance, actual and symbolic, of the great cycles and gradually becoming active participants. It is a process of incorporation and acceptance into the secret-sacred life of fully initiated men. Associated with the stages the initiates must go through are various food tabus. These tabus emphasize the sacred quality of their initiatory state and at the same time signify their lifelong dependence on the sacred essence of the creatures involved. The tabus are on eating, not on killing, and they have a direct bearing on socio-economic activity – withholding from one section of the community, for instance, some food that is available to another section, or encouraging one sort of activity in contrast to another. (See Chapter 3.) Food tabus are nearly always on a personal basis and of limited duration, but some affect a wider range of people and others apply to everyone not classified as 'old'. This is not a question of some (for example, the old) looking after their own interests at the expense of others. It is, rather, a matter of economic balance, even though this is phrased in religious terms and supported by supernatural sanctions.

Secret-sacred activity is controlled by men, whereas in ordinary sacred activity both sexes participate. Male novices are not classified with women. There is simply the recognition that, as males, they can expect to be drawn more and more actively into secret-sacred affairs. Girls face much the same kind of situation, but less specifically, as novices vis-à-vis older women. In the conventional Gunwinggu expressions, men 'go up' to their secret-sacred ground, where the most crucial ritual acts take place, and they 'go down' to the main camp or to any other place outside that ground. This contrast has nothing to do with the actual level of the terrain, as it does in the ordinary way. It is a symbolic contrast, one that applies to that particular circumstance and not to the performers as such – for instance, it is used for the rare cases where women are admitted to the secret ground and the mythical incidents where that ground was temporarily in their hands. A woman who is old, almost blind and 'almost dead', is admitted to the men's secret-sacred *ubar* or *maraiin* ground accompanied by (for example) a son or a 'father' because at that stage of her life the danger is said to be negligible – 'the Mother is no longer jealous of her'. Some women have declined on the score that they were afraid, others have died before they had the opportunity, and probably the total number who have attended is very small. Including three old women who were still living in 1950, on a tentative count at that time twenty-one were reported to have gone to the *ubar* ground, eighteen of these and one other to the men's *lorgun* ground, and thirteen of them to the *maraiin*.

All ritual performance illustrates the interplay of kinship responsibility and obligations. Certain kin serve as guardians of a novice, others aid in revealing sacred objects. Parents, actual and otherwise, have duties to perform, such as providing presents for initiators and participants, or weeping conventionally as a son is taken to the ritual ground. A father may instigate proceedings for his son, the young man's mother prepares decorations for him and is partially segregated or 'set apart' during his initiatory rites, and his wife or betrothed wife observes particular food tabus on account of his ritual state. Ritual sequences are normally arranged by senior members or leaders of territorial units, for example, on behalf of men who want their sons to be initiated.

The performances call for a great deal of preparatory work from both men and women, in assembling food and gifts and in making or refurbishing ritual paraphernalia. Also, they require people – more than are locally available at any one time, in any one camp, and so messengers must be sent out to summon visitors. These visitors are not simply onlookers, but participants and dancers; they are performing a duty and expect to be compensated, and later to have their efforts reciprocated. Moreover, the internal organization of any ritual represents a definition of what members of one moiety and its component semi-moieties should do, in that context, in relation to as well as in contrast to the other(s). Different moieties are essentially both complementary and cooperative.

Control, leadership and rights in performing sacred ritual and making the associated objects are patrilineally inherited, and the eastern Arnhem Land moieties of *dua* and *jiridja* simplify this transmission. A man's significant relatives on the ritual ground are his *ngadjadj* (MB – see Key to Table 4) and *ganggin* (ZS), his *gagali*, and his brothers from the same father. These last are graded for ritual purposes with himself and his father, since elder brothers serve as intermediaries between their younger brothers and their fathers, and are members of the same *gunmugugur*. Excluding them, *ngadjadj*, *ganggin* and *gagali* are of the opposite patrilineal moiety and thus represent ideal helpers and cooperators.

To look at this social dimension in any depth would involve a tremendous amount of detail, and so would a fuller account of myth and ritual. As far as rites are concerned, no two performances are exactly alike, but we shall focus on what the people themselves claimed to be the most important points.

Sacred Myths

The complex framework of role and positioning, defining who does what for whom and in what context and in relation to what others, is supported directly and indirectly, symbolically and actually, by mythology. The mythical ties of the instigators and the leaders are immediately relevant.

The three major ritual sequences apart from the mortuary *lorgun* (the *mangindjeg* rites are subsidiary) are the *ubar, maraiin* and *kunapipi* (or *gunabibi*), and dominating the scene in each of them is the Mother, sometimes called 'Old Woman'. She is essentially a Fertility Mother, responsible for creating much that is on the land and in the sea as well as the progenitors of present-day human beings.

In her guise of Ngaljod, the Rainbow (see Chapter 2), her relevance is very wide indeed. In this form she is sometimes called *gagag*, mother's mother, rather than 'mother', regardless of the affiliations of the speaker. Several women's versions, in particular, insist on her priority – as in this one, from old Ngalmidul. 'She came underground from "Macassar", to Madabir, near Cooper's

Creek, bringing children inside her – people, who later made more people. She made us talk like people, she gave us understanding [sense]. She made our feet, cut fingers for us, made our eyes for seeing with, made our heads, made anger and peace for us, made our belly/intestines, gave us energy to move about – made us *people*. Ngalgulerg [a mythical woman] gave us women the digging stick and the basket we hang from our foreheads, and Gulubar Kangaroo gave men the spear-thrower. But that Snake that we call *gagag* – we would have died of thirst if she hadn't urinated, making water for us. Now, if it's a bit dry, we dig to get water [that she put there for us]. And she showed us how to dig for food and how to eat it, good foods and bitter foods. She told those that she bore first, who became *djang*, those who prepared the territory for us, and they made us. And she put *gunmud* for us . . . [see Chapter 4]. Those First People, she scraped them with a mussel shell when they were born, until she saw their skins were lighter, and she licked them all over . . . And now, when we are inside our mothers she gives us breath, and shapes our bodies . . . . '

As Waramurungundji, the Mother is rather like the Djanggawul (Djang?gau) Sisters of eastern Arnhem Land, although she is said to have come from 'Macassar' (Manggadjara or Munanga) – in other words, as mentioned earlier, from somewhere to the north-west beyond Melville and Bathurst islands. Different versions of her story tell of her adventures on the mainland in company with her husband, Wuragag, and several of his relatives. In one instance she discovered, some time after having coitus with him, that she had forgotten her digging stick, and returned to the spot to find it lodged in the ground. As she pulled it out, spring water gushed forth. Later on, she forgot her digging stick again, and, when she remembered, turned to tell Wuragag. He asked where she had left it. She started to say, 'At the place where we last had coitus,' but before she could utter the last word he slapped her across the mouth, rebuking her: 'If you say that openly, it will spoil the new generation [the people to come].' His prudishness upset her, and (in this version) that was why she left him, taking her daughter. Later she went in search of him, but in the meantime, after many adventures, he had turned himself into what is now called Tor Rock. She herself eventually reached the caves at Benewilngugngug (a Charcoal name), where she and her daughter also became rocks.

RITUAL KUNAPIPI

Within the ganala *trench of the kunapipi. As invocations are called, initiates lay hands upon the central actor. Around the inner sides of the* ganala, *incised designs represent Ngaljod. Oenpelli, 1950*

Kunapipi actor, with Ngaljod and eggs design on his back, awaits the placing of hands upon him. Oenpelli, 1950

Pushing over the jelmalandji *or Ngaljod in the final stages of the kunapipi.*
Oenpelli, 1950

A kunapipi camp at Oenpelli, 1968. Men sit in the shade singing

She instituted girls' puberty rites – one myth reports in detail how she looked after her own daughter at such a time – and she left instructions on various menstrual and other tabus. The place-name itself is in Maung, because she chose that as her final language, but her daughter chose Gunwinggu . . . 'because Maung is too harsh, Gunwinggu is my language.'

In one sense, the creative and ritual leaders who came after the Mother or were contemporary with her were simply her agents. They are not viewed in that way – they are never specifically categorized as agents or as intermediaries. But they differ from her in one important respect: whatever else they created, they did not create human beings.

The major mythical originator of the *ubar* rituals is Yirawadbad, a venomous snake. However, Nadulmi (or Narol?mi; one name for a large male kangaroo) is usually regarded as their principal leader. It is said that Yirawadbad showed him the *ubar* at Wadbal, Junction Bay River, one of the most important *ubar* centres in western Arnhem Land and Nadulmi's birthplace. But also closely associated with it are Balnugnug and Barlgulobi, two Dog brothers, and the Kangaroo husband and wife pair, Gulubar and Garurgen. The Yirawadbad myth exists in several versions, but its main theme remains constant. (See Chapter 2, and Fig. 21; also R. and C. B., 1951*a*: 120-6; 1964: 211.) When his young wife refused to accept him, he turned himself into a snake and killed not only her but her mother as well. To do this, he first worked sorcery on the girl. Then he prepared a hollow log, entered it, and attracted the attention of the two women, who were out hunting. They put their hands into the log in search of the small animal they thought was there, and he 'bit' each of them in turn. Then he emerged in snake form, looked at their corpses, and spoke to himself (and to posterity) justifying what he had done. This was at Gwiugi, not far from Tor Rock.

After that, in the *ubar*-oriented section of the myth, Yirawadbad travelled over wide sections of the country. He was a snake, but he was also a man. At Gumadbari he cut a *magu*, a drone-pipe or didjeridu, and threw it away so that it broke into two parts; one fell at Angu on Cooper's Creek, and the other near Wadbal. The Wadbal half drifted downstream and he found it floating at Gumara, on Junction Bay River; it floated on, and finally dived down at Mandjululg (a mythical Dog name) and became a long reef. At this time, Yirawadbad met a woman named Miralaidj, from the Malag people to the east: significantly, she can perhaps be identified with the younger Djanggawul Sister of that name. The hollow log Yirawadbad made is represented now by the *ubar* drum, the focus of the rites.

After the *ubar* sequence had been handed on to him by Yirawadbad, Nadulmi asked Djig (a bird, something like an owl), 'Shall we show it to women and children?' In response, Djig jumped, throwing his spear at the *ubar* drum, and as it touched the drum the sacred ground spread out: 'We can't show that *ubar* to women and children, it is only for older men!' It is interesting that, although Nadulmi was the leader, Djig and Gudul (mopoke), both associated with hollow trees and logs, are credited with making the hollow *ubar* drum in its ritual form.

Nevertheless, in contrast to Djig's statement, several myth versions claim that women were first in possession of *ubar* ritual or had an equal opportunity to control it. (See, for instance, R. and C. B., 1951a: 122; 1964: 215; C. B., 1965: 269.) In the Nadulmi myth, four Galgbeid Red Wallaby men performed what is now the women's *ubar* dancing, calling out *Gaidba! gaidba!* (or *Goiʔbo! goiʔbo!*) – women's conventional response to the beating of the drum and men's cry of *Gogjei!* Meanwhile, Kangaroo women were busy on the secret-sacred ground. However, 'the men were not good at this [the dancing and calling], and so the women took it over while the men went up to the sacred ground'. In another version also, when men first tried to dance but women did it properly, that is why Djig got angry and said, 'The *ubar* belongs to men, it is not for women!' He threw spears at the women, sending them back to the main camp to dance and call out *Gaidba!* In other accounts the central figure is Garurgen Kangaroo woman, sister of Balnugnug and wife of Gulubar. But from that point onward male and female *ubar* roles are reversed: men go to the secret *ubar* ground, and Garurgen calls out *Gaidba!* from the main camp. Large groups of people come to join her, but 'she drives the men away with her cry, sending them to the secret-sacred ground'. Women's mythical association with what is now men's secret ritual is reported from many parts of Aboriginal Australia. In some areas they are said to have been the original owners of such ritual, and to have lost it only through the trickery of men. (See, for example, R. B. 1952a:

39-40; R. and C. B., 1964: 214-16; C. B., 1965: 268-73.)

Women sometimes call the Ubar Woman Ngaldjorlbu: 'She is like *mai*?, like Ngaljod, she looks like a woman and carries a digging stick. She is like a mother to those boys, looking after them and feeding them – but when they first go there she kills them, and then makes them alive again.' On other occasions, women said, 'She is their wife, she gives them food, and she is jealous of them. They are her husbands, those boys.' But women also say that the *ubar* is 'a mother ritual for all of us'. 'She is our mother.' 'All of us everywhere, dark skin or light skin, people of every place and of different languages – we all call her mother, our true mother, who made herself *djamun* [tabu, set apart] for us.'

Responsibility for the *maraiin* rituals is attributed to two male spirits, Laradjeidja (*jiridja* moiety) and Gundamara (*dua* moiety), who called each other *gagali*. Significantly, they are said to have come 'from Giwidji, east of Milingimbi, near Mululu creek [relevant to the Wulagi and Yanalag language units]'. Mululu is possibly the important Muruwul waterhole, associated with the Wawalag myth of eastern Arnhem Land (Two Sisters and Python or Rainbow Snake – see R.B., 1951*a*.) The two men, Laradjeidja and Gundamara, possessed *maraiin* objects wrapped in paperbark, which they carried in a pandanus basket and 'sold' to people at various places.

Lumaluma the Whale is also a dominant *maraiin* personage. He too came from the east, travelling overland, while accompanying him beneath the ground (some women say) came Ngaljod the Rainbow; and his mythology has many direct parallels with the eastern Arnhem Land Djanggawul. In Chapter 3, we mentioned Lumaluma in connection with abuse of sacred food tabus. He was a powerful and terrifying person, a *dua* moiety ritual leader, with many wives and children. In some accounts, when men and women (that is, the first of the 'new generation' of human beings) were out in canoes, he would capture the women but kill the men and later cook them in an oven. While the meat was cooling he would dance his *maraiin*, and when he had finished he would eat. In other accounts, he ate only children.

His myth is linked with the myth of Laradjeidja and Gundamara. These two erected a *maraiin* shade or shelter at Guwulabulu, on the coast, and Lumaluma in the distance saw smoke rising from it.

He was angry, either because (in one version) one of his wives had been promised to another man and attempts had been made to recover her or because (in another) he was the first to have *maraiin* and 'the others were not performing the rites properly'. He therefore went to Guwulabulu and accused the *maraiin* men of blocking his creek. They rushed away from the ground in fear. Some of their *maraiin* objects they left behind. Others they took with them, as they jumped into a nearby billabong. Lumaluma threw spears at each object in turn, calling the names of different creatures, and, straight away, each of them took the shape that he named. Then he gathered up some of the remaining objects and took them back to 'Murungga Island' in the Crocodile Islands. The *maraiin* men were angry, and planned to kill him. Later they held another *maraiin* sequence, and Lumaluma insisted on attending it against the advice of his relatives. There he was speared to death, in this version by Djinba and Balamumu (eastern Arnhem Land) people. But before he died he showed them all his *maraiin*: he took out all his ritual objects, danced, sang, and called all the sacred invocations and *gunmugugur* names (see Chapter 4). Finally, they buried him and erected a mortuary post to which they attached his stolen wife's armband, but his spirit became a whale (in one version, 'like Ngaljod') and swam out to sea. At Guwulabulu, *maraiin* objects are said to drift in on the tide from those First People who jumped into the billabong in fear of Lumaluma.

In the *kunapipi* myth-ritual sequence, two major characters are the Nagugur father and son, spirit beings in human form, each accompanied by his wife. Sections of the myth resemble the eastern Arnhem Land Wawalag. The *kunapipi* ritual complex extends over much of the Northern Territory, with broadly similar procedures, sacred objects and key words. (See R. B., 1951*a*.) The western Arnhem Land constellation diverges from others in its mythology, more particularly in regard to the principal characters.

The Nagugur myth and related song cycles are very long, and women's versions as well as men's cover unusually large stretches of country. References to fertility abound – the growing of vegetable and plant foods and new grass shoots, the nesting of birds, eggs, and so forth – and the story is rich in symbolic allusions. At various times and places, in the course of their travels, the Nagugur perform parts of the *kunapipi* sequence. They are self-rejuvenating or self-perpetuating – the myth leaves room for differing interpretations. One group comes from 'Macassar', travels from one site to another, terminates its journey, and then continues on as another lot of Nagugur. In one version, the Nagugur carry Ngaljod, the Rainbow Snake (an integral part of the *kunapipi* ritual, here as in other areas): they are said to have taken the Snake from Lumaluma, the Snake's 'mother' (although Lumaluma is usually classified as a man), wrapped up in paperbark as a *maraiin* object.

Wherever the Nagugur go, but not necessarily at every small place they visit, they leave sacred objects and perform ritual 'for the new people'. In some cases, they bury such objects for men to find. The mythology also implies that the *kunapipi* is dangerous and antithetical to other rituals. (See Chapter 7.) For instance, at Dilibam, a little east of the Liverpool River, people died after putting feather-down on their bodies for the performance of the first *kunapipi* there. At Dagaiala, a little farther on, the Nagugur stumbled over a group of *ubar* novices waiting in the tall grass – who smelt them, and vomited or died. The Nagugur were covered with blood and grease. Blood and coitus are two major themes in their mythology. The elder Nagugur is sometimes said to have 'made' male and female genitals.

Also, as in the *ubar* mythology, women first possessed *kunapipi* ritual or were involved in it along with their menfolk. A mother Kangaroo tried to call out ritually like the men (the special *djangarg* or *kunapipi* ritual call), but could not manage it. The Nagugur told her to perform women's dancing, and the male Gulubar called out ritually in her place. This is the 'reason' women are now excluded from sections of the *kunapipi*. (Note the resemblance to part of the *ubar* mythology.) In another context, the wives of the Nagugur were killed because they heard the secret-sacred singing associated with the erection of the *jelmalandji* structure, representing Ngaljod.

As regards circumcision, the myths that justify Gunwinggu rejection of it are not linked with the *kunapipi*. In one account, Waramurungundji first tried unsuccessfully to introduce it. Another myth is interesting for its separation of Gunwinggu and Gunbalang from Dangbun and Maiali. The central character is an old man, Stone-knife-carrier or Penis *djang*, also responsible for cycad-palm ceremonial food. He came from the far side of the Dangbun, circumcising all the boys he could find. Everything went well in

Djalbangur – here placed in Dangbun territory, though often classed as Gunwinggu. Then he came north to circumcise Gunwinggu and Gunbalang and introduce the *mindiwala* dancing, but the first novice he cut, in Gurudjmug, died straight away. Men assembled for the rite flung spears at him and drove him back the way he had come: 'You Maiali and Gundaidnjebmi [Gundjeibmi, Maiali-Dangbun] and Gundjauan, you can do this – but we won't, we Gunwinggu and Gunbalang!' (The word for 'circumcised', *-djoleng*, is ordinarily used for 'cooked' food or 'ripe' fruits; 'uncircumcised', *-gug*, is, among other meanings, 'uncooked', 'raw', 'unripe'.)

Much of all this mythology, like the *djang* mythology proper, is not claimed to be indigenous to the Gunwinggu area. The principal sacred beings all came from outside of it, and some of the longer myths recount events in far distant areas. The *maraiin* mentions groups on the eastern fringe of western Arnhem Land (Gadjalibi, Gungurugoni, Gunavidji, Gundjirbara, Nagara, Burara), and others still farther east (some clans and linguistic units of eastern Arnhem Land, generally called Malag: Wulagi, Ganadi, Yanalag, Djambarbingu, Gubabingu, Ridarngu, and Djinba), as well as the more distant Ngalagan. In the *kunapipi*, the Nagugur not only pass through most of western Arnhem Land and into the eastern cultural bloc, they also visit, among others, the territories of Ngalagan, Mangarei, Nunggubuyu, Wareri (Wadari), and Yangman.

The *ubar* is to some extent an exception, even though Yirawadbad himself came from 'Macassar'. As a ritual sequence it seems to be confined to the western Arnhem Land area, and it may have been the major or even the only sacred ritual initially possessed by these western people, along with the *mangindjeg* bitter yam rites. But there is no evidence to suggest any time sequence, except in relation to the *kunapipi*. We were told that the *kunapipi* we witnessed early in 1950 was the first *kunapipi* shown at Oenpelli, although it is fairly certain that it was performed elsewhere in western Arnhem Land long before that date, especially on the Liverpool.

Warner (1937/1958: 453) reported that 'the ceremonial life of the eastern Arnhem Landers seems to be constantly enriched by cultural waves coming from the south'. Much the same has been true for western Arnhem Land, where the main cultural influences are from the east, south and south-west. The *ubar* and *maraiin* were at Oenpelli in Baldwin Spencer's day. (See Spencer, 1914: 133-44; 218-27.)

The *maraiin*, however, definitely resembles the *mareiin* rituals of the eastern Djanggawul, and the myth itself suggests some close relationship. The *ubar* is actually very similar to the *ngurlmag*, also of eastern Arnhem Land, in which a hollow-log drum called the *uvar* or *uwar* is used (see Warner, 1937/1958: 311-29). Both are associated with a snake (a python), a pigeon is put into the *ubar*, and men dance with snail-shell rattles attached to spear-throwers, while two women climb the forked post erected near the main camp. (The mythology of the western *ubar* is not concerned with the Wawalag Sisters, as it is in eastern Arnhem Land.) And in the special Gunwinggu vocabulary used between mother-in-law and son-in-law, *gungurng*, which includes a number of eastern words, the *ubar* and the *lorgun* are both called '*ngurlmag*'.

Although in this chapter we are concentrating on rite-linked myths, examples from other chapters show that not all myths are directly translated into ritual action, while others again are associated with minor rites or with small sections of the larger ones. The total range is so wide that we have had to be very selective indeed.

Sacred Rites

All of the ritual cycles discussed here, except the *mangindjeg*, have been witnessed by either or both of us at Oenpelli or Goulburn Island. The full series of *ubar* rites was recorded several times, in different sequences, at both these places. As far as we know, the *mangindjeg* rites have not been performed for some years; they are included here because they are still fresh in the memories of the local people, are possibly indigenous to the Oenpelli region, and could actually be revived with little effort if the religious leaders so decided. Various sections of the *lorgun* have also been seen by either or both of us. The tendency today is to telescope its three divisions (noted below), and also to regard it as being much more relevant to mortuary procedure than to the instruction of novices. The *maraiin* rituals have been witnessed by R.B. in considerable detail – but not the full range: they include much repetition. Like the *ubar*, they are still vitally significant to the Gunwinggu; but, also like the *ubar*, they have been subject to deletions and compression, mainly because of the pressures of mission activity and the involvement of the main participants in employment and other

(to page 128)

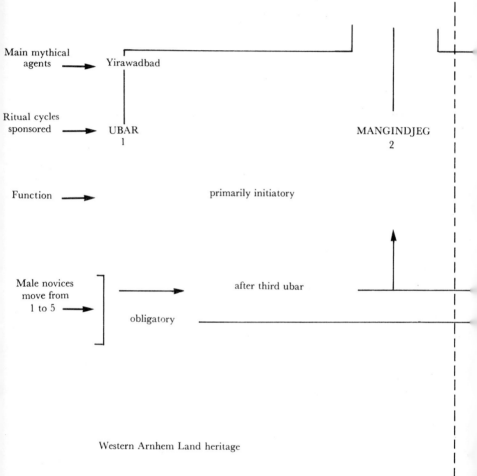

Matrilineal moieties dominant

Core mythology relevant to Fertility  M

Main mythical
agents   ⟶   Yirawadbad

Ritual cycles
sponsored   ⟶   UBAR   MANGINDJEG
                    1   2

Function   ⟶   primarily initiatory

Male novices
move from   ⟶   after third ubar
1 to 5   ⟶
                 obligatory

Western Arnhem Land heritage

Fig. 15. Initiatory rites: sequence and mythical connections.

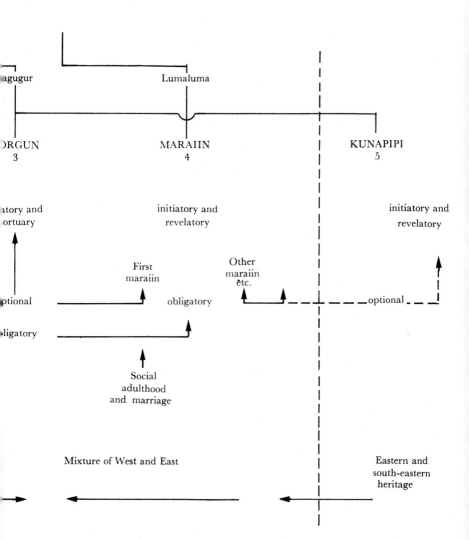

Patrilineal moieties dominant

r Rainbow Snake

agugur   Lumaluma

ORGUN   MARAIIN   KUNAPIPI
3   4   5

atory and   initiatory and   initiatory and
ortuary   revelatory   revelatory

First   Other
maraiin   maraiin
              etc.

ptional   obligatory   optional

ligatory

Social
adulthood
and marriage

Mixture of West and East   Eastern and
                                          south-eastern
                                          heritage

commitments. The *kunapipi* was observed, in its virtual entirety, when it was introduced to Oenpelli in 1950, but we have also seen it in eastern Arnhem Land and elsewhere. On this western side, it seems to have been performed only infrequently in the vicinity of the settlements; but the local people's great interest in it has undoubtedly helped to stimulate, especially, *maraiin* activity.

As far as the *ubar* is concerned, some of the traditional sacred grounds at both Oenpelli and Goulburn Island have been taken over for mission purposes. The *maraiin* stones and grounds, in contrast, are as yet virtually untouched – but, in any case, the *maraiin* rites do not need any specific stretch of ground except on a short-term basis. As regards the *kunapipi*, this has been frowned upon by both missionaries and Administration, possibly in the belief that the *kudjiga* (see later) is a dominant feature of it. Traditionally, it seems very likely that it was, but in recent years this feature has been modified. However, even though the Gunwinggu have largely accepted the *kunapipi*, it remains peripheral to their own religious orientation.

The order in which we review each ritual cycle, from *ubar* to *kunapipi*, corresponds with the sequence through which novices and adults normally pass. (See Fig. 15.) As far as other rites are concerned, they are not in any sense 'big', a word that is used in two primary senses: one, as 'powerful', 'very sacred'; and two, as important and involving the whole community, not just a segment of it. Today, however, this second condition does not necessarily hold, and this is particularly true of rites that are not caught up in the major sacred sequences. The multi-purpose rituals centring on such aspects as increase of a given species, trade, love magic, or death are now performed only irregularly, or out of what would traditionally have been regarded as their proper context.

(1) *Ubar*

An *ubar* sequence should commence at the onset of the wet weather, when the first rains fall. Toward the middle of the year, therefore, in 'cold dry' weather, *ubar* leaders (sing., *nabolggandjari*) begin to plan for it. They spend time in discussion among themselves and with other fully initiated men. Particularly, they choose messengers (sing., *nadulmi*) to go out in pairs to summon visitors who will be the actual participants. (Nadulmi, it will be recalled, was a mythical leader of the *ubar*.) A *nadulmi* does not carry weapons, only a special *malbinbin* message-stick. Whenever they reach a camp, they sing as the mythical Balnugnug Dog messengers did, and women answer with the *Gaidba!* call. Then they enter the camp and stand in front of the men, showing the message-sticks. This should be done at daybreak and sunset for three days. Men say, 'This is *djamun* [set apart, tabu] for us, we shall follow these two to the *ubar*.' 'People are happy to hear it. The women want to dance. They are glad the *ubar* comes.' They get ready to leave, and the messengers continue on to other camps.

In the meantime, the *ubar* hosts prepare the secret-sacred ground (see Fig. 16). This represents the body of the Mother – she is *mandjamun* (set apart). In one version, the prototype of the ground was first made by Yirawadbad, who rolled himself along to make it wide and clean; there are other explanations, too.

The main leader cuts the *ubar* log, and other men go out in search of crane feathers for head decorations. Especially, they collect wallaby fat (or goanna fat). This is congealed and preserved by drying, and later it is warmed over a fire and mixed with red ochre to anoint all the participants, including women and novices. The *ubar* drum is hidden in the sacred shade.

At the appropriate time, visitors arrive, bringing with them novices (whose ages range from eighteen to twenty years). A novice is *nagomdjangnan* ('unable to look yet') or *nagomdudj* (*-gom*, 'throat'; *-dudj*, possibly 'buried'); other expressions are *nagomjag* (literally, 'no throat') or *nagomgerngi* ('new throat', in contrast to an 'old throat', or 'old hand', *nagomgari*). The incoming groups also include girls, for dancing.

The rites proper begin when initiated men go out to the *ubar* ground and the novices are brought to a place near by and hidden in the grass. Men entering the ground are said to be going into the Mother, into her uterus. (Later, when men return to the main camp, if women ask, 'Where has that Old Woman gone, the one who has been singing?' they are told that she has gone away into the bush, and that she has swallowed the novices.) The *ubar* log or drum is also the Mother. The sound is her voice, and, as it drifts to the main camp, women take up the answering cry of *Gaidba, gaidba!* As the women call out, they dance: the novices' mothers and mothers' younger sisters, fathers' sisters, cross-cousins, and *ngalgurng* go round

129

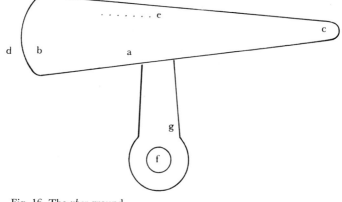

Fig. 16. The *ubar* ground.

Key:
a The sacred shade or hut, called *wangaridja*.
b The sacred Ngaljod head stone, called *mamberiwul*.
c The end of the ground, symbolizing the tail of Ngaljod.
d The top of the ground, symbolizing the head of Ngaljod.
e Where novices stand.
f Participants dance from here on to the ground.
g Symbolizing the arm of the Mother.

and round stabbing at the earth with their digging sticks, symbolically threatening the Rainbow 'so she won't hurt their boys when they go to a billabong or stream'. Their cry is partly to keep away the Rainbow but mainly, they say, 'so that we won't hear the men singing, because that would shame them'.

A series of rites follows. Novices are brought out of the grass by their guardians. In turn, they are taken to sit in pairs, one boy facing each end of the *ubar* with a guardian behind him holding his head. Each boy's hands rest inside the *ubar* opening. To the accompaniment of clapping sticks the *ubar* is lifted at one end, and an object inside it, the pandanus stump used in striking the *ubar*, rolls down and touches one boy's fingers; then the *ubar* is lifted at the other end and the object rolls back to touch the second boy. This re-enacts the scene when Yirawadbad bit his wife and her mother. At this time, novices are told not to eat certain foods, such as barramundi-fish, catfish, goanna, tortoise, crocodile, water-snake, bandicoot, native companion, and emu, turkey and goose and their eggs, or any bitter or dangerous foods. They must be present on three *ubar* occasions before the tabus are rescinded at the *mangindjeg* rite (see hereunder). Also, a novice is forbidden to eat young or fat kangaroo, and the flesh of any kangaroo if its skin has been broken in cooking. If a wild honeycomb breaks, he is not to eat it, nor honey obtained near a mound containing meat ants. He must remain in his hut during the first rains – in fact, he should not even look at this rain in case Ngaljod swallows him.

After these instructions, the *ubar* continues, in one dramatic scene after another. For each scene, the novices are brought to the sacred ground from their hiding place in the grass, and their guardians hold their heads or their testes because 'there is so much power in the *ubar* that they might break'. As they witness the rites, they are warned not to tell any one in the main camp about them, under threat of being killed. They remain on the ground for several nights. Old men bring food for the main participants and the novices, who are not allowed to show their body designs in the camp. Toward the end of the ritual sequences, the sacred shade is demolished and burnt at full moon; men dance through the flames, singeing the hairs from their legs, 'becoming like newly born people'. One particularly interesting feature of the *ubar* is that it includes a licensed clown, an actor whose role is to mock at the other participants on the sacred ground – but they must ignore him completely and go on with the rites as if he were not there.

The final scene brings in an actor representing the mythical being Gulbun, who is really the mythical *ubar* leader Nadulmi; he is painted as the 'Mother one' (*manbaidjan*). He lies full length on the sacred ground, his head resting on a special stone, and underneath him the *ubar* itself is said to lie buried. Men encircle him while clapping sticks are tapped and the drone-pipe is blown, and finally he is lifted up.

Then all the men, crying *Gogjei, gogjei!* leave the *ubar* ground for the main camp, where women are dancing and calling in answer. Two women climb a pandanus palm or 'forked post', the *djumanggal*, said to have been originally one of the forked posts holding up the sacred shade on the sacred ground. They stand upright, holding onto

131

the tree, swinging their snail-shell rattles (*lida*) and calling out *Lida, lida!* while other women dance round with digging sticks. Then they come down, and two men climb up the stand with flexed legs calling the sacred invocations, while both men and women dance round. There are variations on this theme and the scene may be repeated. Other rites are involved, too, and at this time *madgu* moiety men give string to *ngaraidgu* women and *ngaraidgu* men to *madgu* women.

Mothers and sisters of the novices (now called *ngalgomdudj*: feminine prefix used) cry, while other women bring food for the *ubar* men. This is not eaten by women or novices. They eat specially prepared food, because 'if they ate the men's food, the novices would become grey-haired'. Throughout the *ubar*, women closely related to the novices observe very much the same food tabus as they do, and this applies especially to the boys' own mothers. A novice's mother should not raise her voice above a whisper or utter his personal names, 'in case the Rainbow Snake living in the water might hear, and eat him'. She does not use an axe for cutting trees, or her digging stick to get food, and she does not share her camp-fire even with her own daughters – she identifies herself with her novice son almost to the exclusion of everyone else.

(2) *Mangindjeg Rites*

Traditionally, *mangindjeg* rites were held between the *ubar* and *maraiin* rituals, and usually after a novice had seen his third *ubar* sequence. The primary purpose was to break the *ubar* food tabus. (*Mangindjeg* is an edible root – see Chapter 3.)

In brief outline: older men encourage the young novices to sing and then, during the singing, sneak up and seize them, taking them off into the long grass. There they camp together in seclusion. The youths are decorated with head- and armbands and breast girdles, and tossed ritually from one man to another. In the main camp their parents, actual and otherwise, and their siblings paint themselves. The novices are brought back to the main camp, decorated with *mangindjeg* body designs, and covered with green grass. Singing begins, but there is no dancing: fires are made, and again the novices are thrown across them from one man to another.

Later a grass shade or hut is built in the camp, and two of the older youths who have recently completed the *mangindjeg* remain there until the grass dries. Each night the novices are brought down from the long grass and sing around it. When the hut is dry, it is burnt, symbolizing the burning-grass time of the year after which new *mangindjeg* roots are generally available. When the appropriate songs are completed the novices are brought before their parents, their arms are held, and they are given slices of these cooked roots. Heaps of *mangindjeg*, which have taken a considerable time to collect and prepare, are piled up in front of their parents' huts. Later, the two older youths are given spears and throwers and come up to the heaps pretending to spear them. This completes the sequence, and the novices themselves are now called *mangindjeg*.

Spencer (1914: 146-9) describes such a ritual for the Kakadu, but his details differ from this highly summarized account. The Gunwinggu version is said to be of Gundjeibmi origin.

(3) *Lorgun*

The *lorgun* (or *lorgan*) is primarily a mortuary rite, but it is also a sacred series during which novices are instructed. As far as a novice is concerned, his *lorgun* experience may either follow or precede the *mangindjeg*, but he should have been through three *ubar* sequences.

The Nagugur were mythically responsible for instituting the *lorgun*, which is also associated with Moon. In this version of the myth, Yagul, a Red-eyed Pigeon man, is dying. Moon urges him to imitate himself: 'I die, but I become alive again. Here am I now, new!' But Djabo, spotted cat, who has paws like a malignant *maam* spirit's hands, persuades him otherwise. 'No, I shall just die,' Yagul tells Moon, and so that is now the custom of man. In another version, Djabo refused to drink Moon's urine and so deprived men of immortality.

There are three varieties of this ritual: *walalala*, associated with the *dua* moiety *gigig* pigeon, *largan* (*jiridja* moiety *lorgun*), and *barura* (*dua* moiety *lorgun*). The *lorgun* is also called *djunggawon*, a term used for the eastern Arnhem Land circumcision ritual belonging to the Wawalag cycle (see R. B., 1951a: 33), and is said to come from the Dangbun whereas the *walalala* is specifically of Gumadir Gunwinggu origin.

The *lorgun* is held when the moon is waning, some time after a death. A father (for instance) of the dead man builds a sacred shelter, either in the main camp or outside it – a circular construction four to five feet in diameter made of bushes covered with paperbark. He and his brothers or sons, actual or close, cut a tall hollow log. For the *largan* it is short and the 'mouth' V-shaped, for the *barura* it is long with a plain 'mouth' but is hung with lengths of feathered string. It is placed in the shelter. The next step is to send out messengers, carrying a *gadgad* message-stick with feathers attached, inviting various groups to attend the rites. The dead man's immediate kin, including his fathers, collect honey and store it in baskets, and gather yams and lily and other roots. As the visitors arrive, the dead man's mother goes to the shelter and cleans the surrounding dancing ground. Then she calls the men, who come to the shelter and paint themselves as in the *maraiin*. Novices are brought up to witness the dancing. As in the *ubar*, they are told to abstain from certain foods. 'You must eat no honey, and no large fish or meat. Only old people are to eat these. If you catch a large fish or a large animal, you must bring the meat to us! If you eat it, your skin will crack with sores and you will become sick.' Each such forbidden animal and fish is dramatized in dance, while the novices are warned again not to eat large ones.

Finally the hollow log is brought out, like an *ubar*. At dusk, men run from the sacred ground with long paperbark flares, swinging them round the dead man's parents so that sparks fly over them, to let them know. The dead man's bones, that have previously been collected and wrapped in paperbark like a bundle of *maraiin* objects, are unwrapped and red-ochred, and then put into the *largan* or *barura*. The last song sung on the sacred ground refers to the dead man's spirit diving into the water, and invocations associated with his *gunmugugur* are called (these are the *mirindji*). In the meantime, women perform a shuffling dance in the camp, circling around the place where the pole is to be set: the dead man's sisters' daughters, half-mothers, and fathers' sisters.

At sunrise the pole is brought to the main camp, while some women weep and others call out *Bira, bira, bira!* in answer to the men's cry of *Jei!* Others have been clearing the ground and digging a hole ready for the pole (the dead man's sisters' daughters, for instance). Others, again, continue to dance – conventionally, only two now: a daughter and sister's daughter of the dead man – with averted heads and raised hands as if pushing the pole away from them. It is set up and encircled by dancers, and after that the specially collected and prepared food is given to the participating visitors. They also exchange spears, axes, knives, and feathered string baskets and net bags, among other things. In the *walalala*, while the visitors eat, a *ngadjadj* or *ganggin* or brother or son of the dead man walks around singing, clapping his boomerang-sticks while women dance. In the *walalala*, too, but not always in the *largan* and *barura*, the dead man's belongings are taken to the shelter and burnt. The ashes are covered with earth to make a small mound, and on it is placed a notched stick with feathered string if an older man has died, but a plain stick in the case of a young man or woman. This is the *wawal* post, and it is said that the deceased's spirit, or one manifestation of it, can now go to its own waterhole or country. After their first *lorgun*, the novices are called *limbid*. Exchange of goods is an important feature of these mortuary rites, and Spencer (1914: 247-8) mentions it too for the Kakadu. Spencer (*ibid.*: 251-2, 255-6) also briefly describes the *lorgun* of the Mangarei and Mara people, while Warner (1937/1958: 438-42) discusses the hollow-log coffin of eastern Arnhem Land. However, the western Arnhem Land variant is closer to what Spencer reported; in the east, it is not associated with secret-sacred performances, nor with novices.

(4) *Maraiin*

The *maraiin* is really the last in the sacred ritual series of this region, because the *kunapipi* is not correlated with any special stage in a novice's religious development and is, in a sense, additional to the others. For the *maraiin*, a novice must have participated in the other sequences we have outlined, and after his first *maraiin* experience he may marry. But for him, as for other men, *maraiin* activity is expected to continue throughout his life. The rituals are very varied indeed, and so are the objects that are used in them. Between performances these objects are carefully stored away, wrapped up in paperbark bundles, called *dudji*.

If men of a particular territorial group decide to make a *maraiin*, one of them and his close brothers and sons prepare a special sacred shade, and he is the *djirg* or *gandjari*, shade-leader. Usually men of two such groups participate and erect *dua* and *jiridja* patrilineal moiety shades and dancing grounds side by side (see Fig. 17). At the same time, *mulu* message-sticks are sent out, inviting people from other camps to attend. Food is collected and set aside for male

135

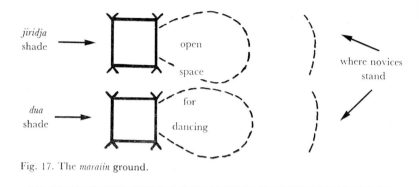

Fig. 17. The *maraiin* ground.

participants; it is called *dagwar*. Men of both moieties prepare their *maraiin* objects: this is an important domain of inter-moiety coopera- tion.

Men and women, painted and decorated, arrive for the rituals. The men go directly to the *maraiin* shades and, as they enter, call the *gunmugugur* invocations. This is a marked feature of *maraiin* dancing and singing, underlining *gunmugugur* membership and ties, among living people and also in terms of the mythical era. *Jiridja* men enter their shade first: the shade-leader is inside, and claps his sticks while the others shake the shade. The conventional utterances while this is being done, not actually singing but more in the nature of chanting, resemble part of the Djanggawul *nara* of eastern Arnhem Land. Then the *jiridja* men emerge on to the dancing ground, and it is the *dua* men's turn to enter the shade. Novices stand before the cleared spaces, feet covered with sand and heads bowed.

The rites continue over several days. Novices are shown the sacred *maraiin* objects as they are brought one by one from the shades. Men emerge to the sound of clapping sticks and singing, either crawling on their bellies or shuffling along lying on their backs as they clasp the *maraiin*, or posturing while holding them. Some are carved wooden representations of various creatures, and others are painted stones or moulded wax representing parts of their bodies. As the novices look at these, they are told not to eat the flesh of any large specimens of these creatures – all large fish and so on must be brought to the *maraiin* men. The posturing actors approach the novices and finally set down the objects in front of them. The novices are told what they are and what they symbolize, and may be given the objects to hold. At each performance, *gunmugugur* invocations are called.

The rites continue until the leaves of the branches covering the shades become dry and fall, and they conclude with the emergence of the most important of all the *maraiin* objects.

After that, all the men come down to the main camp bringing the novices, who are now called *laidgurunga* or *laigurunguni*. They assemble round a pandanus tree or 'forked post', *djambuldjambul* or *mandjanngarl*, where a pandanus platform has been set up. Men, women and novices climb onto the platform and are covered with blankets and mats. Underneath the platform a fire has been lit, and now water is poured onto it so that steam rises. The steaming is said to drive out any sharp claws and nails that have entered them in the course of the rites, from the creatures that were dramatized in *maraiin* form, and to make them of 'strong heart'. It also reinforces the edict that not only the novices but everyone involved except fully initiated *maraiin* men must abstain from eating the flesh of large creatures. Initiated men climb the pandanus and call *gunmugugur* invocations, *dua* men first and then *jiridja*. Women dance the *madjidji*. The men's final dramatic dancing concerns the *dua* water goanna and the *jiridja* crocodile, who dances with his sacred basket held in his mouth. Next, men move around the camp and dance outside each hut or shelter, underlining the fact that the entire group has been involved in the rites – everyone present has participated in one way or another. Then, to the accompaniment of clapping sticks and the calling of invocations, all the people together go down to the billabong and wash. The mythical precedent for this scene was mentioned earlier in this chapter: Laradjeidja and his companions, frightened by Lumaluma, jumped into the billabong at Guwulabulu.

Just as in the *ubar*, the novices' mothers, full sisters, fathers' sisters and mothers' mothers, especially, must observe the same tabus as the novices do, and the sanctions that women mention in this connection are supernaturally based but policed by human agents. 'If anyone breaks the tabu, he/she may die.' The *maraiin* leader(s) would be upset 'on account of his sacred basket [with the *maraiin* things inside it] – "Why did he upset [do harm to] my *maraiin*? Shall we kill him?" ' And, women say, 'When we hear the clapping sticks tapping once, then again, very slowly, [to let us know] the men are coming down from their ground – then we don't move about, or stand up and look at them, or call out to each other in front of them, or laugh: or those whose *maraiin* it is might throw spears at us as we sit, all of us women together, gathered at the *mandjanngarl*. . . . ' It is women's responsibility to teach this proper behaviour to children, as part of the ideal rule of respect for and deference to sacred things – and, above all, anything in the sphere of the secret-sacred.

A man who has been through only one *maraiin* sequence is not allowed to accept food from his wife or betrothed wife until the ritual paint wears off. After he has seen two sequences he is permitted to give her small animals and fish, not large ones 'in case he gets broken up and lame'. Older men tell him, 'If you give such things to your wife secretly, you may die,' and so (women say) 'he is afraid and doesn't give her any'. Later, after he has participated in several *maraiin* rituals and the food-sharing tabu is lifted, it is to her that he should first give kangaroo and other meats, fish, and honey. After that he can give food to his *ngalgurng*, and then to his father.

The repertoire of *maraiin* songs is wide and some of them, as already noted, have eastern Arnhem Land parallels. There are also parallels with the eastern Wawalag mythology, with the Yulunggul and Moiidj Rainbow Snakes. *Maraiin* songs deal with seasonal changes and with fertility generally, with *gunmugugur* significance, and territorial ownership. The shades on the sacred ground symbolize the Mother's (or Ngaljod's) body, from which the *maraiin* emerge. The mass of detail surrounding the objects is complex, especially in reference to 'finding' them. This is done through dreams. For instance, in the case of a particularly large catch a *maraiin* leader may 'find' a stone object, a 'heart' or 'tongue', within the creature's belly. In such circumstances only *maraiin* initiates may eat its flesh, away from the main camp, and before they return to the camp they must brush warm branches over themselves or wash themselves to dissipate the dangerously strong sacred aura attaching to them.

(5) *Kunapipi*

This very widespread ritual complex was reported by Spencer in 1912 (1914: 162, 164-6, 213-18) and has been discussed in more detail by Warner 1937/1958: 290-311) and R. Berndt (1951*a*). In its southern forms it is associated with both circumcision and subincision. In eastern Arnhem Land, circumcision is practised but not included in the *kunapipi* cycle and there is no subincision. In western Arnhem Land, Gunwinggu do not traditionally circumcise or subincise. In both areas the *kunapipi* is recognized as an 'imported' cult but its importance is not questioned.

When a *kunapipi* sequence is about to commence, messengers (*gagawar*) go out to summon visitors. A Gunwinggu performance is most likely to be instigated and directed by visiting southern people, for example by Maiali-side Gunwinggu, Dangbun, or Rembarnga. Other visitors come to be initiated as novices or to have sections of the ritual revealed to them. The sacred ground which is the centre of the rites varies in shape. In many cases, and in conventional terms, it resembles the *ubar* ground, but the arrangement shown in the sketch (Fig. 18) is apparently more usual for western Arnhem Land. The *ganala* is a trench two to three feet deep, symbolizing the uterus of the Mother, or Ngaljod (or Yulunggul) the Rainbow Snake, or both. (For other interpretations, see R. B., 1951*a*: 43.) On the inner walls of the *ganala*, snake designs are incised. It is said that in some cases a *nanggaru* hole is dug on the sacred ground, representing a sacred waterhole and also the Mother's uterus.

The distinctive long-drawn calling begins, and men bringing novices (*walg*) come up to the sacred ground. 'The Mother is calling them, they will be swallowed by the Snake.' Simultaneously, bullroarers are swung – *maralbindi*, either male or female. The female ones are ordinarily used, the *mumana* (or *ngalmamuna*, the Mother's name, a non-secret word) or 'Mother one': they are classified as *dua* and made by *dua* men, but said to be really *jiridja* because the Nagugur were *jiridja*. The bullroarer is also called her *mai*ʔ (or 'meat'), like the Rainbow and its ritual representation the *jelmalandji* (see below). Its sound, as it is swung, is the voice of the Snake, the female Yulunggul: 'She comes out, she calls them, she talks, she goes with them to the sacred ground!'

There are three major ritual-song divisions: *djamala*, *gudjiga*, and *warimulunggul*. The first covers ritual sequences centring on the

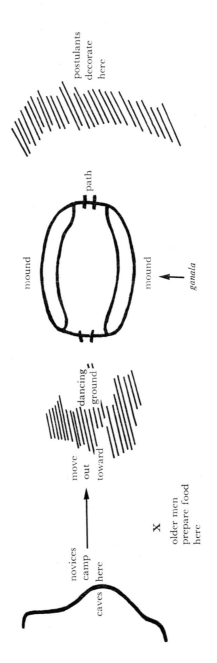

postulants
decorate
here

path

mound

mound ← *ganala*

"dancing ground"

move
out
toward

X

older men
prepare food
here

novices
camp
here

caves

Fig. 18. The *kunapipi* ground.

ganala and the *jelmalandji* and the instruction of young novices. The second conventionally includes ritual coitus, but the songs may be sung without that accompaniment. The third covers all *kunapipi* singing and ritual carried out in cooperation with women or in the main camp: all *warimulunggul* singing is 'open' or public.

On the sacred ground, postulants dance out various sequences relating to creatures mentioned in the songs. They emerge from where they have been hidden, move toward the *ganala* and enter it – they have been 'swallowed by the Rainbow' and have 'entered the Mother's uterus': they are sung over, and the cry of *Kunapipila* . . ! rings out. Before they witness such acts, novices have sweat rubbed on their eyes, and this is done afterward to the actors themselves.

A long series of rites follows, until the time comes to erect the *jelmalandji*. The *jelmalandji* emblems at Oenpelli early in 1950 were about nine feet high, much smaller than those seen elsewhere. The larger one is *jiridja*, the smaller *dua*, but often only one is used in a ritual although conventionally two should be. At first, the *jelmalandji* is erected near the *jiridja* shelter: *dua* men are led before it and embrace it and throw bunches of leaves in front of it. Throughout the night, women call from the camp. Food is brought up at intervals: it is sacred cycad-palm food.

Then follows a possum dancing series. Actors with erect paperbark penes dance around the *ganala*, filling it in with earth until only a shallow depression remains. The *jelmalandji* is erected at the head of the *ganala* and novices are told, 'There is the Rainbow!' They embrace it, and all rub themselves against it. Later, they all red-ochre themselves, surround the *jelmalandji* and push it down.

All participants are now painted over with blood, on a base of red ochre mixed with termite mound. (In the 1950 Oenpelli *kunapipi*, half a kerosene tin of arm-vein blood was used among approximately forty to fifty participants.) Young novices, lying in the grass some little distance away, are seized and also painted with blood. Symbolically, this means that all of them have been inside the belly of the Snake. While this is happening, ritual crying continues, along with the swinging of bullroarers. All the men now wear white headbands (*maralbibi*). They leave for the main camp, where a *djebalmandji* (or *djebanbani*) has been erected on the outskirts – two forked posts with a connecting ridge pole, covered with branches (see R. B., 1951a: 53-5). This is a special shade, associated mythically with flying foxes, and it can also represent the Mother's uterus. Two men perch in the forked posts and call out ritually, while novices are hidden under the branches and hold on to the ridge pole 'like flying foxes'. Singing begins, and women come to the *djebal-mandji* and lie down around it covered with mats and blankets. Men dance round them. Then the women begin to leave, and men continue to dance as the novices are brought out from under the branches and go away with the women.

Finally comes an exchange of sweat, and more ritual calling. Tabu-ed food is given to the participants. Just as in the *maraiin*, married men are not permitted to sleep with their wives yet or share food with them – not until their paint rubs off entirely – because Ngaljod would resent it. The novices camp together on one side of the main camp. About two days later, all the participants and onlookers, men and women, as well as novices are painted with fat and red ochre, with body designs of male and female Ngaljod and her eggs. Payments are made to the *kunapipi* directors and an exchange of goods takes place between visitors and local people.

The *gudjiga* section of the *kunapipi* is traditionally performed at full moon. Men sing and dance on the sacred ground. The songs relate to ceremonial coitus, mythically connected with the Nagugur and their wives, but, as noted, this does not necessarily take place.There are two major variants: the north-eastern (noted in R. B., 1951a: 47-53), involving ritual exchange of wives and coitus with tabu-ed relatives, and the southern, in which an unmarried and presumably virgin girl is deflowered with a boomerang by a man who calls her *gagali*, and then has coitus with all the male participants regardless of kin relationships. The second is the type known at Oenpelli. Conventionally, once this is completed the girl's betrothed husband leads her away to the main camp, returns to the sacred ground and buries the sheet of paperbark on which she was lying, then reports to the other men who have been singing close by. In the meantime, the girl's mother has painted her daughter and herself with red ochre, and when she is ready she calls the men to come. They leave the sacred ground and enter the main camp, encircling the girl and calling out ritually. This sequence underlines the importance of fertility in the *kunapipi* rituals, and also serves as an initiatory rite for the girl.

Under this subheading, all we want to do is to draw attention to some procedures that fall more obviously toward the magical end of the continuum. In so far as these can be separated out from religion in the conventional sense, the distinction probably rests on two points: (a) they are more narrowly centred, socially speaking – geared explicitly to the interests of specified persons and specified units rather than to those of the society in general; and (b) the connection between means and desired ends is also more specific and more direct – the end is believed to follow more or less automatically from the action (rite, spell). The simplest increase rites and weather-influencing rites have sometimes, therefore, been described as predominantly magical rather than predominantly religious.

Most of the 'big' rituals (*ubar, lorgun, mangindjeg, maraiin* and *kunapipi*) emphasize increase of natural species, but others do the same in a smaller way in reference to specific *djang* sites. For example, merely marking a white stone Tortoise *djang* site with a charcoal band 'sends out Tortoise spirits' to increase that species. At Nimbarbir, near Oenpelli, the territorial leader of a Long-necked Tortoise site should break leaves over the rocks while he calls on the Tortoise spirits to emerge. At other *djang* sites, a common rite involves spraying out water from the mouth and calling for the relevant species. Djinganendji, on the East Alligator River, site of a 'White Rat' *djang*, needs a slightly more elaborate rite. The holes or burrows, turned to stone, are cleaned, and a fire is made near by. Fat and skin from a corpse should be burnt to attract the spirit Rats from inside, who are believed to smell this and say, 'Maybe grandfather or grandmother is there outside!' The performer of the rite makes tracks around the hole to indicate where the spirit Rats should go, and at the same time calls the names of those places. At Gabari an Orphan, *namalaidj* (see Chapter 2), rested a large bag of *mandaneg* roots which turned into rocks. Now, Gunwinggu say, the *gunmugugur* head should go there in the dry season, break a stick and hit the rocks, calling the names of places in which they should grow, and, after the wet season, women will be able to find plenty to dig.

Also under this heading come rain-restraining songs, *jira* (yira), sung by men with white hair and said to come from the Ngalagan. Although Ngaljod's qualities of protection and benevolence are emphasized in certain contexts, she (he) is also dangerous and feared as being responsible for rain, storm and floods. This aspect is dominant at the beginning of the wet season, and that is why *ubar* novices should not go out in the rain but remain in a hut. The *jira* are sung to ease or ward off rain and lightning. But while they represent an attempt to control the destructive qualities of Ngaljod, the songs themselves tell of the first rains, grass growing, increase of various creatures, eggs, growing yams, and fertility of the country in general. Some Gunwinggu, therefore, fear that singing *jira* songs in a time of heavy rain will actually have the opposite effect and encourage the Rainbow further.

Gunwinggu interest in fertility and in relations between the sexes does not take the form of love magic, though they know about this from their neighbours. For instance, so far they have taken no interest in the *djarada* rites and songs that have proved popular in some other parts of the north. (See C.H.B., for example, 1965: 238-65.) They favour a more direct and practical approach, including the stimulatory variety of gossip songs.

Sorcery is another matter. It appears in numbers of myths as a major or minor theme, and in several rock paintings illustrating mythical and quasi-mythical incidents: in one, a man rejected by a girl he wants paints a partly human figure on a cave wall, calling her name and 'singing' for an eagle or other bird to eat her heart within so many days. This course of action is a potential threat in ordinary life, where sorcery is taken as an empirical fact. (See Chapter 7.) In between a threat and an accident, illness or death, is a screen of inference. The event itself is 'proof' of sorcery. Gunwinggu and other western Arnhem Landers believe that sorcery procedures are available, and that they are actually used by anyone who wants to harm someone else, with or without advance warning. But because they are also believed to be necessarily private and secret, witnesses are very rare and evidence is overwhelmingly circumstantial and retrospective.

In one believed-in rite, the central feature is an appeal to Nagidgid, the mythical patron of sorcerers. This type of sorcery procedure also requires the sorcerer to come into direct physical contact with his victim. (A sorcerer is always assumed to be a man, although a woman may help by supplying material for him to work on.) He spears his victim in the neck and collects some of the blood in a paperbark container, then he heals the wound with a heated spear-blade while he invokes Nagidgid, asking him to give the victim temporary life, or a temporary appearance of life. The maximum period Nagidgid allows is three days. In the Gunwinggu view, such a person is already dead. His body goes through the motions of living, but it is only an animated corpse. (The stem -*gid* is used for this state of 'living death'.) The sorcerer also specifies the agent of the victim's public or obvious death: a snake, shark, crocodile, the Rainbow, or even his (or her) own spouse. If anyone behaves recklessly in a potentially dangerous situation and is subsequently killed – for example, walking carelessly where there are almost certain to be snakes – people will think back and say, 'His soul [spirit] must have been stolen, or he wouldn't have done that.'

A simple sorcery technique is said to be more usual. This implies an appeal to Nagidgid, but has the advantage that it can be used from any distance and at any time. All the sorcerer needs is something that has been in close contact with the victim, especially personal leavings, and if he does not want to take immediate action he can store this away for years. Then he merely heats it over a fire, calling the victim's name and uttering the appropriate spell, specifying the agent of death.

The most effective sorcerers, in local belief, are those with the most 'power'. A man with a reputation as a sorcerer may be called *mangorang*, but (as the prefix *man-* suggests) this is more a hypothetical category than a label for any actual person or type of person. Occasionally, the term is applied to a *margidbu*, a native doctor or 'clever' man, to indicate a secondary role. But, except in myth, a *margidbu* is more often defined as entirely benevolent and beneficent, concerned with healing and helping – for example, in illness or a difficult childbirth, or in dealing with ghosts. (See, for example, C. H. B., 1964: 267-80.) By the late 1940s and 1950s, fewer than a dozen middling- to high-powered living *margidbu* could be identified among the Gunwinggu and their neighbours, with a larger fringe of men considered to have only 'a little power'. An exact count was impossible because some of them had very localized or fluctuating reputations, and there was uncertainty or disagreement on others – whether they 'really had power'. By 1966, almost all of the more easily identified *margidbu* were dead, and even more vagueness surrounded the diminishing number of marginal ones.

Moon was a *margidbu* because he has the secret of eternal life – he dies, but comes back again in the same shape. The most powerful *margidbu*, in real life and in myth, are credited with other marvellous feats: not only healing the sick, but also travelling through the air to distant places, including the sky, and seeing local sites 'as they really are' instead of the more humdrum scenes that ordinary people see. Some have their own personal Rainbow Snakes that they can summon without danger to themselves. They are said to obtain their power from ghosts, especially from a dead 'father' of the same *gunmugugur*. But this 'initiation' and most of their more outstanding exploits are private affairs – like acts of sorcery, they are reported but not witnessed by anyone else. The association between songmen and their spirit-familiars is private too, since it nearly always takes place in dreams. Ordinary people are told about it (for instance, about dream encounters with a Rainbow Snake or the ghost of a dead child or a blue-tongue lizard or a frog), and they hear the songs and the prediction of future events – the messages that the songman makes public.

The *margidbu* complex and the sorcery complex are both individual-centred, and both carry further two related themes that are present in different shape and with different content in the circumstances of sacred ritual. One is the notion of secrecy and partial exclusion; the other is inequality of knowledge and power.

It is clear that the Gunwinggu and their neighbours were exposed to varying points of view, and this exposure was relatively sustained. People from different areas met, not only for specifically religious rites, but also during the comings and goings of ceremonies that were oriented toward gift exchange and trade.

We have already mentioned the exchange of goods that takes place in the course of *lorgun* and other rituals. Usually it is not seen as part of the main business of the gathering. It is simply that people who have come long distances take advantage of the meeting to engage in ordinary trade, arrange marriages and settle disputes. Nevertheless, expectation of payment for any services rendered is well entrenched. In all sacred ritual, people who are shown objects, hear songs, or see dances must pay. Novices and their parents pay for being initiated. Visitors, summoned to participate in a ritual, expect compensation.

There were also, traditionally, ceremonies that were multi-purpose but held ostensibly for trade. These are the *djamalag, rom, midjan, wurbu, mamurung* and *njalaidj*, each of them associated with the production of distinctive articles and with a specific area. Altogether, they cover virtually the whole of western Arnhem Land. In the *rom*, specially made objects are danced with in the main camp where local people and visitors have assembled, and some of the dancing is not unlike sacred *maraiin* dancing. The *midjan* is much the same. The *wurbu* includes aspects of increase; after a rite centring on native companion (birds') eggs, dilly-bags full of eggs are presented to the visitors. The *mamurung* is sponsored by the father of a boy whose hair is cut for the first time or who (for example) gets his first honeycomb or kills his first goanna or tortoise. A small object, such as a moulded beeswax goanna, is sent as a symbolic message inviting people to attend the ceremony. In the *njalaidj* (see Chapter 2; also R. B., 1951*b*: 156-76) actors wear feather-down stuck on with blood, and conical headdresses, and their dances are strikingly similar to sections of the *kunapipi*.

Religious belief and ritual in western Arnhem Land have been especially receptive to influences from neighbouring regions – in songs, rites, myths, practices and rules. Nevertheless, in all instances, even in the *kunapipi*, contemporary rites are validated by mythology that is connected somehow with the local scene – if not rooted specifically in that region, at least in an area not too far away. It is given a local flavour. The myths themselves are flexible and expansible – an important point in an expanding Gunwinggu culture. Interrelationship of myth and ritual is vital for Gunwinggu religious momentum: rites without mythical substantiation do not constitute religion in Gunwinggu terms. Not all myth is necessarily reflected or acted out in ritual; Gunwinggu mythology is much more wide-ranging in content. But a great deal of it concerns, either directly or indirectly, the great Ngaljod – one aspect of the concept of the Mother as both Protector and Destroyer.

In the *ubar, maraiin* and *kunapipi* rituals, men enter the Mother – in the shape of the sacred shade, the sacred ground, the *ganala*, and so forth. At such periods they are all *with* (within) the Mother, and so, in spirit form, are all the creatures that were ritually dramatized. Novices return to the main camp 'reborn' to a new social status, a new stage in their progression through life. Fully initiated men are revitalized, too: they have been in direct association with elemental forces. The power that they have released is primeval, basic, and dangerous – but they have endeavoured to protect themselves, and their women and children, through careful performance of the appropriate rites and the myth-songs which themselves re-create the creative era. And women, whose role in their traditional religion is supporting and submissive, have helped to maintain what is seen as a pre-established pattern – not only through their own complementary ritual acts, but also in their role as providers of sacred food.

Chapter Seven

Conforming and Non-Conforming

THE RELIGIOUS SYSTEM and the system of social control among the Gunwinggu are certainly not the same thing, but they do coincide to a considerable extent. Values and beliefs that are part of the religious complex, or derived from it, underwrite a great deal of what could be described as mundane or secular behaviour, and not only in the borderline sphere of magic and sorcery. They substantiate divisions along sex and age lines and the behaviour that goes with them. Specifically, they substantiate leadership based on religious authority.

Leadership and Control

This leadership is most clearly defined and most visible in the context of sacred ritual, and least so in the conduct of everyday affairs. But it is not irrelevant in those affairs. It is the ultimate source of authority and control. Leaders whose power to command rests on their imputed access to the 'supernatural' and the sphere of the secret-sacred can intervene even in trivial matters. This does not mean that they *do* intervene to any extent. A lot depends on the circumstances. But even more important is the judicious use of their authority so that it is not put to the test too often. Because secrecy and mystery are such a vital part of it, and because there is no organized body of persons assigned to upholding or reinforcing it, it could actually be weakened by attempts to impose it in circumstances where its major sanctions were believed to be irrelevant or lacking. Another factor is personality. A man of middle age or older

149

may be fully initiated and well informed on sacred ritual procedures and symbolic interpretation – but unless he has the incentive and the drive to validate his status he remains at best a secondary leader, someone who is approached for advice and information but does not emerge as a major figure. To do that he needs to be not only forceful but physically active, and a reputation as a native doctor, a *margidbu*, is also an advantage.

Special terms apply to various ritual leaders, but an all-round leader is simply a person who 'looks after' his group. (*Gawo ?nan*, someone who 'looks after', 'sees to', 'cares for'.) The position is informal, and it is most relevant to the camp complex focused on a range of sites over a fairly confined area of contiguous small territories. It can be shared among two or three men of approximately the same status, with the most forceful and active of them not an isolate, but a first among equals: and discussions among such men are not, or were not, confined to religious issues.

But religious leadership in the fullest sense has been drastically affected by outside contact, with the imposition of outside control. Its teeth have been drawn: the sanctions and threats that upheld it have been weakened or removed altogether. The sphere of religious authority has shrunk to the narrower zone of ritual performance and myth interpretation and their extensions in the field of graphic art. A religious leader in this changed situation is little better than a master of ceremonies, or a man who knows more about such matters than other people do. It is a mistake to suppose that, because this is so today, the same state of affairs existed traditionally (that is, before the full impact of outside influences), when the overall system of socio-political control was totally different.

The basis of social control was acceptance of the normative order and, on the whole, of the existential order. Protests were made within the system and not against it – or, rather, there is no evidence of any challenge to the system as such. The essence of the system was assent, agreement on the rightness of the rules and unquestioning acceptance of the supernatural or spiritual order which supported them. The key to its practical working out lay in the social control and organization of sacred ritual – that is, (i) domination by senior men, (ii) younger to middle-aged men acting as junior executives and handling most of the active work, (iii) women, also differentiated on the score of age and experience, having limited authority and limited autonomy in certain fields, and (iv) responsibility for pre-adolescent children resting with adults of either or both sexes according to circumstances. This arrangement, tightly organized in the ritual context, was superimposed more loosely on the entire range of activities outside it. Relations between old, not-so-old and young had overtones or undertones of senior-junior or superordinate-subordinate, either obvious or latent.

The result was not so schematic in practice, if only because of variation in personal interests and abilities – but then, Gunwinggu themselves did not expect it to be. Outside the core of basic assumptions and shared premises, they anticipated some diversity – not in definitions of right and wrong, but in their implementation. The degree of flexibility rested with the people immediately concerned in any particular case: how they assessed the situation, and what they did about it. Even in regard to deviant behaviour, behaviour formally regarded as wrong, there was no clear-cut sequence of wrong action followed by penalty.

In general terms, most adults can give a coherent account of the proper course to follow in all of the circumstances they are likely to encounter. Such accounts are built up from a variety of sources, from direct precept to the more discursive oral storehouse of myth and story; but, of course, the content of that storehouse is not limited to ideals.

Myth and Conduct

Obviously, Gunwinggu myths (see Chapters 2 and 6) are not such a ready guide to social behaviour as they are to 'living with the land', economically and ritually. Creation myths and *djang* stories are rich in illustrations of bad as well as good behaviour, sometimes explicitly identified as such and sometimes not. Evaluation may be implicit in the myth itself (for example, a bad action leads to punishment, or a good action is rewarded) or articulated in comments or omitted altogether. Just as in real life, many characters and actions are neither wholly good nor wholly bad, and the denouement itself may reflect that mixture.

The Lumaluma myth (see Chapters 3 and 6) is an example. Lumaluma was killed because he used a sacred tabu for personal ends or because he ate men or children; but he was also a benefactor, a religious leader who introduced some of the most important sacred rites. Wuragag's record was mixed, too. In several versions of his myth, the final episode shows him covering himself completely with rocks because 'he was afraid men were coming to kill him', and, even now, 'If we light grass fires near him we can hear him calling out, frightened, from inside the rock.' When the reason for his fear is mentioned, it is attributed to guilt – because he had taken a girl who was betrothed to another man. Nevertheless, he accomplished his own transformation without the help of any intermediary, including Ngaljod.

In other myths the Rainbow is an agent, not merely of fate, but also of punishment. Characters confronted by storm and floods cry out, 'We have gone wrong!', or the final disaster is revealed as a natural consequence of displeasing the Rainbow. Despite that, people trying to help the Orphan whose crying attracts the Rainbow meet the same end as his tormentors do. In this ultimate circumstance, the innocent are hardly distinguishable from the guilty. The outcome is the same for both, and the implication is that, in the long run, it does not matter whether they kept the rules or broke them. Perhaps we could read into this a parallel with Gunwinggu views of the afterlife, which say nothing about punishment or reward for actions performed during a person's lifetime. In that respect, death and its aftermath are the same for everyone.

Up to that point, however, moral judgments apply. In the same way, even *djang* stories where the conclusion is hardly in doubt allow some scope for evaluation and comment. A character with a grudge who deliberately smashes a tabu stone to bring the Rainbow and destroy people who have offended him, can be compared with a native doctor, a *margidbu*, who summons his personal Snake for private vengeance – except that the first case implies suicide as well, not a traditional Gunwinggu feature outside the spheres of myth and song.

In reporting mythical incidents conventionally regarded as wrong, a speaker sometimes allows facial expressions and changes in tone to tell this part of the story without any extra words. One myth from old Ngalmidul, for instance, included a dispute between a man and his wife's mother, his actual *ngalgurng*. This man wanted his wife's full sister, too, but she was betrothed to his younger brother because full sisters should not share a husband. 'And so, when he brought home kangaroo meat, he hung it up on a tree for a time and didn't give it to his mother-in-law, and he stopped his wife from giving her any of the yams she got. His mother-in-law was annoyed: "Why are you keeping back that kangaroo instead of giving it to me quickly? If it's because of my younger daughter, you're mad [your mind is going round]!" He replied sharply, "Don't talk to me like that, or I might spear your younger daughter if you can't send her to me [for even a little while]!" ' (This was at Mawulgudji, in mixed Maung and Gunwinggu territory near the King River. All of the characters eventually became birds: the elder brother is the *bugbug* rain pheasant and the younger is the *djuri*, whose coloured feathers are used in making sacred *maraiin* string.) Ngalmidul paused at the critical points; she pulled down the corners of her mouth, rounded her eyes, and waited for the audience to respond with shocked murmurs before going on with her story.

Other storytellers are more explicit. Women telling the Orphan and Rainbow story spoke disapprovingly of the people who neglected or teased the child or did not keep forbidden things out of his sight. In the story of old Nawulabeg (see Chapter 3), the reason his 'wives' left him was that he would keep having homosexual relations with the elder girl's little boy whenever the two of them were alone in camp: the narrator added, frowning, 'If he wanted to do that, he could have used his dog!' But we have suggested already that sequences like this last one, particularly when they are expanded with dramatic detail, come into a special category. They are part of Gunwinggu erotic mythology, which seems to stimulate teller and listeners, whether by design or otherwise, just as the blunter erotic songs do.

All of the stories of the sort discussed above may be taken as a guide to conduct in a negative sense, by providing a bad example; but that applies to many others, too, including more straightforward and unembellished incest stories.

One of the best-known bad-example myths is also one of the most important ritually – the Yirawadbad story. (See Chapter 6.) Apart from its ritual associations, it has the same theme as a number of others that focus on a double triangle in social relations: man–mother-in-law–betrothed wife, and man–betrothed wife–betrothed wife's sweetheart. It also carries a double caution: (a) a young wife who rejects her betrothed husband, even if he is old and ugly, is liable to be punished, and (b) a woman who does not see that her daughter marries the right man and stays with him cancels out her special relationship with her son-in-law. Also, the repercussions can affect more than the people immediately concerned: Yirawadbad, in his snake form, expresses hostility to everyone, even though girls are his favourite victims. The warning to girls is reflected in actual incidents, past and present. So is the warning to mothers-in-law, but less often and less explicitly, and recognition that one set of actions can have community-wide consequences is spelt out only in specific instances. But some side remarks on the myth, from elderly men as well as from women, condone the girl's stand 'because her husband was old, ugly, and bald' and so it was natural for her to prefer a young sweetheart.

This tolerance of sweethearts – in general, and for oneself – comes out more openly in another myth where Yiriu, before turning into a rocky hill near the coast, proclaimed with his last words: 'I'm Yiriu, standing here with a long nose. If I had remained alive, no woman would have been able to resist me, whether she was right for me or not – they would all have fought over me!'

Myths reflect in varying ways the socio-cultural context, the status, and even the personal interests of the people who tell them, and they contain 'ought' statements that can be singled out as guide-lines for behaviour. They are also assumed to influence conduct, but a direct cause and effect connection is easier to guess at than to demonstrate convincingly. We cannot go into these details, especially since the material is so abundant, but the importance of myth as a traditional 'charter' as well as a repository is quite clear – if only from the commentaries and interpretations that are a living part of it.

Going through the Life-cycle

In everyday living, rules of behaviour are largely kinship rules. (See Chapter 5.) Because kinship recognition covers the whole population in any person's interactory perspective, it is like a mesh or grid spread over the total content of activity, dividing it up in terms of interpersonal relations.

Children are introduced very early to this orientation, but the teaching process is deceptively casual. A baby is always in the company of other people – parents, grandparents, older brothers and sisters, or other close relatives in the same camp constellation. Even before he can sit up, they handle him and talk to him, using kin terms to identify themselves and anyone else near by. They treat other features of his environment in the same way, pointing to specific objects, animals (especially dogs), and so on and at the same time repeating the appropriate words. By the time he can run freely he is expected to have a vocabulary of basic everyday words, and to be able to apply the main vocative terms and the simplest reference terms to the people he sees most often. Mistakes are not directly corrected and he is not punished for making them. People simply reiterate words, phrases, and kin terms in the proper way, confident that he will imitate them. This consistent teaching might not seem to extend to toilet training. Adults show no concern when small children urinate over them, and even children well into the 'running about' stage can expect to have someone else attend to covering up urine and faeces for them. Gunwinggu and other western Arnhem Landers are traditionally fussy about this. Any kind of excrement is potential sorcery material and should be concealed, and when a person cannot attend to it himself the responsibility devolves on his close kin. For children, the principle is actually the same as in language-teaching and teaching about kinship – an emphasis on imitation and example, simultaneously showing and telling what to do. The argument in this case rests, not on cleanliness, but on self-preservation.

Various phases are singled out in an ordinary life-cycle. One term refers to a child before birth, and then for several weeks afterward – during which time 'he lies on his back' and later 'he turns over'; his mother carries him under one arm in a curved pad of thick paperbark or holds him against her breast. 'He crawls'; 'he sits'; 'he stands', grasping an upright stick some close relative has put in the ground for him. 'He goes, he falls' – takes a few steps and falls again. Even before this he can expect to be carried astride someone's shoulder or neck, supported by one hand until he has learnt to hold on. 'He runs about'; 'he grows bigger', but still expects to be carried or breast-fed on demand.

Both parents are recognized as contributing to a child's growth, from the very beginning of its life, but in different ways. Pre-natal tabus fall most heavily on the mother, but the father shares in them too, and it is to him that the child first appears in spirit form. If a woman of child-bearing age, or her husband, finds edible things or creatures that are unusual in some respect – very small, thin, large, fat, numerous, tame, or otherwise odd in appearance or manner – other people say, 'She must be pregnant.' But the dominant emphasis, where this is concerned, is on the pre-natal bond between a child and its *father*. The father or his sister may see (for example, in a dream) the child's spirit riding on a fish or a crocodile or a buffalo, 'bringing good things to its father'. The foods associated with such an occasion, vegetable as well as meat, are identified as the child's *gaingen*, 'flesh-concerning' (*gain* = 'flesh'), but there is no tabu on eating or killing them. Nor do they seem to have any connection with the *gunmugugur* or moiety or semi-moiety affiliation of either parent. The child himself may not remember any of them in later life, although his parents (and possibly his grandparents) will probably be able to list them in detail, with the circumstances in which they were identified as *gaingen*. Some adults do recall being told about their own *gaingen*, and can show on their bodies the mark where the weapon struck that particular fish (etc.), but they seem to be more interested in their children's and their contemporaries' children's. Possibly, children's lack of interest in such matters is related to the fact that there is nothing they have to do about them – no action they need take, for instance.

The two main dimensions a child must learn to deal with are the social (other people) and the non-human, and the idea of what is normal in both of these is highlighted in a negative way by the behaviour of children who do not respond to teaching. Comparisons are sometimes drawn between children born at about the same time, or between older and younger children, but only very approximately. An 'abnormal' child is one who deviates well outside the customary pattern or becomes fixed at one stage: for example, if he cannot stand, let alone walk, when his peers are already running and playing together, or if he cannot speak intelligibly when they are quite fluent. Several cases are reported in genealogies from the recent past. The abnormalities range from slight disabilities to fairly severe ones, but the worst-affected children, aside from those afflicted with straightforward physical deafness and dumbness, have rarely survived beyond puberty. To explain such abnormalities, people usually say that one of the parents must have broken a tabu or somebody with a grievance has worked sorcery on the child or a malignant spirit has taken away his ability to understand and communicate.

For Gunwinggu, understanding comes through listening. A person with 'blocked ears' has 'no sense, he can't think'; and associated with this is loss of power to communicate in speech — having no 'tongue', a word that has a double meaning in Gunwinggu, too (tongue-as-organ, and tongue-as-language). The symptoms are believed to show up in early childhood – although in some respects they have a parallel in adult sorcery victims. There are stories of native doctors, *margidbu*, effecting dramatic cures, but none of these has been authenticated. And the threat that a malignant spirit will kidnap a child or take away his tongue is a sanction against a wide range of naughty behaviour. A 'deaf' child relates only minimally to other people. And he cannot discriminate between what is edible and what is not (he tries to eat stones and earth) or between what is dangerous and what is safe. This last applies not only to snakes, crocodiles, bitter foods, and the like, but also to the food tabus that carry a comparable threat of punishment for non-observance.

Apart from the literal reference to blocked ears, the usual term for a person who is more or less consistently abnormal in this sense is *bengwar* (*ngalbengwar* for a female; *-war* is *-wari*, 'bad', 'wrong', 'not good'). The stem *-beng* means 'mind' in the sense of the machinery for storing and assessing information and acting accordingly: to remember is to carry or to have in one's *-beng* ('I remember', *ngabenggan*). And another kind of deviation is signified in the expression *-bengwabun*, or *-bengwabom*; *wabun* means 'going round', 'circling', or 'spinning'. A person whose 'mind is going round' is either dizzy or silly – not as drastically as if he were *bengwar*, and the upset may be temporary, but the implication is that he 'doesn't know what he's doing'. This is said of normal children and adults who say or do something that is regarded as both stupid and wrong.

Ordinarily a child gradually learns to take responsibility and in the process becomes more obviously independent and self-reliant. It is a limited independence, because interpersonal cooperation is basic to the Gunwinggu way of life, but in fact its smooth working rests on intelligent participation.

In the first place, then, a child makes a working adjustment to *people*, starting with his immediate family. The first kin term a child learns, Gunwinggu say, is *garang*, 'mother'. Mother's sisters and co-wives, grandparents, and his own older sisters are temporary substitutes, but until he is weaned his own mother is particularly important to him. Even if other mothers breast-feed him or dip their fingers in honey for him to suck, this does not take the place of a single, continuing, and specifically personal relationship. The word *malaidj*, translated as 'orphan', does have a broader range of meaning, especially in 'swearing'. Directed abusively at someone else, it implies, 'You're a person without close relatives!' Applied to oneself, it expresses dismay or despair. In ordinary speech it can be applied to a fatherless child, but, above all, it refers to a motherless one. Later in life the definition of 'own mother' is expanded, in line with the widening range for other close relatives, but not at this early stage in a child's experience. Even in the ideal situation where a close sister of his mother is married to his father and has cared for him almost since birth, she is viewed simply as the best available, not as an almost identical replacement. The crisis is poignant enough for a girl, but the use of the masculine form *namalaidj* in all our versions of the Orphan and Rainbow story is more than a convenient way of suggesting that the child could be of either sex. It underlines the bond between mother and *son*, most conspicuous if the boy is an only child or youngest child, with weaning delayed accordingly.

Not that weaning in general is seen as a problem. Children are introduced early to solid foods – honey, fish, lily roots, bones. The Orphan and Rainbow story reflects this too, although the Orphan seems to be usually between about one and four or five years old – old enough to have formed a personal attachment, but not old enough to be relatively independent. Women claim that children stop drinking milk of their own accord as they come to like other foods better. But they also recognize sibling rivalry, in themselves in retrospect and in their own and other people's children. And they concede that a second-to-last child is discouraged by the sight of a new baby drinking in his place, or, failing that, by threats and slaps from his own mother. The process of emotional separation from his mother is slow and uneven, even though it is moderated by the presence of other relatives, and though the father becomes increasingly significant, even for a girl.

*ng spirit beings on bark at Oenpelli, 1958. These have mythological significance and
Mangerdji style*

Painting a kangaroo. Gunwinggu X-ray style. Oenpelli, 1958

Painting an anthropomorphic sorcery figure. Gunwinggu style. Oenpelli, 1958

Waramurungundji, the Fertility Mother. Feathered ornaments hang from her head, a net bag at her back, and a dilly bag from her elbow, and she holds a digging stick. Her heart is shown above the centre of her body. Artist: Old Wurungulngul, Maung, 1947

Wuragag, husband of Waramurungundji. He wears feathers in his hair and a hairbelt, and carries a spear. The bottle on his head, he found in the course of his travels. He was eventually metamorphosed as Tor Rock. Artist: Old Wurungulngul, Maung, 1947

Nadulmi in his Kangaroo manifestation, as ubar leader. A dilly bag hangs from his neck; he has a beard, and white crane feathers attached to his head. His body is painted with a special design called gunmed, used by ubar actors. Two malbululug grass night birds are his companions. Artist: Midjaumidjau, Gunwinggu, 1947

Nadulmi as a man, painted to represent the 'Mother one'. He lies full length on the sacred ubar ground which symbolizes the Mother's body, resting his head on a special stone; on the right is an 'arm' of the Mother, entrance to the ground. Artist: Ngaiiwul, Gunwinggu, 1950

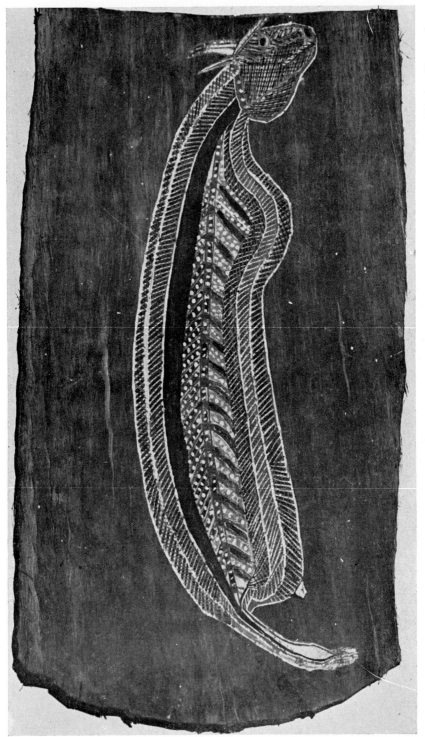

Ngaljod, the Rainbow Snake, who followed Gumadir creek until she came to Gabari, where she swallowed a man named Najugjug and his dog. She was later

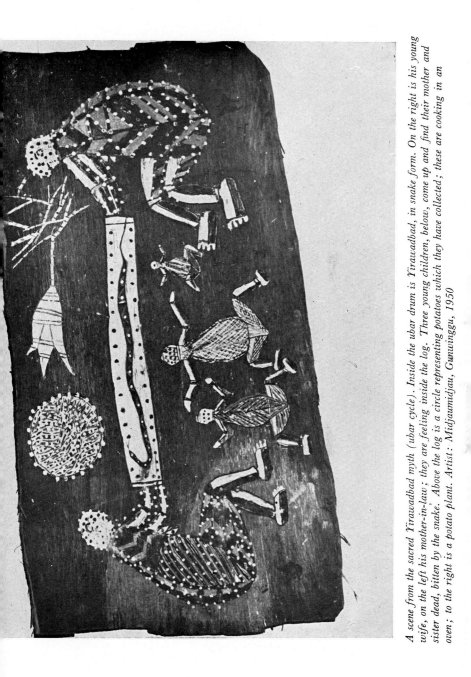

A scene from the sacred Yirawadbad myth (ubar cycle). Inside the ubar drum is Yirawadbad, in snake form. On the right is his young wife, on the left his mother-in-law; they are feeling inside the log. Three young children, below, come up and find their mother and sister dead, bitten by the snake. Above the log is a circle representing potatoes which they have collected; these are cooking in an oven; to the right is a potato plant. Artist: Midjaumidjau, Gunwinggu, 1950

Namalaidj (orphan) rests his bag full of round mandaneg *bitter roots on a flat stone (above the bag). He holds a fly whisk. The* mandaneg *were metamorphosed as stones at Gabari, near Cooper's Creek. Artist: Ngaiiwul, Gunwinggu, 1950*

Ideally, a child's parents speak the same dialect of the same language. If they do not, and if by some chance the close relatives of either have not learnt the other's language, this makes things harder for the child – because Gunwinggu say that children learn first from their mothers and that the father's language, if it differs, comes, later. Some continue to keep their 'mother tongue' in first place, without switching priority to the father's language on the way to puberty. This is perhaps more likely in a matrilocal situation. (One of the most clear-cut illustrations is the eldest son of a 'true' Gunwinggu [Danig] father and a Maung [Merwulidj – that is, Maiirgulidj] mother, living in Maung territory; he cannot speak or understand Gunwinggu, and even expresses active antagonism to it. His mother can understand Gunwinggu but does not speak it. Her husband learnt Maung quite early, but he was able to teach some Gunwinggu to all of his children except the eldest.)

Aside from language, children are taught that in some respects they are aligned with their father, in others with their mother. A man may tell his son or daughter, 'You and I are one – we are of one *gunmugugur*, like my father and his sister, your *mawa*.' On other occasions, the child's mother points up the contrast: 'You and I are one – we are of one *gunmud* [moiety, semi-moiety, matrilineal subsection cycle], like my mother and her brother, your *gagag*.' The contrast is projected into the future, with *gunmugugur* continuity underlined for boys and *gunmud* continuity for girls, but not so single-mindedly that they lose sight of cross-linkages and oblique influences in the past and in the present. These emerge indirectly through talking about individual persons and their inter-relationships, but most children absorb genealogical information half-heartedly and in patches.

Other adult–child relations include conventionalized joking-exchanges between *gagali* and *ganjulg* of opposite sex. The actual content is usually simple and some of it is quasi-erotic. Gunwinggu say that children have to be shown how to take part in this – what to say and what not to say, and when, and which *gagali* and *ganjulg* are *not* joking partners.

Nevertheless, children are also expected to play together, and although much of their play foreshadows involvement in adult affairs there are no formal pressures in that direction. Teaching about kin tabus begins early, but adults are realistic about performance. The first such tabu to be seriously implemented emphasizes the

prohibitions *and* the obligations between *nagurng* and *ngalgurng* –
the mutual commitments that are focused on the giving and
accepting of a *ngalgurng*'s daughter as wife. The appropriate relatives
in this category, those between whom the existing tie is closest and a
future tie already anticipated, may be shown to each other, if they
live near enough, as soon as they are able to take consistent notice
of what is said to them – conventionally, at about the 'going and
falling' stage. Most often, whether or not they have any full brothers
or sisters, this is treated as a paired relationship: 'She will make a
wife for you', 'You will make a wife for him', and so on. If they live
in the same camp, they may play together at first – even at 'husband
and wife' if their parents or grandparents or mothers' brothers are
not too strict. More often they are called apart, reminded of their
special relationship, and advised to choose other playmates.
Conventionally, they should be learning the special vocabulary that
underlines their relationship, since they are not supposed to communicate in ordinary language.

Brother–sister avoidance is even less firmly enforced in early
childhood, on the grounds that siblings should first learn to stand
together. They are told to keep watch for each other in case of
snakes or other possible dangers, and a girl is expected to act
quasi-maternally toward a younger brother. At the same time, they
are warned that one should not eat food the other has caught or
collected, that this is a mutually supporting avoidance relationship
with wider implications. A boy is told by his mother that his sister
will 'make a child for us, for our side', and that it is in his own
interest to protect her – as well as to discipline her if necessary.
They are told not to touch each other, not to call each other's
names, and not to demonstrate openly the affection they are supposed
to feel for each other.

These are the most conspicuous kin restraints. By the time their
nasal septums are pierced – traditionally when they are between
six and nine years old – children are expected to observe the restraints
and also to be able to see them in a larger context of relationships –
and to have some idea of the system behind the specific and tangible
referents.

In the second place, by that stage a child should have learnt to
make a working adjustment to *things*. There is no obligation yet to
attend to kinship commitments, which are still handled by his

parents. Before this, both boys and girls have had to observe certain food tabus (such as not eating bitter roots), again primarily the responsibility of parents, expecially mothers. But this piercing of the nasal septum, usually done casually by a *gagali* or a *ganjulg* with no ritual formality, is the first real experience of event-centred food tabus, and of prohibition on handling axes, spears, or digging sticks.

After the nasal piercing, boys and girls more often play separately. A boy still has some way to go before being initated as an adult. A small rite, the cutting of a lock of hair, would once have marked the killing of his first fat goanna or fish, and after he has hunted with his father a small ritual feast should mark the spearing of his first kangaroo. He cannot marry, however, traditionally, until he has been through the *ubar, lorgun,* and *maraiin* series. He is called by the various labels for 'novice' or 'initiate', or the general terms for 'young man', 'unmarried man' and later, 'married man'.

Once the septum is pierced, a girl, in traditional terms, is marriageable or almost so, and may go to her husband without waiting for puberty. But whether she is married or not, the public rite of re-entry into the main camp after her first menstrual seclusion, accompanied by song and ceremony, formally marks her transition to adulthood. Even though she is labelled 'married woman', she is also categorized as 'young or adolescent woman' until she has borne a child; different labels apply if the child dies or if she reaches middle age or menopause without one. The onset of old age, signified by greying hair, brings a change of term – the same for men and women except for the sex-indicating prefix.

By the time a person is past middle age he will have accumulated at least 2 or 3 principal personal names, and usually more; but he is also likely to have given at least 2 or 3 away, preferably to close relatives in the same *gunmugugur* (to brothers' sons, sons' sons, etc.) but also to others. If any of these people should die, the name reverts to him, so to speak, but in any case he may continue to keep it as an alternative name even if he does not use it. The same applies in the case of a woman. Gunwinggu personal names are mostly separate for each sex, except where they refer to places or sites. Nicknames are not usually given at birth, but acquired at any time from early or middle childhood onward. Some, again, are simply place-names, but many of them point to physical characteristics or disabilities (the prefix *ngal-* being added for a female, except for animal and bird names); examples are Biddubbe ('Clawed fist'), Djagu ('Left-hand'), Mamig ('Shortie'), Bambal ('Baldie'), Djebwi ('Possum'), Magagur ('Pelican' – having big feet), Ngalgulerg (name of a short, stockily built mythical woman whose breasts developed before she reached puberty), or ordinary words for 'blind' or 'deaf'. Others are comments on behaviour: for example, Dangwog ('Wordy-mouth') or Wogwari (a person whose speech is 'bad', in the way he articulates it or in the content of what he says), Nawoneng or Nanguluminy or Ngudjawog ('Yarn-spinner'), Djanmal (having a slightly lisping way of speaking, described as sounding 'like *laad laad laad*'), Wirindji (a large and aggressive mythical 'cannibal woman'), or Nawurgbil ('Hawk' – applied to a woman who, according to gossip, would single out a man, circle around him, swoop in to catch him, and then start looking for another). Other nicknames again commemorate incidents in a person's life; and, if they are dramatic enough, they can displace others as substitute names – 'Spear-in-the-back', for instance. In this last form, a nickname can be bestowed on a person quite late in his lifetime; and this is the most specifically individual type of name, as contrasted with the traditional names that are inherited and transmitted in a more or less invariant form. Name transmission gives an extra dimension to an existing tie (for instance, between a woman and her brother's daughter); but it also helps in the establishing or confirming of new ties, especially now that personal names are being spread more widely outside the *gunmugugur*. Genealogies collected between 1947 and 1968 show many of the same personal names recurring, still being bestowed on children by patrilineal kin or from patrilineal kin who are now dead; but they also show that the basis of transmission or selection of personal names has been broadened considerably even within that period, as regards not only matrilineal kin but also purely nominal or category kin.

Generally speaking, children are highly valued. They are indulged and petted. The comments on the Orphan and Rainbow story typify the view that it is almost impossible to deny a child something he really wants even if he should not have it – for example, bitter foods, or new-season's fish from a partly tabu billabong – and that the easiest and best approach is to keep such things away from him. In return, children are expected to help and support their parents in old age. The nurturing–dependence relationship is reversed, in a cycle which takes in, though less centrally, the grandparent–grandchildren's generations as well. Because kinship on the basis of territory or merely of category is a partial substitute for close genealogical ties, elderly people with no close living descendants can always expect someone younger to accept active responsibility for them.

But attitudes toward the old are ambivalent. They are respected for their experience and knowledge, and they have certain privileges, by way of relaxation of food and kin-avoidance tabus. Elderly men who were religious leaders, provided they are not senile, are listened to with some attention. Old women are helpful in minding small children, and once they are assumed to be near death they can be taken to the men's secret ritual ground without fear of supernatural reprisals. On the other hand, they are disparaged for being ugly, no longer sexually attractive, smelly (one expression for them can be so translated), weak, and eventually a burden.

Keeping the Peace

Everything would be all right if people behaved properly and obeyed the rules, so Gunwinggu sometimes say. But they match this with a strong conviction that at least some of them will not. The information a person accumulates by the time he reaches adulthood, therefore, includes conventionally accepted means of defining and coping with offences – and also, though this is not admitted in so many words, committing them.

Response to any breach of the peace is inseparable from the question of who committed it, or is believed to have committed it. It is relative to age, status and social relationships.

Where children are concerned, for instance, it is predominantly a domestic matter. A mother is responsible for her children while they are small, but, if she beats them too often, she herself stands a very good chance of being beaten by her husband for hurting 'his' children. It is easier to use preventive or conciliatory tactics, like coaxing and persuasion, and, if that fails, to 'hit them with words' or make threatening gestures. An alternative was mentioned in case material and myths, but we saw no examples of it: to put the spirit of a disobedient child symbolically into a tree or into a patch of ground and then thrash the spot vigorously, preferably with the child's knowledge – a threat to the child, and an emotional outlet for the parent.

In one reported case, a little boy accidentally killed a baby (his own FZDS: see Fig. 19), but very little was done about it and there was no question of compensation.

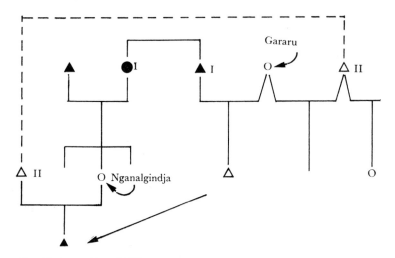

Fig. 19. An accidental killing.

Key:
See Fig. 13.
Gunmugugur affiliations: I = Wurig, II = Madjawar.

Note: In this small camping unit, the two men (Nganalgindja's husband and Gararu's husband) were both Madjawar. Gararu's husband's father and his brother and their wives were sometimes in this group. The incident took place near Maganjir, in Madjawar territory.

The baby's mother, Nganalgindja, said some years later (in 1950) that she had put him to sleep and left him in his paperbark carrier near the edge of a billabong while she dived for lily roots. Several children were playing near by. One was her little MBS, whose mother was Gararu; his father was dead. Another was his elder 'sister', the daughter of Gararu's second husband from another mother who had eloped and left her behind; she was being reared by Gararu. Suddenly the children called out to Nganalgindja to come quickly, the baby was hurt. A fishing spear, flung by the boy in play, had struck him in the head. By the time she reached the spot, the boy's 'sister' had pulled out the spear and blood was pouring from the wound. Then the girl turned on her brother and beat him quite severely. His mother and stepfather did the same when they came home to camp that afternoon, and refused to allow him any food until the next morning ('he had only grass to eat'). But Nganalgindja did nothing to punish him. 'He didn't mean it,' she said in retrospect. 'He couldn't see the baby there, in the grass.' She gashed her own head in grief and would not eat: 'I just wept, all night and all day.' The following night, the baby died. (He was given the full sequence of mortuary rites: the corpse exposed on a platform, the bones collected after drying but in this case kept in a basket, food assembled for a mortuary ceremony during which Nganalgindja and her husband washed themselves ritually; and then the whole group moved out of that area, 'away from that country where our baby died'.)

The excuse of unintentional killing would probably not have been enough to block further action if the offender had been an adult, *unless* he was closely related to the dead child and its parents. In this instance, there was not only the factor of close kinship but also the extenuating circumstance that the culprit was a child.

Gunwinggu are reluctant to discipline other people's children, and this applies to grandparents too. Even casual and neglectful mothers resent outside interference, especially with a son. A mother is expected to be warmly protective of her children as long as she is able, whatever their age, and to defend them against gossip and physical attack. And she is likely to start a fight with any woman who seems to be leading her son astray, deflecting him from a properly arranged betrothal or marriage.

Responsibility of parents for children is most complete when they are very young, but because the nuclear family is not easily isolated as a unit this is a matter of degree. In addition, some authority is delegated to children themselves. A girl helps to mother a younger brother as well as a younger sister, and the role of a brother in disciplining a sister, already mentioned, is a strategic feature of social control; his role extends into the next generation, where he can exercise combined disciplinary and protective power in relation to his sister's children.

Even small upsets within a family unit – between children, children and parents, husband and wife, co-wives – can spill over into the wider field of kinship. Gunwinggu have a lively sense of individual separateness and resent any intrusion they consider unwarranted, but they put no premium on privacy in so far as that implies withdrawal and reticence. Openness and frankness are 'good'. Secrecy among close relatives and friends is not, except in the religious sphere. If an argument is going on in one part of the camp, others near by know about it: there is no attempt at concealment. People either listen or ignore it, or appear to ignore it, or wait to choose their moment for joining in.

The main areas of trouble fall under four headings:

(1) Domestic issues, such as preparation or sharing of food, use of firewood, slapping of a child or a dog, or refusal to get water.

(2) Other arguments over property, such as the killing of someone else's dog (rare).

(3) Betrothal arrangements; extra-marital affairs without a spouse's consent; elopements.

(4) Breaches of tabu; infringement of secret-sacred rights or rules (rare).

Disturbances under the first heading are often very noisy while they last, and they may even go on intermittently for up to a week or so; but in the ordinary way they are contained within the domestic group and spears are not used, or not used in earnest. This applies to most minor dissension between husband and wife, and between women – provided no more deep-seated grievances are involved.

Men keep out of women's quarrels unless they have a pressing personal reason for intervening. Older women may try to resolve the trouble by reminding the combatants of their kinship roles. But if those centrally involved are determined to fight and take no notice of 'brother' warnings, and if no brother is near enough to take notice or allow himself to be drawn in, then what could have remained a camp skirmish may be regularized into a conventional combat. Two opponents take up their digging or fighting sticks and confront each other in the middle of a group of onlookers and supporters. One grasps her stick in both hands while the other stands with head bent forward and hands clasped in front, taunting or daring her. They do this in turn, and the winner is the one who first incapacitates the other – for example, by wounding her in the head, breaking her arm or knocking her to the ground.

A small camp fight can have further repercussions if it revives old grudges or exacerbates new ones. Gunwinggu themselves, including women, often cited 'women and corpses' as the outstanding causes of conflict, in mythical or quasi-mythical as well as contemporary situations. Old Mangurug suggested that the reason the Woraidbag are virtually extinct was that 'they were always fighting over women – not over dead men and their killers, but only over women. That's why all of them are dead and their country is empty of people. If we had done the same, we would all be gone now, too.' And for Gunwinggu and other western Arnhem Landers, as well, the suggestion is that 'corpse trouble' was itself very often a consequence of 'woman trouble', or quarrels about betrothal and marital relations. This suggestion seems to be based on a sprinkling of cases where a man has been fatally speared by another who wanted his wife or a woman has been speared for refusing to elope. But quarrels over women do not usually go so far.

Betrothals, and Elopements

Betrothal arrangements are the subject of a great deal of discussion. Much of it is about people who are already born and not just future possibilities, and that in itself indicates a margin of choice. It also implies that, the ideal notwithstanding, in many cases a girl's betrothal is not finalized at her birth. Even if it has already been arranged, interested persons can still find scope for negotiation; and if the girl herself objects, that complicates it further – as in this example.

In March 1950, Biliridj (Marin *gunmugugur*) was about eleven years old and her betrothed husband, Djawida (Gunumbidj), possibly forty-five to fifty. The two were 'proper *gagali*', but not genealogically close. Both her parents were dead, but she called Gulamarmar 'father' (Djelama; current husband of Wurgamara – see below). Djawida had been pressing for the marriage to be finalized. One night, her MFZDs, Djunggubulbul and Gunbagunga, tried to send her to him. (Her brother was married to Gunbagunga's daughter.) She refused to go, on the grounds that she didn't like him and that he already had two wives, one of them her own sister. Her mother's brother, Ngambaiinga (Gurulg; father of Waiula – see below), supported her, but Djawida struck her on the back with his spear-thrower. She ran for protection to the camp of Gulamarmar's mother Mangguwai (Mingalgen), her father's mother's close sister. Gulamarmar took her part, shouting, 'I won't give her to you, you've already got her elder sister!' Djawida retorted, 'Well, don't expect me to give you *manme* or *mai*ⁱ or kangaroo meat. You can find another man if you like, to give her to!' Djunggubulbul and Gunbagunga woke the girl up and tried to send her to Djawida's camp, but she cried and resisted. Shouted recriminations went on for several nights. Ngambaiinga's main argument seemed to be that 'you [Djawida] didn't give us any of your sisters' daughters, or I could have given you *our* sister's daughter'. Because this was close to Oenpelli mission station and because both Gulamarmar and Ngambaiinga took Biliridj's part, nothing more was done to force her to go to Djawida.

By 1958, in fact, Biliridj was married to Djunggubulbul's son Dubungu (Born), whose first wife had been a daughter of Wurgamara by her first husband (Djelama). Biliridj's own father's mother was Born. By 1966 she had six children and her elder sister, Djawida and Mangguwai were all dead.

Emphasis on the ideal type of marriage, formally arranged by kin, goes hand in hand with an emphasis on romantic love. The general climate of opinion regarding extra-marital affairs is permissive. A recognized code of behaviour applies between sweethearts, *mararaidj*. They send messages to each other through go-betweens, exchange small token gifts, and sigh sentimentally about each other to trusted friends. Erotic scratching and biting are appropriate signs of their affection, and they demand wholehearted loyalty regardless of any prior attachment: 'You are my *true* wife/husband!' The duration of such episodes varies. Some dwindle away after several weeks, and a few end in elopement. In other cases somebody, usually the spouse of either or both, decides to make a public scene. After that, the relationship may continue surreptitiously on the same footing or be dropped in favour of another, or the result may be a marital re-shuffle.

The Yirawadbad myth and others that deal with this theme support the established principle of marriage arranged in the proper way, and show what can happen to a wife who rejects her chosen husband in favour of a sweetheart. The gossip songs, in contrast, insinuate that it is possible to have both of these simultaneously – a spouse *and* a sweetheart – or, failing that, a sweetheart *as* a spouse.

Early in 1950, and for some little time before and after, these temporary liaisons were very much in fashion. Three main songmen and a few others were kept busy reporting them, in short dialogue-style songs that did not identify any individual characters by name. This left room for gossip and speculation, which in turn provided more song material. Tolerance of sweethearts normally stops short when it comes to one's own wife or husband. The injured person is expected to make at least a show of rage and jealousy once a liaison becomes public knowledge – not before that, however, unless a man becomes ill and therefore suspects his wife is being unfaithful, or he dreams about her, or his mother hears rumours and decides to intervene. Some men are chronically or spasmodically jealous, even to the extent of forbidding their wives to take part in ordinary ceremonies, and accusing them of potential infidelity if they show any interest in gossip songs. Skirmishes and shouting contests precipitated by this may result in bruises or minor wounds, or a broken bone or so, but not usually in any fatal injury. Women rarely assault men, whereas a man may attack his wife as well as her supposed sweetheart, and her mother's brother may do the same. So may any man who calls her 'sister'. This is essentially punishment rather than retaliation, but its extension outside the immediate triangle of spouses-and-sweetheart leaves more scope for going beyond the rough-and-ready estimate of an appropriate penalty. Although such disturbances are worked out in terms of kinship (consanguineal and affinal), in all of them there is a point at which somebody who is not deeply involved steps in and separates the contestants, declaring that the matter has gone far enough.

An elopement sets in motion the same kind of response in a more heightened form, and with more action in proportion to words. The outcome depends on a combination of factors – the relationship of the people concerned, the response of the woman's husband, and where and for how long the couple try to seek refuge. In a few cases they claimed that they wanted only a short interlude together, though without the husband's consent. In others their aim was a more permanent union, particularly when the husband's claim to his wife was disputed.

Two main issues arise in connection with elopements. One is the relationship between the two persons themselves – how far this conforms with the rules governing marriage and sexual relations generally. The other is their relationship to other people, especially the woman's husband or betrothed husband. The first is of wider concern, because of its moral implications. The second centres more on personal claims, and public opinion is less relevant than kin support.

In one case that would almost certainly not have been tolerated traditionally, the eloping pair were of the same semi-moiety, *jariburig*. She is *ngalwamud* and Ngalngbali, he is *nabulan* and Madjawar, and they called each other MB/ZD, but their genealogical connection was not close. Her father was Nawundurba and her mother's mother Mandjalima (Fig. 13). His father's sister was the mother's mother of Balada, the father's mother of Mandjuraidj (Fig. 20, Note b). Both of them had been correctly married to other people. Her husband was a Wurig man, a son of Mareiiga in Fig. 14. His first wife was a Marin woman, a sister of Ngalgindali's mother's second husband (Ngalgindali in Fig. 13).

We met the eloping pair first in 1945 at a small buffalo station near the Mary River. They told us they were afraid to go back to the Oenpelli area. He claimed that he would be killed, and that his own relatives, including his full brother, would not protect him because the union was so wrong. By 1947 her 'first husband' was dead, but it was not until shortly before 1958 that he brought her back to Oenpelli, and by 1961 he himself was back in the area to stay. After some arguments they were accepted without penalty, although in 1966 the marriage was still being talked about as intrinsically wrong. The fact that they had no children made the reconciliation easier. His first wife had been married for a long time to another man, but he kept the second (Badmadi – or Djulbin – from the Maiali-Djauan side.)

Another intra-moiety union was a source of continuing upsets at Oenpelli in 1949-50. Nama is *ngalwagaidj* and *jarigarngurg*, a daughter of Mangurug and Mikinmikin (Fig. 14). After her first husband's death another marriage was arranged for her, but by 1949 she was beginning to show openly her preference for Namuwongudj, *nagangila* and *jariwurga*, and finally left her husband to live with him. They called each other *gagag*. Her mother expressed shame at this, but did not actively oppose it. (The fact that he was Mirar like herself did not seem to influence her, because his main affiliations were Gunbargid and Maiali side.) Nor did Nama's father – perhaps because of his Yiwadja orientation, since intra-moiety unions are said to have been quite acceptable in Yiwadja tradition. Nama had no children at the time, but in 1951 bore her 'sweetheart husband' a daughter. When that happened, they moved away toward the Pine Creek area. Her 'first husband' had expressed disgust at her behaviour but he took no steps to recover her: the gloss on this, by 1958, was that he had 'given her away'. By 1966 the Nama-Namuwongudj union seemed to be accepted *in absentia* as an established fact, and their daughter was betrothed to one of Gurindjulul's and Manggudja's sons.

In a fairly recent example, one of Gurindjulul's and Manggudja's daughters, Minyaiwi (born in 1946), ran away to Croker Island with a young man whose sister was married to one of her brothers. She left her little son behind with his father, Balada. Balada's first betrothed wife's father was a Ngalngbali man, brother of Nawundurba (Fig. 13), and her mother, a Durmangga woman, was a close daughter's daughter of the Wurig siblings shown in Figs 13 and 20 (including Gararu's, Gurweg's and Mareiiga's first husbands). After this first wife died, Gurindjulul and Manggudja gave Balada (in 1949) their eldest daughter, who had been tentatively promised to him, and she later bore a child. He killed her suddenly as she slept one night, during a mental blackout. Nevertheless, after a time they gave him Minyaiwi. They were upset at first about the elopement, but by the time she was pregnant with her third child (born in 1966) from her 'sweetheart husband' they had forgiven her. Her 'first husband', Balada, has not tried seriously to recover her, even though she has now returned to Oenpelli; he has another wife, a daughter of Nawundurba and daughter's daughter of Mandjalima (Fig. 13).

The central figure in another case was a young Wurig woman, Melenggir, whose first betrothed husband died while she was still a child and the second not long after their marriage; he was also married to her eldest sister, Wurgamara. Melenggir then married his brother, Djurubinyin. All of these men were Djelama. Djurubinyin's other wife was a daughter of Mareiiga (Fig. 14) and was

Djelama too, because Mareiiga's husband had lent her for a while to a close 'brother', but Mareiiga's 'true husband' and the father of her other children was Wurig.

Melenggir eloped with her second sister's husband, also Djelama, and that sister accompanied them, but he eventually brought her back because he was sorry for her husband. His full sister had been married for a time to Melenggir's brother. Later, Melenggir eloped twice with a Dangulu man from the Margulidjban area, who brought her back, first for the same reason, and the second time because his mother was afraid of trouble. They called each other *'gagali'*. But after that Djurubinyin refused to take her back, saying that he had always been generous in letting her sweetheart have her and so there was no reason to steal her. She therefore settled down with her 'sweetheart husband', but not long afterward there were fresh disturbances. Her sweetheart husband's half-brother from the same father came to Oenpelli to claim her on the grounds that one of her 'uncles' (Barbin; not a close mother's brother but a quite influential man) had promised her to him; the 'uncle' actually wanted a girl, Waiula (Gurulg), over whom the newcomer himself had some control as an uncle.

A great deal of argument went on about this at the end of 1949 and the first part of 1950, exacerbated by several factors. The daughter of Melenggir's eldest sister, Wurgamara, had died leaving a baby girl, and Wurgamara wanted Melenggir to stay and help look after 'our daughter's child'. Wurgamara was upset too because Waiula, wife of one of her sons, was openly having an affair with his younger brother, and because another of her sons was serving a term in Darwin gaol for a spear-killing. Djurubinyin's other wife was also in trouble. She had previously been the centre of a small storm when he accused her of having as sweetheart a young man she called *gagag*. The boy had been hurt in that fight, and now his close mother and father's sister were afraid the same thing would happen again and so they both turned on her.

However, Melenggir finally went with her 'sweetheart husband' to Maningrida, where she is reported to be still living with him. By 1966 she had four children, but by 1958 he had already taken a second, younger, wife.

In a number of reported cases of elopement in the past nothing seems to have been done to restore the *status quo*, and the couple simply remained together as husband and wife. One possible answer was sorcery.

Un-natural Death

Sorcery explanations are retrospective. (See Chapter 6.) When the hazards of illness, snakes, crocodiles, buffaloes, sharks, drowning, and so on, claim a victim, the immediate query is, 'Why this person, and not that?' For a girl whose betrothal arrangements were changed, the answer is that the first betrothed husband was angry and resentful. A rejected suitor or husband has a respectable precedent in Yirawadbad, who used sorcery as the first part of his revenge. In one recorded case, a woman is said to have been killed for taking some fish an old man had put aside as tabu for the *maraiin*. (The woman left a baby son – Balada, in Fig. 20; and when the old man himself died, nearly twenty years later, it was said that the boy had now been able to avenge his mother's death.) In another case, a man who had eloped with a woman of the same semi-moiety but a different dialect was fatally bitten by a snake – because, people said, a close brother of the woman's husband was sorry for him and decided to punish the interloper.

Gunwinggu believe that no creature is really dangerous to a whole person, one whose soul is intact. He can be bitten or injured but he will not die. Thus, old Mangurug told how a native doctor once cured her easily when she was bitten by a poison snake, 'because I was not sorcerized (*-gid*), I was strong!' (or 'hard', the word that is used for rocks and hard ground, and for 'hard' Gunwinggu). Had she died, that would have shown it was part of a prearranged plan and not an accident. Nevertheless, people try to keep clear of venomous snakes and the like, if only because they can always name someone with a possible grievance against them – that is, a potential sorcerer. Even where the physical cause of death seems obvious, the question of 'who was responsible' remains to be answered: in a fatal spearing, the man who threw the spear is not necessarily the 'real' killer.

The Gunwinggu origin of death myth (see Chapter 6) asserts that death is inevitable now, but need not have been. In everyday affairs the same kind of argument is raised, but *within* that framework: it is natural for all human beings to die provided they are ready for it, that is, provided they are very old. Otherwise, death is *un*-natural and somebody must be to blame. This holds for infant deaths and stillbirths, but in their case there is the possibility of rebirth through the same mother. (She may take steps to encourage this, such as eating a dead child's fingernails or carrying the corpse or some of the bones about with her or burying it in a termite mound.) Responsibility for illness and death among the very young and the old is still ascribed to human agents, but they are likely to be accused of neglect rather than sorcery.

Anger is therefore, along with grief, a conventional feature of mourning, and accusations and threats are a normal part of a camp upset after a death.

Old Gurweg (see Fig. 20) died suddenly one morning just before dawn, in February 1950. She was very frail and had been ill for some weeks, so her death came as no surprise, but the timing of it was. The main Oenpelli camp was almost deserted. Nearly everyone was some distance away at the *kunapipi* ground, waiting for the concluding rites when the novices 'emerge from the Snake'. Later in the day, as women wept, several of Gurweg's *namud* angrily charged others with neglecting her.

The main accusers were Balada and Marwana, who called her 'mother'. Especially, they threatened to kill their 'sister', Garidjala, claiming that she had been 'following another man, one to whom she hadn't been properly betrothed so that they had only been stealing each other', and that she 'hadn't been looking after her own mother, her big mother, but always leaving her to go to other places' – 'not saying to herself, "Someone might kill my mother, my own mother, and I should be there to look after her." ' Garidjala's husband at that time was Mikinmikin (Fig. 14), who was oriented toward the Yiwadja-Maung side, whereas her father's people had a Maiali-Djauan orientation.

The upset lasted intermittently for a few days, but nobody seemed to take the threats or the accusations seriously. They were probably, at least in part, an expression of self-consciousness or guilt at the circumstances of the death. (As several people said at the time, 'She died while we were away, and we didn't know about it! We were not there!') However, by 1966 Garidjala had left Mikinmikin and had a new husband, a Mirar man from the Maiali side (whose sister was married to a son of Mareiiga – see Fig. 14). (By early in 1968, Garidjala was dead.)

174

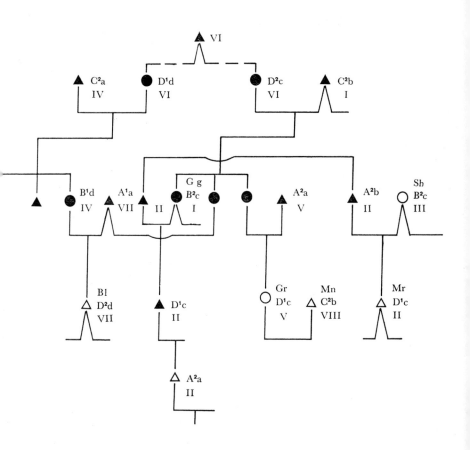

Fig. 20. Argument following a death.

Key:
See Fig. 13.
Gunmugugur affiliations: I = Barbin, II = Wurig, III = Ngalngbali, IV = Danig,
    V = Wadjag, VI = Madjawar, VII = Mandjulngoin, VIII = Maninggali.
Abbreviations of personal names:
    Bl = Balada   Gr = Garidjala   Mr = Marwana
    Gg = Gurweg   Mn = Mikinmikin   Sh = Gararu

(a) Gurweg and her two sisters were said by some people to be 'really Danig', perhaps because they called Balada's mother and mother's brothers 'sister' and 'brothers', or perhaps because of some closer liaison between their own mother and a brother of Balada's mother's father. Gurweg's father was also the father of Mareiiga (Fig. 14); Mareiiga's first husband and Gurweg's first husband were full brothers.

(b) One of Balada's mother's brothers was the father of Mandjuraidj (Fig. 13, Note a), whose first husband was the son of Gararu by her second husband. Gararu's daughter, Gadjibunba, first married the elder son of Balada's other mother's brother, and after his death went to his brother.

(c) The wife of Gurweg's son (Djelama) went after his death to Namaragalgal (Fig. 14), half-brother to Gurweg. Her sister's first husband was Wurgamara's brother, whose father was a brother of Gurweg's first husband; her third husband was a Marin man, brother of Gurweg's son's son's wife.

Public quarrelling like that after Gurweg's death provides an opportunity to express the right sentiments and, ideally, it clears the air. It serves an expressive purpose rather than an instrumental one, even though some of the accusations are made in earnest.

Circumstantial evidence alone does not convict a person, though it can help to build up a case. Hard evidence comes from other sources, such as clues found during an inquest (ideally, organized by a native doctor) or otherwise. One kind of clue is a small object among the dead person's belongings (that may have been wrapped into a bundle and hung on a tree) or in his hair, said to reveal the semi-moiety of the 'murderer' (for instance, charcoal, *jariburig*; stone, *jarigarngurg*). Or the information is disclosed in a dream, still without mention of any personal name. The final identification comes when someone, preferably a *margidbu*, considers the evidence in the light of the whole situation and the people connected with it, usually a little time after a death when their emotions have cooled down. The guiding question is, 'Who had a motive? To whose advantage was it that this person should die?' There is no suggestion of killing for its own sake. The assumption is, always, that no normal person works sorcery to kill another without a reason which made sense to him at the time.

Once the 'murderer' has been identified, it is for the deceased's close kin to say what should be done next. They may choose sorcery. This might be interpreted as a wait-and-see policy, on the grounds that sooner or later the 'murderer' will meet with an accident or fall ill or die, and then, by implication, they will be responsible. Alternatively, something from the dead person's belongings – a small piece of dilly-bag or clothing or hair, or the sorcery clue itself – is bound on to the shaft of a spear, partly exposed but not obvious. This revenge weapon is carried about by a close relative of the dead person such as a man's brother or male *gagali* – and then given to someone who has a reputation for being 'dangerous' or aggressive (*nabang*: see Chapter 3 for other uses of this stem, -*bang*), someone who is 'good at fighting', 'and that thing makes him hot (angry) so he has to spear the right man'. The substance itself is said to lead him to the 'murderer', whether or not any positive identification was made beforehand.

Revenge and Settlement

Revenge and counter-revenge on this individual self-help basis can continue indefinitely, through open attack or alleged sorcery or a sequence of both. The sequence can be halted at any point, however; for instance, by a spearing that is deliberately intended *not* to kill. But direct feud killings and even ordinary spearings in the heat of a quarrel are becoming very rare now that police action is almost impossible to evade, as western Arnhem Landers learnt from several reported cases during the 1940s.

One revenge killing, late in 1943, took place quite close to Goulburn Island mission station. Two Gunwinggu men (one Danig, one Marin) pretended to be on friendly terms with a Maung-speaking man (Gadbam), who had Gunwinggu affiliations; one called him 'elder brother', the other *gagali*. They waited for an opportunity to get him alone and speared him in revenge for a sorcery death. Then they weighted down his body in a stream with a heavy log, but otherwise made very little effort to conceal what they had done. One of them served a gaol sentence in Darwin for it. In addition, both of them were obliged to take part in a formal peace-making or 'running the gauntlet' rite, the *maneiag*. This is very similar to the *magarada* of eastern Arnhem Land (the *makarata* described in Warner, 1937/1958; see also R.M.B., 1965*b*). An accused man, or a substitute in the case of a woman or boy, backed up by close male kin, confronts his accusers, who throw spears at him to wound but not to kill. Ideally, this settles the matter and puts an end to the feud, but in practice there have been exceptions – where the accused was deliberately killed or the quarrel was exacerbated instead of being resolved.

Stories involving *maneiag* settlement come from mythology as well as from case-history material. Another feature of both myth and quasi-historical accounts, however, has no counterpart in the immediate past – that is, the raiding party or war party. Accounts of raids come also from Kakadu and other Gunbargid groups in the west and from beyond the Liverpool River in the east. They contain enough detail to show that, whether or not western Arnhem Landers actually took part in such expeditions, they have a coherent tradition of what was involved in them.

The basis of alignment in this kind of enterprise was linguistic and territorial – it did not rest directly on kinship. Message-sticks would be sent out to summon allies. Occasionally, armed men would meet in open fighting. The more usual pattern was one of surprise attack before dawn after elaborate preparations – making and repairing weapons, painting spears and bodies, sending spies ahead to locate the intended victims and report on their movements; then stealthily surrounding the camp-complex in a circle, touching hands to check that there were no gaps between the raiders, and, on a given signal (a bird call or a whistle), rushing on the sleepers with a distinctive fighting cry a little like the men's *maraiin* call of *Ngugwaaa!* Descriptions include the killing of all who could not escape except (sometimes) girls, and in a few instances the 'warriors' were segregated from women and children before and after an attack.

One such episode was said to have taken place possibly a hundred years ago – when the father's sister of a woman who was about fifty in 1950, and the mother's father of one who was about thirty, were about eight or nine years old. A number of Gunwinggu from Mabidjul in Gurudjmug came down to Gumadir, joining other Gunwinggu there as well as some Maung and Gunbalang, and sent a party eastward to kill a group of Guru speakers. On its return they all gathered together at Bobonggi (a Leech and Barramundi-fish *djang* site) near the sea, 'eating fish, and various vegetable foods [listed] including lily roots, and kangaroo, various meats, and honey', while they watched the tracks leading eastward and waited for the revenge expedition; men stood guard all night, expecting trouble.

They do not seem to have done this thoroughly, however, because the account goes on to tell how Guru speakers sent messengers to gather men from Gugaidjiri and then came westward to surround the sleeping camp at Bobonggi on a moonlit night. Children and young people mostly escaped, some by climbing up into leafy trees, others by hiding in the water and holding onto roots just below the surface. The boy and girl identified in this account, both Gunwinggu from Gurudjmug, burrowed into a patch of soft ground where children had been digging in play, and covered themselves with earth leaving only their eyes and nostrils exposed. ('They could feel men moving about over their heads, as they lay there in hiding.') When the attackers had used up all their spears they went away. Some survivors returned and took the children, 'those orphans', back to Gurudjmug. 'The children all wept, and it was only when they became adults that they stopped thinking about it.' The account goes on to say that then, to avenge their parents' death, young Gunwinggu and Maung men sent message-sticks east to Gunavidji country, and 'to us in Dangbun country that stick came running' (the narrator otherwise identifies herself as Gunwinggu from Mandaidgaidjan), and so Dangbun men came down from the rocks, making weapons. They left their wives and children in Gurudjmug, and set off to kill a group of Guru people. 'If we don't kill them, they may think they've scored over us!' (Or this could be translated as, 'They might claim a victory over us . . . . ') 'And so they balanced the score.'

The points emphasized in the last two remarks are typical of several accounts. One, the shame of being a loser while the winner boasts of his prowess, comes up also in individual fights and camp quarrels. The second, the desirability of maintaining a balance, keeping the score even, is raised in regard to marriage exchange, too, although not so consistently or so definitely. (See Fig. 14.) It is most explicit in conventionalized *gagali* joking. For example, if one man pretends that he wants to claim his *gagali*'s sister or *gagag*, an appropriate response is, 'You've nothing to pay me with!' (Literally, 'You have no exchange commodity' [*jurmi*].)

From these reports of revenge attacks it is not feasible to make even a rough assessment of the number of people involved. Even descriptions of the last case, where the story of the hidden children seems to have been passed on to their own immediate relatives as an exciting event, are too far removed from eye-witness accounts to help in that direction. Also, the larger the size of the camps concerned, the better the story. But small-scale revenge and raiding parties may very well have been a feature of the area. This would be quite compatible with such aspects of the culture as emphasis on fighting ability, on revenge, and on balancing accounts. The pattern is also something like that of the traditional warfare of eastern Arnhem Land.

The Non-empirical

Whether or not they took place as reported, these sequences are straightforward. But when it comes to tabus and the non-empirical generally, the range of possibilities is more or less hypothetical. At one extreme are avoidances and prohibitions affecting individual persons; at the other are those believed to have wider repercussions. Cutting across these categories is another distinction, depending on whether the tabus relate to everyday life or to the context of sacred ritual. Examples of breaches of tabus are few and far between. On the face of it, at least, people just do not go near forbidden waterholes, or eat foods that are tabu at a particular life-stage or in a particular ritual setting. Or, if they do, the matter is kept quiet – but this seems unlikely. People in the same camp complex know as much about one another's tabu commitments as they do about their own, and anything more than a small evasion would be almost impossible to conceal.

There is less public concern over potential infringements when the penalty falls directly on the person responsible and that person's children. When a woman is pregnant she and her husband are warned, among other things, not to eat dangerous (*nabang*) meats or bitter foods that might kill the child. And she should keep well away from all pools and streams, for fear of the Rainbow – other women should get water for her. Babies are especially vulnerable to attack from the Rainbow. In rainy weather, or if she goes anywhere near water, a mother should paint herself and her baby with yellow ochre or termite mound. And a menstruating woman should not touch or even go close to a pregnant woman or a baby, or walk about in the camp, or go near a waterhole that other people are using. Traditionally, she should stay in seclusion, with a fire burning constantly in her hut or shelter to keep the Rainbow away. Now, however, mothers of small children complain that young women when menstruating sometimes deliberately conceal their state, and that when they wear clothes and live on a mission station or in similar surroundings other people cannot always tell. Several suspects were mentioned during an alarm early in 1950, when a couple of babies were ill. There was a lot of angry discussion exhorting 'everyone' to behave honestly, without dissembling. No proof was demanded or offered, and the impression was that these warnings should be enough. But several women claimed that their 'brothers' would spear them or punish them in some other way if their babies died. Because a woman's brother takes a special interest in her children, he can discipline her if she neglects them.

Such tabus, therefore, carry two kinds of sanction. One is believed to be automatic: for example, a breach leads to the death of a child or to the death of all the fish in a billabong. The other is the threat of intervention by other people: for example, what a child's parents might do to a girl who had been careless or what a man might do to a sister. Human-intervention threats are more explicit in secret-sacred affairs. Men, as custodians of these affairs, take their position seriously and women show every sign of accepting it. The case of the tabu-ed fish (mentioned earlier in this Chapter) is interesting in that no direct action was reported to have followed the 'theft' – perhaps because the fish had been put aside in readiness but not actually declared tabu. This implies more flexibility in interpreting and dealing with such breaches than in, say, the Western Desert region. Even though belief in sorcery makes this (that is, sorcery) more than a nominal sanction, it is nevertheless a secondary one.

Conversely, in a few isolated cases the screen of the secret-sacred is said to have been drawn over incidents arising out of kin feuds and private grudges.

One of these is said to have happened at Oenpelli before it became a mission station, possibly in the early 1920s. A man disappeared suddenly after leaving the main camp for a *maraiin* sequence, and was not seen again. He had no close kin in the area at the time to take up the matter, and his wives could not get beyond the rumour that it was 'something to do with *maraiin*'. In 1950, one of the widows and several close relatives of the other men involved were talking about the episode, and the essence of their story was this. The victim (Bedbed territorial group) had been called to join in a *maraiin* rite, but this was a ruse. As he sat on the sacred ground being painted, a Djelama man who called him 'long-way brother' (both were of the *nabulan* subsection) suddenly speared him. He tried to crawl away but was attacked by the others, all Gunwinggu men. According to the 1950 account, it was a revenge killing, 'paying back' for the death of the Djelama man's father's sister – three children had reported seeing this Bedbed man killing her by sorcery. The dead man's body was concealed, and so was the fact of his death: the women were given evasive replies. But the news leaked out, partly because the explanation of his disappearance was not convincing, and partly because one of the Djelama man's wives told the other what she suspected. His close relatives south of Oenpelli heard the rumours, and did not accept the *maraiin* cover as an excuse for secrecy. They came in a revenge expedition and met the others in an open spear fight, during which the Djelama man was wounded in the side. (He did not die, however, until a few years later.) The issue was declared settled.

Plainly, awe of the 'supernatural' and respect for the authority deriving from it can co-exist with recognition that leaders do not always act impartially – that personal interests can influence their behaviour even in the context of sacred ritual. The Lumaluma myth, for one, reflects this acknowledgment.

In a very different set of circumstances, the death of an apparently healthy man was attributed to the 'supernatural' danger attaching to a religious cult.

Early in 1958, we returned to Oenpelli after an absence of nearly eight years. Several people had died in the interval, and among them was a middle-aged Dangbun-side Gunwinggu (Durmangga) man who had been a novice in the 1950 Oenpelli *kunapipi* sequence. According to reports from his widow and from others, he collapsed one day, bleeding from the nose, but with no other sign of ill-health or sorcery. They did not accept the mission explanation of heart failure. Nor did they blame his widow or her previous husband's relatives, even though she and the dead man had eloped in a sweetheart match as close *ganjulg*, cross-cousins, a long time before. Instead, they interpreted the suddenness of the death, the nose-bleeding, and the lack of any visible death agent as clear proof that the *kunapipi* was dangerous to strangers. Strong hostility was expressed to the *kunapipi* complex, not in itself, but as something that belonged elsewhere – not traditionally associated with Gunwing-gu or with the land on which Gunwinggu had settled: 'It doesn't belong to us,' and 'It doesn't belong to this place.' The same opinion was expressed independently at Goulburn Island in 1961, where people worrying about the risk attaching to *kunapipi* parti-cipation cited the example of 'that man who died at Oenpelli'. (The topic came up during a camp quarrel, when a Maung man who had 'learnt about the *kunapipi*' from mainland Gunwinggu threatened to summon the *kunapipi* snake to attack anyone who struck his children.) By 1966, however, antagonism to the *kunapipi* seemed to have diminished and at least some Gunwinggu were actively involved in it again – as they were, also, during our 1968 visit.

Checks and Controls

In camp disturbances and in feuding within an area, people deal with one another as known and identifiable individuals even if they have few intimate contacts. In the revenge raids, the units involved are presented as socially and linguistically distinct. Kinship links between attackers and attacked are not mentioned. Nor is there any reference to the possibility of individual neutrality or selective killing (as in the Eastern Highlands of New Guinea, where neutrality in war goes with certain relationships). They treat each other as non-kin – in other words, as being outside the range of ordinary restraints and obligations.

The contrast between kin and outsiders is sometimes narrowed to one between *close* kin and outsiders – the *namud* in contrast to all others, even though the *namud* itself is so loosely defined in composition and in size. Kin obligations and rights are not always exactly balanced, but they are reciprocal. Belonging to a circle of close kin implies emotional security, as well as tangible help in goods and services. It is provocative and insulting to taunt a person with having no relatives to support him. ('You are alone, you have no *namud*!') Normal people do not stand alone: they belong with others, to whom they are committed in a variety of ways. But even the closest consanguineal ties are not once and for all relationships established for ever on the basis of birth alone. People must work to sustain them. Close kin demand more from one another than from outsiders, and must give more in return. They are alert to one another's shortcomings, ready to challenge any failure to meet an obligation. A person with a grievance against a close relative may say, 'You're treating me as if I'm not kin to you. All right, I'll *behave* as if I'm not!' (The word for 'not kin' in such cases could be translated as 'different', 'not of the same kind', 'strange'.)

One evening early in 1950 Medeg, a young Wadjag woman, came back to camp with a couple of basketfuls of long yams she had spent almost a day in digging, and put them down in a heap by the fire ready for cooking. Her close sister's young daughter, Ngalmagu (Danig), about nine years old, kicked at them idly with her feet, and as they were brittle new-season's roots they broke into small pieces. Medeg almost wept with rage and hurt. Her reaction was, in effect, 'Nobody would do this to a close relative, and therefore it's obvious you don't regard me as one. So that's how I'll regard you!' The child's mother, Gadjibunba (Madjawar), defended her, and the two women fought with sticks. Gadjibunba's mother, Gararu (Ngalngbali), who was Medeg's dead mother's full sister, finally managed to stop them – by urging Medeg to remember that she was also the girl's 'mother' and should help Gadjibunba in rearing her, and by suggesting that some man who called them both sister might be near by and might hear the disturbance. Medeg countered that she was the injured party, that the girl did not want her as a mother, that Gadjibunba and Gararu had followed this up by showing, in supporting the girl, that they did not want to be sister and mother to her, and therefore she herself could no longer respond to them as their mother, sister and daughter. She was still brooding about this nearly a week later, after a public reconciliation when all four agreed to restore their relationship.

Threat of withdrawal from the circle of active cooperation carries some weight in circumstances like these. Within the *namud* range, sorcery is very rarely a threat. Sorcery accusations are nearly always directed outside it, except where affinal ties have been superimposed on consanguineal ties. Gunwinggu claim that the ideal marriage, between actual *gagali*, strengthens and perpetuates existing genealogical bonds, but they recognize that it also introduces new sources of dissension – as in the mythical precedent of Yirawadbad. Close kin do argue and quarrel, but efforts are always made to prevent them from going too far. Rarely, one of them is badly wounded or killed in a sudden flare-up before anyone can move to prevent it. Pressures based on kinship provide support for individual combatants. The ideal of taking the part of close kin regardless of any broader issue of right or wrong supplies a comfortable measure of security: in a crisis, there is nearly always somebody who can be called on to help. Problems arise when all of those involved are close kin. But the closer they are, the harder it is to back one unreservedly against another.

A clear example of this was a quarrel between two brothers over a girl (Waiula: see 'Elopement' section) who was married to one of them but having a sweetheart liaison with the other. Her husband was against the liaison, and angry at the rumour that she wanted to change spouses. The mother of the two men (Wurgamara) was distraught with anxiety in case one of them should be hurt or killed. She and her close brothers and her husband concentrated on trying to resolve the dispute and avoid bloodshed, and neither brother was able to mobilize active support against the other. The outcome, eventually, was that the girl remained with her husband and curtailed the liaison – or at least did not maintain it openly. (In one instance of fratricide, possibly in the 1920s, the brothers were Maung, with close Gunwinggu kin and Gunwinggu wives. The reason for the killing was that the dead man had been secretly associating with the other's wife – who was actually not a 'proper' wife but had eloped with him, leaving her old Gunwinggu husband. No action was taken in this. In another case a Gunwinggu [Djelama] man who knifed his full brother in the stomach was immediately killed by his own relatives to 'make it even'.)

When choice is more clear-cut, it is easier for a disturbance to spread. In this way kinship loyalties exacerbate conflicts instead of helping to resolve them. But in such circumstances, too, the assumption is that someone will intervene to check the disruption – someone who will stand outside the perspective of a single kinship role and take a less partial view. This is more likely to be a senior person than a junior one, and the more weight he carries, the more effective is his intervention – or the more effective it would have been in the past.

Even in the past, presumably, seniority was not immune to challenge. Physical weakness with advancing age meant loss of status for practical purposes, whatever religious knowledge a man possessed. A spear is the conventional symbol of maleness, as a basket or dilly-bag is of femaleness, and a religious leader was expected to be able to handle his weapons as competently as anyone else, if not more so. The system of tabus (apart from kin avoidance) rested as much on human 'policing' as on the supernatural sanctions that went with them; and it was men, not women, who were principally responsible. But, to cite the Yirawadbad myth again, it was recognized that even men well up in the religious hierarchy were vulnerable in one major respect – that is, women.

Older men, so Gunwinggu and other western Arnhem Landers say, prefer young wives, but this preference need not be reciprocated. The tradition of sweetheart relationships, sustained and stimulated by gossip songs and perhaps culminating in elopements, points up the potentiality of contests between older and younger men, and in these contests the older is not necessarily the winner. He may bow gracefully to the inevitable, or he may take the initiative and give his wife away to someone else before a crisis develops. If he is a *margidbu*, or an outstanding songman whose spirit dream-familiars are especially respected, this last course is more probable, with the tactful understanding that he could keep a wife or even reclaim her if he wanted to. Case material sometimes gives the impression that women are the Achilles' heel of leaders and aspiring leaders, young as well as old. Men may try to use women as pawns in marriage and sweetheart arrangements, but women often refuse to play it their way, and 'break up the game'. Nevertheless, women also provide spectators and audience for men's fighting, singing and song-making, and didjeridu-playing, and, though often indirectly or at a distance, for the sacred rites in which men's participation is so much more conspicuous and enveloping.

As far as formal control goes, older able-bodied men with ritual status and maturity of experience are senior to younger men, and older able-bodied women to younger women. Age for age, and still at this formal level, men have seniority over women, and adults of both sexes are senior to children. Informally, as we have seen, women's part in mundane life is more equally balanced, and in domestic affairs and in marriage arrangements they appear to have the advantage. Some middle-aged women go very much their own way, and a few younger ones have the reputation of not being afraid to fight back if their husbands hit them. As children learn in the course of growing up, men and women are expected to play different roles, and their areas of jurisdiction are different although overlapping. Sex differentiation counts least for up to a year or so after birth, and decreases again in old age, but ghost stories suggest that it remains relevant for at least a short time after death.

The various phases of the life-sequence are associated with broadly defined expectations regarding involvement in social and ritual relationships. No two people respond to these expectations in exactly the same way, but the possibilities for variation, and deviation, are limited. Traditionally, the range of alternatives has been circumscribed. There is concentration on certain kinds of offence, and this contrasts with a complete absence of others, even conceptually. People do not quarrel over land. Stealing, except in sexual relations (for example, stealing a wife), was not seen as a problem. Apart from dogs, and occasionally food or small belongings, property offences were relevant only in this sense of 'persons-as-property' – mostly women; men are not usually spoken of in those terms.

Both conformity and non-conformity were patterned within a predictable range. Differences and the idea of differences could be incorporated without major dislocation. In the social dimension, Gunwinggu have adopted the subsection system and, more recently, named patrilineal moieties. Ritual innovations include circumcision and the *kunapipi* cult, and different mortuary customs. Spatially, Gunwinggu have moved over great distances, well outside their traditional home territories, and this movement must have intensified not only interaction, but also intermingling, between them and other western Arnhem Land groups. Contact with outsiders, however, has had an overwhelming impact in the last few years, and the changes resulting from it are extensive and profound.

Chapter Eight

Gunwinggu and the Outside World

IT PROBABLY DOES not need saying, these days, that the industrialized urban world has no monopoly on courtesy and dignity in social relations – that they can be just as much a feature of a technically simple non-literate society as of any that rests on a more complex economic and material base. The Gunwinggu and their neighbours illustrate this very well. In ordinary living they are socially perceptive, sensitive to one another's responses, and not necessarily because they are interested in seizing an advantage or getting the better of someone else. This is something over and above the obligations and rights that link them in reciprocal relationships. Such relationships are certainly ego-oriented – they hinge, in part, on what is done by and for a person himself, or herself. But also, and even more significantly, they are *alter*-oriented – they hinge on what is done by or to or for someone else. A woman and her brother are concerned with how other people behave in relation to their *jau* (yau; her son or daughter, his nephew or niece). A man and his sister have the same concern for their *gulun* (his son or daughter, her nephew or niece). And so on. Kinship obligations involve watching other people's interests even more than watching one's own. This implies an awareness of other people's relationships within a certain range, an awareness that is made explicit in the *gundebi* series of kinship terms.

'Our Gunwinggu Way'

The distinction in Gunwinggu kinship terminology between ordinary and more polite forms of reference has a parallel in other spheres.

In everyday conversations, a blunt demand is couched in one style and a more polite request in another: 'Do this!' as against 'Would you do this?' – or, as English-speaking Gunwinggu translate it, 'Would you please . . . ?' or 'Would you mind?' The second form is used more consistently in talking to persons senior in status, genealogically and otherwise, such as close father and father's sister and mother's brother, but in fact it seems to be preferred in most face-to-face situations. Even when the verb form itself remains a direct imperative, it can be softened to imply diffidence. The more forthright approach predominates when a speaker is angry or exasperated or impatient, or giving an order to his wife, and quite often when adults speak to children. A sorcerer is said to address the spirit of his victim in this way, in his compulsive spell. And, except facetiously, the same approach is always adopted in speaking to dogs.

Gunwinggu includes a number of ways of expressing diffidence, hesitancy or doubt, and these are sprinkled through ordinary conversations. Something of the same impression is conveyed in *djang* myths. Characters ask each other for guidance: 'Where are we going?' 'What are we to do?' The conventional question and answer pattern relating to place-names is different, because it seems to be a device for drawing the listeners' attention to the more important places. Two other features might seem to suggest lack of confidence. Many characters 'go wrong': they make mistakes, such as taking the wrong turning and losing their way, and not only in the escarpment area. And, exceptions notwithstanding, the predominant emphasis in their final emergency is on their helplessness and on the inevitability of the whole course of events. But this assumption, and others like it that could be drawn from myth, need much more discussion.

Gunwinggu vocabulary provides a number of ordinary alternatives, less direct than the more basic terms but with meanings that are quite clear in the right context. For example, the direct term for husband is *nagobeng*, or *nabiningobeng* (and likewise for wife, with the feminine prefix). But it is much more common to hear people using a male or female pronoun followed by the expression, basically, 'we-two go [together]', or 'we-two sleep, or camp [together]'. (Even in polygynous unions, the personal relationship between husband and wife is emphasized.) Two ways of referring to sweethearts use ordinary words meaning 'meeting each other' or 'looking at each other'. Other ordinary alternatives, in conventionalized form, refer to animals, reptiles, and so on. A snake is a 'creature [*mai*ʔ] that crawls on the ground'. A buffalo is 'that creature with ears' (horns). A goanna is 'that creature with claws' (literally, finger or toe 'nails') and a long-necked tortoise is 'that creature with a shell'. (The same word stem is used for the tortoise's shell and for the nails on human fingers and toes.)

Attaching different prefixes to one word stem can give it a different connotation, over and above the simple male–female contrast. The Rainbow Snake is distinguished from ordinary *mai*ʔ, and even from other ritually significant *mai*ʔ, by the feminine form of the 'gender' or sex indicator, for example, *ngalbu*. (See Chapter 2.) But, interestingly enough, in one way of referring to the *ubar* woman this feminine prefix is not used. It is replaced by the prefix *man-*, one that in ordinary speech marks off such things as vegetable foods, but also classifies objects or characters or concepts as belonging to the ritually sacred dimension. (An example is *manbaidjan*, the 'mother' or 'big' one.) On the other hand, the conventional term for sacred rites in general takes the prefix *gun-*: *gungamag*, for instance, which means simply a 'good' event or thing but is often used with this specific connotation.

Figures of speech provide another contrast between more and less direct ways of saying things. Expressions *not* included under this heading are those that have no special symbolic meaning but are merely examples of Gunwinggu verbal categorization – the conjunctions and contrasts which, together, provide a verbal picture of the Gunwinggu world. For example, the 'bone' of a stringybark tree is the bare trunk, exposed when bark has been removed for canoe- or house-making; the same term, *-murng*, refers to human and animal bones, but also to the kernel or seed of a fruit, and so on – in other words, to a hard core or skeleton. Other expressions are almost but not quite accepted as straightforward labels without any double meaning – a number of kinship terms, for instance. Others again are polite substitutes for more direct forms. And others are open to personal choice, in ordinary conversation and in song composition –

with the proviso that in local convention songmen do not compose songs, but transmit them from such sources as dream-familiars.

The usual term for betrothed wife (not betrothed husband), *gulbagen*, seems likely to lose its literal meaning of 'blood-concerning' and become a mere label, now that changes are taking place, not only in the practice of betrothing a girl at birth but also in the ideal itself. This direct allusion to afterbirth blood contrasts with the more polite avoidance of the word for blood in reference to menstruation, and particularly to menarche. The word is sometimes used, but Gunwinggu prefer to say 'a stick [or a bamboo spear] pricked her foot', or 'she is sitting down with [an ache in] her back'. Similarly, where a living person is concerned the stomach and abdominal organs are freely mentioned, both literally and as a seat of emotions: 'his intestines grew hot', or 'went wrong', means that he was angry or upset. This is not polite in reference to a corpse: its organs are simply a 'palm-leaf basket'. In another example, from myth, a husband who planned to spear his eloping wife and her sweetheart anticipated the result by speaking of them as 'my two corpses' or ghosts. To be ingratiating or deceptively friendly is to 'give softness', using the same word stem as for tangible things. In place of the ordinary word for deceiving or tricking someone, an alternative expression is to 'turn [one's] hand'; but to 'hide [one's] hand' is to act with secrecy.

Interest in food, and eating, comes out in reminiscences and comments on what foods are available in various places, and in discussion on topics like pre-natal 'totemism'. Symbolically and indirectly it extends into other spheres too, for example as an alternative way of alluding to sexual intercourse. 'I eat your nose!' expresses affection or pleasure. 'Eat your mother's bones!' is an insult to be repaid by violence or sorcery, but, in the first person, 'I eat my mother's bones!' is an exclamation of self-reproach. 'What's eating you?', 'What ate you?' and 'What did you eat?' are traditional equivalents of 'What happened to you?' or 'What's wrong?' 'A spear bit him' means 'He was killed by a spear'. 'She bit their hand(s)' means 'She died'. 'Let him eat grass for ever!' is a threat to kill.

Songs are a favoured medium for this kind of oblique reference. All the series owned by individual songmen include straightforward songs that leave nothing to the imagination; but they also include a great many others made up of indirect allusions and hints, glancing sideways at the scenes and the characters they draw upon without actually confronting them.

However, while all of these expressions and themes and song styles are found in Gunwinggu, they are not exclusive to it. Their closest parallels are within the same region, but others can be traced well beyond the boundaries of western Arnhem Land and adjacent regions.

This is the case too with rock and cave paintings. Galleries of rock art are scattered over much of the Australian continent, but an especially rich belt stretches from the Roper River and eastern Arnhem Land westward to the Katherine–Pine Creek area of the main North-South road and across to the Kimberleys. Many of them are only now in the process of being recorded. As a result of population shifts, the country surrounding a large proportion of the galleries is either almost empty, or inhabited by people from other areas who cannot identify meanings exactly or who read their own meanings into them.

The paintings are excitingly varied in subject matter and style, in single figures or superimposed in a kaleidoscope of lines and colours. 'X-ray' designs with stylized representations of the internal organs of fish and kangaroos and so on are characteristic of western and south-western Arnhem Land and beyond to the Katherine River. Gun-winggu share this style with their Gunbargid and Maiali-Djauan neighbours. In another distinctive series, sometimes called *mimi* (or *mi ʔmi*), stick-like human-type characters are caught in arrested movement on the rock surfaces, walking or running, or in hunting scenes. The most striking of them are outlined, not in ordinary ochres, but in blood. According to stories, *mimi* spirits still live in remote areas among the rocks where human hunters have met and talked to them, and in a few accounts it was *mimi* themselves who put their own likenesses on the cave walls. Mostly, the paintings are traced to a mythical origin – as in the Ngalmoban story (Chapter 3). Some of these are associated with sorcery. In other examples, men are said to have painted figures and designs to illustrate stories they were telling, either secret-sacred or *djang* or quasi-historical.

Paintings on stringybark were used for the same purpose, or for display during initiation rites, or occasionally and more casually in decorating the walls of wet-season huts. Some of them resemble rock paintings in topics and in style. The actual rock paintings do not seem to have had much ritual significance, at least in the recent past. The emphasis has shifted to bark paintings, but, although they are being made in greater numbers than before, their ritual significance has not kept pace with their production. The last decade or so has seen a tremendous increase in outside interest in them, partly because of the more highly organized mission-sponsored expansion of this field in eastern Arnhem Land. Western Arnhem Land, so far, cannot match these developments on the eastern side.

For several years, missionaries at Oenpelli discouraged the production of bark paintings, for sale or otherwise, on account of their traditional religious associations. Their views have changed now, at least to the extent that they are seen as marketable commodities. One famous eastern Gunwinggu artist, Balilbalil, had, returned to Oenpelli by 1966. But another, even more famous, Midjaumidjau, an elderly Gunwinggu with Yiwadja-Maung ties, has settled more or less permanently at Croker Island. In the late 1940s he made several attempts to keep his Yiwadja wife on the mainland, but her parents succeeded in taking her back to the coast because, they said, 'We are saltwater people, not bush people.' He followed her to Croker, and set up house with her in the Maung-Yiwadja hut constellation. One of his brother's daughter's daughters, Minyaiwi, also moved to Croker Island when she eloped from Oenpelli, leaving her small son behind in the care of his father, her 'first husband'. (See Chapter 7.) She and her 'sweetheart husband' did not join the main Gunwinggu camp either. (By 1968, both of them were back at Oenpelli.) In 1966, they shared a separate multi-family dwelling with a group of other Gunwinggu and Gunwinggu-affiliated people, some of whom used to live at Oenpelli. Two of the men are artists who occasionally make bark paintings to sell through the Methodist Mission centre in Darwin – an elderly Yiwadja-Margu, and a young Gunwinggu from the Gunbalang side.

Goulburn Islanders do not have the same opportunities for making and selling barks, and the few artists there are mainly Maung. At Maningrida, arts and crafts with a traditional flavour are officially encouraged, partly because they are now a cash-earning commodity and partly because of their current and potential appeal to the world outside. But in practice, probably more even than at Oenpelli, professionalization in this field has to compete with intensified work and training programmes. In any case, Gunwinggu are in a minority there. (Hiatt, 1965:12, notes that in 1960 Gunwinggu made up only 3 per cent of the total population.) Some of them lived for a time at Oenpelli before the establishment of Maningrida drew them back to the Liverpool River.

As far as art styles go, paintings and other material from the Maningrida–Cape Stewart area combine several features that appear in more distinctive combinations farther east and farther west. In a typical north-eastern Arnhem Land bark painting the 'canvas' is almost completely covered and the whole design is enclosed in a frame-like ochred edging. In a typical western Arnhem Land bark, the design stands out against a plain background with no frame outline, and naturalistic representations of human, anthropomorphic, animal, fish and bird figures predominate. (See R. B., ed., 1964b.) How much of this broad western Arnhem Land style and its 'X-ray' extensions can be identified as specific to Gunwinggu, or any other such language grouping, is open to conjecture. Western Arnhem Landers themselves point to a distinctive Mangerdji style with characteristic head shapes and facial and other features. Its prototypes can be seen on rock walls in what was formerly Mangerdji territory, including Oenpelli. But the last adult Mangerdji man who painted in that style (he died at Oenpelli in the early 1960s) claimed that his own mother and mother's father were 'true Gunwinggu' (Murwan *gunmugugur*). Barks painted these days by people using the Gunwinggu label are not easy to distinguish from the work of Maung, Yiwadja and Gunbalang artists on the one hand, and of those with a more southern Maiali-Dangbun orientation on the other. What seems to be developing is a composite overall style, one in which stylistic differences among individual artists are becoming increasingly prominent – without yet departing very far from accepted conventions in subject matter and treatment.

Nevertheless, people who identify themselves as Gunwinggu sometimes claim that a distinctive set of traditions and norms goes with the same label – 'our Gunwinggu way', 'our rule', in contrast to others. This happens more often in reference to specific features: 'crossing' the two matrilineal moieties in marriage, marrying *gagali*, a woman giving her daughter to her *nagurng*, and so on. Or they say, simply, 'This is what we do,' without specifying who 'we' are. Conversely, in regard to other things, 'that is not our Gunwinggu way', 'We don't do that' or 'We don't say that'. The main examples they gave, in talking about this, were circumcision and subincision, marriage within the same moiety or semi-moiety, use of eastern subsection labels, burying a corpse instead of exposing it on a platform, or neglect of precautions concerning the Rainbow Snake. Some included the *kunapipi*, too (see Chapter 7), and a few included the *maraiin*.

Linguistic clues are crucial in this connection. The larger language names provide an overall framework, and small speech contrasts help to reinforce it. Gunwinggu and Maung are not mutually intelligible, but they share some fields of interest in which terms and names are the same – or almost the same. The differences are small, but distinctive. In subsection terms, for example, where Gunwinggu say *nagudjug*, Maung say *nawiug*; in language names, where Gunwinggu say Gunbalang, or Balang, Maung say Walang; in personal names, where Gunwinggu say Ngalgindali, Maung say Ngalindali; and in ritual names, Gunwinggu *ubar* is Maung *uwar*. In this small section of their vocabularies that they hold in common, they themselves can quickly identify a Gunwinggu accent or a Maung accent, and so can other western Arnhem Landers who do not speak either of these two languages. A Gunwinggu utterance virtually never commences with a vowel – *ubar* is pronounced almost like *wubar* and *igurumu* almost like *jigurumu* (yigurumu); and the Gunwinggu prefix *ngal-* is almost always feminine. In the first respect Gunwinggu differ from the Maung, and in both respects from Mangerdji and, they say, other Gunbargid conventions.

A full account of the contrast between languages and the place of the smaller and more localized dialects at this formal level is a matter for linguists. The operational perspective we adopted was based roughly on intelligibility – how far we could go with a reasonable knowledge of 'core' Gunwinggu (a long way with Maiali, a fair way with Dangbun, considerably less far with Gunbalang, and almost no distance with Maung, Yiwadja, and the Gunbargid language group). In practice, communication is simplified because so many people, including Gunwinggu, are bilingual, and because Gunwinggu itself has become widely accepted as a second language, learnt either as a mother tongue or in the course of trade or ritual or other gatherings. But fewer Yiwadja speak Gunwinggu, unless they have close kin ties in that direction or live in a predominantly Gunwinggu environment.

These two last points, kinship and propinquity, alone or in combination, are significant in the majority of cases where people (other than core Gunwinggu) claim Gunwinggu identification or speak Gunwinggu as a second language. The nature of the kin ties varies; but if a person's mother or mother's mother or father's mother was Gunwinggu or 'half-Gunwinggu', this can influence his (or her) current orientation. For example, one woman at Oenpelli in 1950, Midjara, was more often referred to as Dangbun than as Gunwinggu, by herself and by others. Her paternal territory (Durmangga territorial group) was actually the same as the paternal territory of others who were usually referred to as Gunwinggu; but her mother (Djorolam) was from the Rembarnga side of the Dangbun, not the Gunwinggu side, whereas the others' maternal territories were core Gunwinggu.

Core Gunwinggu themselves, when they were asked how they would identify a Gunwinggu person, replied that they would require him to do one or both of two things: (1) Belong to a *gunmugugur* acknowledged as Gunwinggu (that is, be Gunwinggu by virtue of descent), and (2) speak Gunwinggu either as a principal language or at least as often as any other. The first condition, as we saw in Chapter 4, is open-ended – not so much in regard to personal affiliation, but certainly in regard to the fit between *gunmugugur* and language categories. The second represents a sort of operational test, especially for people without the qualification of paternal descent. For example, an early missionary brought to Oenpelli a man of part-Aboriginal parentage whose mother's territory was in the Katherine area (Wadaman language). He settled down there, married (his present wife is Gunwinggu), and speaks Gunwinggu as his major language. For all practical purposes he is now usually said to be Gunwinggu, but in 1947 and in 1949-50 he was usually not. In other cases, people who use Gunwinggu as a secondary language but lack the paternal descent requirement are often spoken of as half-Gunwinggu, or 'Gunwinggu, perhaps!'.

These larger language labels cannot be dismissed as a product of the contemporary contact situation. The process of fusion and differentiation must have been going on for a very long time. It seems very likely that traditionally, before the most intensive wave of outside contact, language divisions were much smaller and tied more closely to territorial divisions made up of clusters of adjacent *gunmugugur*. But because people met for religious ritual and for trade and other ceremonies, the boundaries were not watertight, there was a certain amount of coming and going, and a certain amount of intermarriage – which has made for fairly widespread kinship connections. Even in the case (Chapter 5) where a man disagreed with his wife on the betrothal of their daughter and distinguished 'north' from 'south' Gunwinggu, he and his wife were actually connected by genealogically traceable links. And although his mother's affiliations were Maung and her father's were Dangbun, his father and her mother came from the adjacent Gunwinggu areas of Gumadir and Gurudjmug.

But Times have Changed

Quite a long time has gone by since this region had its first recorded contact with the outside world, and people now identified as Gunwinggu began moving out of their home territories.

One of the few myths that could possibly refer to the early picture of disease and depopulation is the Wurudja (Poison Island) sickness *djang*. (See Chapter 1.) Wurudja, a mythical boy from that island who spoke Margu and Garig, came to the mainland with his uncle, his mother's brother. His uncle warned the local people not to touch the boy's head or to wake him when he slept, and the boy avoided even the taste of ordinary mainland foods. But local women found him irresistible and so their husbands were jealous and killed them as well as the boy, 'secretly, by sorcery'. When the boy's uncle took the death message to his parents, his father transformed himself in spirit into a sickness 'like hot ashes', and as he died he called the name of the place where his son's 'murderers' were living. Sickness rose up, like a wind, in search of them. 'They saw dawn coming as though sun and moon were rising together. It was that sickness coming after them' – like smoke from mosquito fires, like fine hot ashes, burning their lungs when they breathed. Their territory was denuded of people: 'only the ground remained'. Of course, this could commemorate the impact of a volcanic eruption in the Indonesian islands, not far away, but people have reported similar symptoms in influenza attacks. Influenza and measles still take a toll in sporadic epidemics through Arnhem Land. And some northern Gunwinggu said, 'When sickness strikes us, hot sickness from coughing, from wet ground, that's where it comes from . . . !' (The myth is different in Maung accounts, but they are even more emphatic about the dangerous quality of the island.)

The Gunwinggu were among the more fortunate groups that did not collapse under the first strong wave from the outside, and many of them went on with their ordinary lives almost as if they could continue to make a choice.

One reason they were able to do this was the position of the Northern Territory itself in relation to the rest of the Australian continent. It was sparsely populated, and separated from the more densely settled south by a large area having only poor communications. The pioneering era continued in the north long after it had gone from the south, and even now it has not entirely disappeared. Establishment of the Arnhem Land Reserve created an official buffer between the people of that region and others, although policing of the boundaries was difficult. It was designed to protect them from outside exploitation until they could look after their own interests, not to keep them from moving out. And, in fact, numbers of them did move out – from curiosity, or following relatives, or to evade punishment or revenge.

Since the early 1950s the pace of change has accelerated. The sudden growth of the non-Aboriginal population of Arnhem Land is one sign of the south's post-war discovery of the north. Aborigines are encouraged to visit not only Darwin but also southern cities, for medical treatment or for training. The Northern Territory's reputation for casualness and leisurely living has been shaken, in the course of developing a new image. Developments include improved communications between centres within and beyond Arnhem Land, radio connections, regular weekly or fortnightly air services, and all-weather roads. Oenpelli in 1966 still had only two small alternative dry-weather airstrips, but by early in 1967 a road had been completed between Oenpelli and Maningrida, continuing the earlier dry-season road between Oenpelli and Pine Creek, and there was talk of pushing the road through to Yirrkalla on the far north-eastern corner of Arnhem Land.

Schools have been expanded at Oenpelli and at Goulburn Island as well as at Maningrida, and on Croker Island full-blood and part-

Aboriginal children attended the same school. The teaching and learning of English have been spreading through these formal channels, and other informal ones such as patients returning after leprosy treatment. People who still speak little or no English are mostly middle-aged and older, but the increase in staff and visitors at all the places mentioned is changing this picture too. The jump in the Aboriginal population is less dramatic than on the eastern side of Arnhem Land. But the proportion of children to adults is rising at Oenpelli as well as at Goulburn Island, and this is a pointer to the future.

The situation now is very different from what it was in 1946-50. Oenpelli and Goulburn Island were small settlements then, with a staff of half a dozen or so non-Aboriginals. Small planes could land in good weather. Methodist mission boats linked Goulburn Island with the eastern Arnhem Land stations and, via Croker Island, with Darwin. Very few full-bloods were camped on Croker, mainly transients and usually well away from the main settlement. In 1946-50, all the emphasis was on a holding policy – gradual development, preventing a repetition of what had happened earlier. But even then, western Arnhem Landers had aspirations that they could not realize by relying solely on their own traditional resources. Gunwinggu were infiltrating other areas and nominally absorbing people from other language units, but at the same time their knowledge of their own distinctive traditional past was dwindling.

The visible changes today are outward signs of a revolutionary difference in approach to Aborigines throughout Australia. Official policies are geared to the aim of assimilation, with two parts to it: Aborigines, including Gunwinggu, are encouraged to adopt a generalized Australian way of life, and they are promised equality within it. In western Arnhem Land now, education and health are under direct government control and mission policies and programmes are affected in varying degrees. But one-way assimilation in general has come under fire from several quarters, because the stress on similarity and absorption is interpreted as a threat to Aboriginal identity. The strongest opposition to 'assimilation' has come from the south, mostly from people of part- or full-Aboriginal descent with no first-hand experience of any traditional Aboriginal culture. In the north it is not an issue so far, except in a very small way. But it may become so in future, and for quite the opposite reason

– that many of the people concerned have not only had some contact with outsiders, but are still close enough to traditional Aboriginal culture, their own or someone else's, to see that there is more than one side to the question. Also, because Arnhem Land was a reserve where Aboriginal interests were officially the prime consideration, pressures toward change were deflected or softened. The Aborigines who lived there were able to keep something of their own culture to substantiate their sense of separate identity.

Another factor has been the Methodist Mission policy of 'building on what was best in the Aboriginal culture' instead of destroying it. This was attempted at Goulburn Island, but it was a long time before it came into favour at Oenpelli. (See C. B., 1961.) Missionaries there not only disapproved of infant betrothal, they also tried to discourage marriage between adolescent girls and middle-aged or elderly men and to ensure that the partners were of much the same age. Until the late 1950s, Oenpelli was committed to the dormitory system, and this provided a little nucleus of children to work on. As regards adults, too, the mission orbit was narrow and concentrated on a fairly small number of people. This meant that in practice there were areas of privacy for both sides – for missionaries and for Aborigines. The main sections of the Aboriginal camp were just far enough away from the mission houses for evening ceremonies and singing to proceed undisturbed; and so, up to a point, could quarrels and arguments. But this was a consequence of *laissez-faire* and of language difficulties, rather than a deliberate policy of tolerance. Interestingly, in the last few years Goulburn Island and Oenpelli seem to have been reversing their approaches to Aboriginal traditions. This is not because of any alteration in Methodist policy as such. It simply illustrates the obvious point that the practical working out of policy, in such circumstances, depends very much on the attitudes of the people on the spot.

A feature common to both stations, however, is the curtailing of polygyny. This is almost certain to affect the practice of arranged betrothal. Several men have been blocked from marrying girls betrothed to them on the grounds that they already have other wives. Some of the opposition comes from the first wives themselves, who have been encouraged to favour monogamy. Younger women in particular say they prefer it, even though co-wife jealousy was not really conspicuous in this region. One consequence has been some upset in the marriage market in and around these settlements. Already it has led to a circumstance that seems to have no traditional precedent: that is, a number of unmarried girls have borne children whose fathers are not publicly acknowledged, even though in most cases – among Gunwinggu and Maung, but not Yiwadja – other people identify them as the 'right fathers', the girls' betrothed husbands. When people avoid mission settlements these days, the reason is not likely to be that they are forced to attend church services there. Some of them, at least, are wary of the prospect of any interference, however well-intentioned, in their marital and extra-marital affairs.

Gunwinggu (and Maung) views on the structurally ideal type of marriage and on the grading of alternatives have hardly been shaken. This does not mean that everyone strives to achieve the ideal. It is certainly a matter for concern among parents and mothers' brothers, but sweetheart matches and acceptable alternatives to the ideal also represent a fairly long-standing tradition. What is important is that the majority of pre-adolescent girls are informally betrothed or the centre of informal negotiations with betrothal in view. One can only speculate on how far their experience in the school situation will affect the outcome in future, especially since outside pressures emphasizing free choice in marriage have such well-established traditional counterparts. (A fuller discussion of marriage in this region, with a breakdown of betrothal and marriage figures, is given in C. B., n.d.[2].)

The categories of social alignment outlined in Chapters 4 and 5 appear to be just as important in social relationships as they were a few years ago, although the content of obligations and rights has altered to meet the new situation.

The range of goods has been affected more obviously, so far, than the nature of the services people expect or demand of one another. Introduced foods have not entirely replaced fish, various meats, geese and ducks, lily roots, and so on. These continue to be popular whenever people have an opportunity to get them, though not at the expense of flour, tea, sugar, and other now 'essential' foods. For non-edible goods, however, the substitution is almost complete. Such things as tobacco, clothing and blankets, soap and hair oil, torches and lamps, are necessities now, and the range of commodities is widening. Some people are employed for wages, on mission or government or buffalo stations, for instance, whereas others are not, but Social Services benefits (old-age and invalid pensions, maternity allowance, child endowment) partly offset this. If a person earns more or has access to a larger assortment of goods (through visits to Darwin or Adelaide, for example), his contributions to kin are assessed accordingly. Reciprocity does not mean exact equivalence, or equivalence in kind. Sharing food supplied by someone else can be paid for by, say, preparing or cooking it, or by some other service like supplying water or firewood or minding children. But some areas of kin-based action are no longer relevant. Traditional mortuary rites have become the exception instead of the rule, and the paraphernalia associated with them are rarely made or used. Girls' puberty rites seem to have lapsed, too (one such was held in 1950), and most babies are born in hospitals or nursing posts or within easy reach of them.

Nevertheless, kinship remains important. The traditional social categories are still basic to all interaction among the people themselves that is not initiated or sponsored by others (for example, Europeans). Adults continue to teach them to children, with the same general assumption as before – that they cannot be expected to remember everything they are told. In the Oenpelli elementary school in 1966, even the two higher classes were very hesitant about their individual semi-moiety affiliations, but all of these older children replied promptly when we asked them, in an open session, to name the subsections and identify their own. Adults claim that children always master the subsections before the semi-moieties, and it is true that in 1950 pre-adolescent children did not show any more interest in *gunmugugur* than they do now.

Along with this goes a continuing concern with sacred ritual and ceremony. It is diluted to some extent by preoccupation with other affairs, but still strong, and it has even been partially revivified. After a long period without a *lorgun*, for instance (see Chapter 6), one was held at Croker Island in 1966 as the final rite for a young man who had died a few years before. (News of his death came to Goulburn Island when we were visiting there early in 1961.) An *uwar* series at Goulburn Island in 1965, however, was prompted from outside. We had talked with people there early in 1964 about the possibility of a performance so that it could be recorded for the Australian Institute of Aboriginal Studies. Both this and the Croker

Island *lorgun* were filmed.

Renewed interest in Aboriginal culture from a research and recording point of view coincides with increased government and commercial enthusiasm for its tourist potential. Mission stations throughout Arnhem Land have been under pressure since the middle 1940s to admit tourists, but now it is stronger and on a much bigger scale. So many unheralded visitors without official permits to enter have been crossing into the reserve by the dry-season road that Oenpelli mission has agreed to regularize the situation by sponsoring guided tours of local cave paintings. Oenpelli is especially vulnerable because of the attraction of buffalo- and crocodile-shooting in the area. From time to time there have been rumours that the reserve *as* a reserve would be abandoned, rumours reinforced by the granting of bauxite and other concessions on the north-eastern side. Official plans for developing Maningrida as a 'show-place' are one aspect of a wider concern with building up open, not closed, communities throughout the whole region.

Interest from these two perspectives (of research and tourism) complements the growth of emphasis on Aboriginality as something important in itself. This 'Aboriginality' is being defined on an Australia-wide basis. In practice, it means that distinctive local cultures may have no place in this general scheme except as symbols of Aboriginal identity in contrast to any other kind. More specifically and on a smaller scale, something of the sort – identification through contrast – can be identified in the Maung situation, and it seems to be developing in the case of Gunwinggu too.

The composite culture that is coming into being in western Arnhem Land as a result of contact among Aborigines, and between Aborigines and others, is for many people and in a variety of circumstances identified by the label of Gunwinggu. Mission sponsorship of Gunwinggu a few years ago set an official seal on what was already an expanding language of inter-Aboriginal contact on this western side of Arnhem Land. People who spoke some other language among themselves taught that language first to their children; but no systematic information is available on linguistic patterns in family and camp situations – whether those children learnt Gunwinggu at all, and how much the adults themselves used it. Both Gunwinggu and Dangbun women at Oenpelli in 1966 claimed that Dangbun children were becoming so accustomed to talking Gunwinggu in the school playground that they were forgetting their own language. But the spread of fluency in English is bound to diminish the usefulness of Gunwinggu as a trade and contact medium. Even a revival of Aboriginal nationalism may work against it, as the resurgence of Maung has shown. The population is too small to support any of the vernacular languages as a primary or sole means of communication, even if western Arnhem Landers could agree on the choice of one of them.

Another question that has a bearing on this will certainly become more important in future – Aboriginal land rights. This is no longer a dead issue. Mineral finds, discussion of royalties, and alienation or potential alienation of sites have given it a new twist, with political implications. (See R. B., 1964a: 258-95.) On the plains of western Arnhem Land, it is likely to concern buffalo and pastoral leaseholds or fishing and hunting zones rather than mineral leases, but in the escarpment country it could be another matter. Sorting out titles to shared claims could be a means of restoring or sustaining social affiliations, with at least indirect reference to socio-linguistic identity. It is difficult to see this in terms of the smaller territorial linguistic units when the larger language names have become so widely accepted. Nevertheless, as far as land claims go the larger names are really irrelevant. Whether a person is truly Gunwinggu or not does not signify. It is the localized territorial affiliation that counts. The Gunwinggu may have been essentially an inland people, as the persisting contrast between salt and fresh water, coast and 'bush', suggests, and as Maung and other coastal groups explicitly say. But the Gunwinggu label now covers groups from Gumadir and other coastal (not island) territories, and this does not seem to be a new development. It is a means of wider social identification – not superseding more specific ties between people, and between people and land, but setting them in a different context.

Mobility and 'Transformation'

By the late 1940s, the Gunwinggu seemed to have achieved a workable balance between matrilineal and patrilineal descent. The subsection system, so we are led to believe, had been introduced some time before. Whatever its more specific effects have been on marriage and behaviour patterns, it has reinforced matriliny, just as the growing acceptance of patrilineal moiety names from eastern Arnhem Land in recent years has underlined the importance of patriliny in religious as well as in territorial terms. Whether either was dominant at some earlier period is an open question. They served different purposes, and the cross-cutting linkages between them meant that they were complementary in more than a nominal sense.

In the 1940s, also, Gunwinggu seemed to have reached a working balance between what they were getting from outside sources and what they could get for themselves, from their own environment. Even people living more or less permanently on mission stations spent some of their time in hunting, and collecting vegetable and water foods. Except for tobacco, if they had been left to their own resources they could probably have managed quite well. They could have continued to meet their subsistence needs from what was available to them locally. But they did not see the situation that way, because their conception of the necessities of life had altered, and the process was a cumulative one. It was, of course, an expansion of their own traditional orientation, in which self-sufficiency in food resources went hand in hand with trade and ceremonial and ritual connections and exchanges over a wide area. New things and new items were being incorporated, and were leading to some modification in what was there before.

The mythical characters who moved about in the region were flexible in their linguistic orientation, and they nearly always ended their stories in places some distance away from where they began. They set out without a very clear picture of their future, under the influence of some compelling force of destiny outside their personal control, and in their final transformation they became something very different from what they had been before.

There is a partial parallel here with the real-life story of the Gunwinggu and their neighbours, including their *balanda* neighbours, in the contact situation. They do not draw it themselves, not explicitly, in looking back at their own past. But perhaps they will one day, if the present signs of reviving interest in their own traditions are anything to go by – although this is not so much a revival of interest, as the reversal of a trend in the opposite direction. The content will undoubtedly change even from what it is now, but that is a normal feature of traditions.

The mythology of this region has been attuned very closely to the circumstances of mundane living as well as of sacred ritual. These circumstances have been undergoing radical changes, and even more radical changes lie ahead. Individual myths may survive for a long time, to enshrine a sentimental view of the past or as esoteric religious material. As far as entertainment goes, stories about ghosts and giants and the like seem to be just as popular as ever, perhaps because they are told *as* stories. But if mythology is to be anything more than this – if it is to remain part of a coherent tradition – the long-term answer may lie in what it has to say about the land, especially in validating claims to specific sites or specific areas. This is not the same as talking about mythical themes, or the relevance of myth to moral rules, because themes need not be tied to specific sites. (The Orphan and Rainbow theme is one obvious example.)

In Chapter 3 and Chapters 2 and 6 we saw two different forms of relationship to the land.

One emphasizes the practical side. The myths include an enormous amount of material on topography and natural resources, confirming and documenting and supplementing everyday experience. An important part of their message is the information they provide on bitter or dangerous foods and creatures, and dangerous localities. In the past, this kind of information was directly related to survival. To take one instance, the outline of resources in Chapter 3 shows how many root foods need special handling to make them not only edible but tasty, and how to use such things as twine, bark, and timber and other local materials.

Classifying Gunwinggu as 'hunters and collectors' is convenient for some purposes, but only as a first step. As it stands, the phrase can give the impression that their way of life was simple, unimaginative, and essentially parasitical – at best, an example of 'intelligent adaptation'. (Gunwinggu children's songs show the creatures that they comment on in much the same light – clever and resourceful in adapting to their natural environment, but only in a very crude and limited way.) It is true that the region is fairly fertile, compared with some, but its advantages rest on much more than a favourable combination of climate and natural resources. Gunwinggu and other western Arnhem Landers have worked hard to achieve them. The work involved in collecting and hunting and preparing food is only a very small part of their effort. What is significant is their very detailed study of *everything* available in the region, animate and inanimate. Over and above the question of locating food and other supplies, the record of that study includes the end-results of a great deal of practical experimentation, showing how this and that resource must be treated or modified to make it useful or edible, and what it is best suited for.

Given what they had to draw upon, they could not have done more than they did. Theirs was a discriminating and thoughtful adaptation, one that could hardly have been bettered. Even if agriculture had been possible in their environment, it would not have ensured a more varied or a more comfortable life. Now, however, the need for such a detailed record has diminished, and the myths and songs that perpetuated it no longer seem so vital. (Kinship and marriage rules will probably meet this fate eventually.) What people want from the land now is not what they wanted from it a few years ago. They are not committed to it in the same way.

But the second form of their relationship to it has only been weakened, not drastically altered. The influence of the sacred, the non-empirical, affects even people who do not participate actively in religious rites. Introduced views of the land (and its products) as impersonal and inanimate – secularizing views of it – have made some headway. But even adults who have forgotten most of the actual content of their own traditions retain the feeling that there is more to the land than its physical appearance – just as a normal human being, one who is not sorcerized, is more than a physical body. This is a feeling about the land in general, not just nostalgia for their own territory. The negative or threatening aspects of nature – storms, floods, crocodiles, and so on – symbolized in the Rainbow Snake and other mythical figures, probably reinforce the feeling. So do stories about sorcery, and about the marvellous feats of *margidbu* (native doctors). All these are 'proof' of the reality of the powerful and dangerous forces that lie just behind the visible and tangible world of everyday life.

Gunwinggu and their neighbours in western Arnhem Land share the same overall orientation in this respect. Their premises are almost identical. On many other things, too, they 'speak the same language': kinship, betrothal and marriage rules, relations between men and women, child-rearing, the need for balancing and reciprocity, and, in fact, social relations generally. They diverge in the procedures and techniques they use to translate these premises into action, but not so much that they cannot communicate at this general level, once practical difficulties of communication have been overcome (for example, the barriers imposed by specific languages). Smaller contrasts and differences are significant in other circumstances, but the basic likeness has made it easier for people in this area to choose one local label rather than another – say, Gunwinggu rather than Maung, or vice versa. It has faciliated marriage among them, too, making the intra-marrying population much larger than it was before. The likeness, or assumption of likeness, has undoubtedly been enhanced by outside contact, because the contrast between individual units or 'tribes' was negligible when compared with the contrast between all of them together on one hand and Europeans on the other. Whatever the position was like even fifty years ago, a full description of Gunwinggu now must be an account of Gunwinggu in the context of 'peoples of western Arnhem Land'. It is only in that context that they really take shape as Gunwinggu.

This preliminary study has focused on a number of related themes that are of prime importance to the people of the region. These are relations between man and land, both in mundane and in more or less sacred terms; between man and man, the social dimension; between man and the non-empirical, the sphere of religion; and between local man and alien man, the contact situation, in which we see the impact of the wider world, and the transformation it has brought about. In addition, there is the problem of tribal identification. It is conspicuous here, in this coastal mainland area of long-intermingled local groups – but not only here. (See R.B., 1959: 82-107.) In other regions, too, the more-encompassing 'tribal' names were probably convenient identification labels over a wide range of contacts, while the significant units for most purposes were smaller, locally based, descent and residence groups. Tribal names have become more important in inter-Aboriginal relations as mobility and mixing have increased. They have also become virtually indispensable in relations between Aborigines and outsiders.

What is happening now is just as dramatic and intriguing as anything that has happened in the traditional scene, although in a very different way. The trend toward still wider identification is inescapable. So is the dilemma of choosing between two divergent possibilities. One is generalized-Australian identity, which until recently was the single official goal. The other is *Aboriginal*-Australian identity, an emphasis on Aboriginality, membership in a dissimilar-but-equal minority along with other people of wholly or partly Aboriginal descent from all over the Australian continent. This is sometimes phrased as a choice between assimilation and integration, but both of these terms are used very loosely. The labels are incidental, but the dilemma promises to be a real one. So far, it is not articulated as sharply as this. For many Gunwinggu and other western Arnhem Landers, young as well as old, it is still quite localized, a problem of tension between 'old' and 'new' – between local Aboriginal (*binin*) ways and *balanda* ways. Nevertheless, it is inherent in this very question. And it is foreshadowed in the current scene outside western Arnhem Land, too, as part of the larger issue of relations between Aboriginal and other Australians.

Chapter Nine

Perspective

AT THE BEGINNING of this volume we asked, 'Who are the Gunwinggu?' To some extent this question has been answered. We know where they are to be found, and we have seen that on the fringes of their area – leaving aside those who have virtually or completely moved 'out of the system' – dual or superimposed identification as Gunwinggu, usually at the expense of other identifying labels, has provided for the Gunwinggu a nominal ascendancy unequalled by other smaller groups that have been less obviously oriented along migratory lines.

In other words, two factors are relevant to this social identification. First, as far as the smaller groups are concerned, the range of situations in which their own traditional identification is significant is smaller than that in which Gunwinggu identification is not only expedient, but a part of everyday thought. Secondly, there is the problem of what is 'true' Gunwinggu. A very large proportion of the people who acknowledge this label, actually, when pressed, give it a hyphenated or composite form (for instance, 'Gunwinggu, Maiali side'): both levels of response reveal that the language they generally speak is an important criterion. This means that they nominally subscribe to what passes for Gunwinggu culture. More significantly, it implies that a large part of their social interaction takes place with Gunwinggu speakers. Nevertheless, the hard core of 'true' Gunwinggu has nearly always been distinguished as Gurudjmug, Gumadir and Marganala (Murganella) Gunwinggu, and, very possibly, Margulidjban as well. Historically, as far as we know, these 'district' divisions represent Gunwinggu home territories.

Throughout the greater part of Aboriginal Australia it seems highly likely that, irrespective of any other differences in custom, the language a person speaks is more important for broad identification than anything else, and this seems to be true too in the Gunwinggu case. As we have seen, in terms of culture and especially in relation to myth and ritual, symbolism and emblems, 'true' Gunwinggu elements are not so clearly marked. There is ample evidence to show that Gunwinggu have been receptive to external pressures as far as these cultural items are concerned. Much could be said for the view that Gunwinggu culture is composite, certainly as far as a large part of religious myth and ritual is concerned. In this respect, syncretism is marked. At the same time, as we have seen, the Gunwinggu propensity for incorporating and acknowledging members of smaller entities within its broad perspective, if not actual boundaries, means that socially the category of 'Gunwinggu' is, to an appreciable extent, heterogeneous. The overriding common element binding various persons and units together is the Gunwinggu language: and the language itself has provided a distinctive mould or style for the Gunwinggu culture – making it 'Gunwinggu' even if many of its roots lie elsewhere; making the people concerned 'Gunwinggu', even if their origins are diverse.

The genius of the Gunwinggu, the 'true' Gunwinggu, has been their ability to assimilate incoming ideas and put them to work as if they were their own. They have also moved out of their home territories, but it is a mistake to think of them as migratory or indeed as really being migrants in the strict sense of the term. They did not relinquish rights in those home territories, nor did they sever their spiritual ties with them. They simply expanded: and the reasons for this do not seem to have been shortage of land, or a search for better hunting and food-collecting country, or even that they were forced to do so through pressure from farther east. Rather, their increased mobility was, in part, a direct result of alien contact in the west, and of depopulation and detribalization of the original western Arnhem Land and 'buffalo plains' peoples; and, in part, due to the attractions of the alien settlements. But they moved only so far. The limits of their extended territory, which in the process they Gunwingguized, are the western and south-western boundaries of the Arnhem Land Reserve. Beyond that, although many of them did in fact go farther afield, is not regarded as being Gunwinggu territory even by adoption. Also, when they did move out of their home territories, they did not go among strangers or move into unfamiliar country. Both people and country were already to some extent familiar through their mytho-ritual constellations. The tradition of inter-Aboriginal contact was already firmly established, so we are led to believe, and enshrined in the movements of ancestral and spirit beings. Even more importantly, the people they came among were those with whom they had traded over long periods. (R.B., 1951*a*: Fig. 1.)

Man and Land

In western Arnhem Land, among the Gunwinggu, a marked emphasis on matriliny distinguishes the organization of social relations, and this has only indirect linkage with territory. That tie is left to the *gunmugugur*, a named unit of patrilineal descent. Its basis is an *estate* in Stanner's terms (1965*a*: 2), a 'traditionally recognized locus' that constitutes the 'home country', the ancestral land wherein reside the spirits associated with two or more sites. Agnatic members form a patri-descent group, distinguished by a specific name and by *igurumu* (see Chapter 4). The *gunmugugur* usually comprise a number of localized sites ('small names') within a larger and more inclusive territory ('large name'). For instance, in the Aboriginal map in Fig. 2, a number of sites around Gabari are owned by members of the Djelama *gunmugugur*, but these sites are located in the more inclusive area known as Gurudjmug – and Gurudjmug people are, ideally, considered to be bound by close kin ties. Similarly, in the map in Fig. 3, three *gunmugugur* groupings are noted, all relevant to Gumadir and regarded as being 'of one *family*'; so also in the Fig. 4 map, where the big name is Margulidjban, but since this area is larger than the others, it is not so much a family of *gunmugugur* which is indicated, as a 'community'. To some extent, this resembles the Gidjingali situation (Hiatt, 1962: 279-81; 1965: 19), although the Gidjingali are structurally different, belong more closely within the north-eastern Arnhem Land organizational orbit, and are more obviously patrilineally oriented. Among the Gidjingali, a number of sites are owned by one or more patrilineal groups, which *in toto* make up a 'community'. Among the Gunwinggu, a number of sites are owned by one *gunmugugur*, which in turn belongs to a larger territory, also associated with other *gunmugugur* which have separate estates. These estates of the larger named territory constitute a region, its members forming what could perhaps be called (in Hiatt's terms, 1965: 24) a community.

It is highly likely that, in the past, Gunwinggu forming a community did interact more frequently with one another than with those outside; but they did not restrict themselves to the territory of their own *gunmugugur* – or, for that matter, to that of their community – for purposes of hunting and food-collecting. It is true that they focused on their *gunmugugur* sites for various purposes, but not necessarily for food. Local supplies would have been too limited for that. For one thing, the boundaries of *gunmugugur* were not in any sense hard and fast. (See also Hiatt, 1962: 285.) In the maps in Figs. 3 and 4 we do have tentative boundaries drawn, but these are only rough demarcations: the *gunmugugur* were actually focused on specific sites. The *range* (to use Stanner's term, 1965a: 2) was the tract over which these groups hunted and foraged for food, and included the estates of others as well as their own.

In this area, however, estate and range were not co-extensive, not even approximately so, and from the evidence available it would seem that people moved over a much wider space – particularly in recent times, whatever may have been the case historically. Even prior to 1947 people had been moving away from their *gunmugugur* territories, and the settlements at Oenpelli and Goulburn Island were becoming major foci of interest. This meant, in turn, that changes were taking place both in social organization and in economic imperatives. But also before 1947 and even since, although less markedly so, emphasis was and is still placed on the *gunmugugur* as the territory of a patri-descent group; and this tie with the estate is, pre-eminently, religious. A strong spiritual association between man and his natural environment binds him intimately to the land, his own land, his 'home' (even though he is resident elsewhere), his place of origin if not of birth. This attitude is basic to Gunwinggu thought, and has not decreased in importance. The *gunmugugur* is still the local descent group, even though its members may be physically removed from its sites. In this area, unlike some others (for example, parts of the Western Desert), Gunwinggu are not cut away from their sites – they can still visit them occasionally, and numbers actually do so.

On the other hand there was, traditionally, the hunting and foraging group. This has sometimes been called the *horde*. We shall not retrace the discussion that has centred around the composition of such a group (see R.B., 1959: 98-104; Hiatt, 1962: 267-86, 1966*a*: 81-92; Stanner, 1965*a*: 1-26). The Gunwinggu *local descent group*, the *gunmugugur*, is an exogamous unit: both men and women should find their marriage partners (and their sweethearts) outside it. The members of each such group are linked to the sites of their estate by mytho-totemic ties and its men have responsibilities toward some of them, especially in terms of rites. Members of two or more estates incorporated under a regional label could be spoken of as a 'community' (in terms of population this would vary from, say, twenty-five to seventy-five or one hundred persons). Traditionally, estate land was not transferable. It was held in trust collectively by its members, in a time perspective that looked backward indefinitely into the past and forward into the future. Membership of the *gunmugugur* was, ideally, not transferable either. We have no examples of formal 'naturalization' or 'adoption' of a person of one descent group into another descent group (see Stanner, 1965*a*: 15; Hiatt, 1966*a*: 91), although we do have a few cases of confusion at the individual level regarding membership of a particular *gunmugugur* rather than another. The usual reason is that a growing child may have one or more stepfathers who do not have the same *gunmugugur* as his or her actual father, the genitor.

The question of 'residence' poses some difficulties. It has usually been designated as being patri- or viri-local (Stanner, 1965*a*: 3, 16). In one sense, this is perhaps so as far as the Gunwinggu are concerned. Even with the emphasis on matrilineality, after marriage a man may continue to live with or adjacent to his father's family and his own brothers, and a wife go to live with her husband and husband's family. However, the suffix '-local' may be misleading, since residence is not necessarily on the estate of the father or the husband. As a family group the husband and his wife or wives and their young children would certainly camp on or near it, especially, and traditionally, in the course of a wet season, since all such areas contain traditional and habitual camping-places. It is more likely that a family would camp on any of the estate lands within the area covered by the big name, the community, or sub-region. Furthermore, face-to-face 'co-resident' or 'co-mobile' groups (hordes) formed and re-formed, mainly for the purpose of exploiting the natural environment, and moved across country in a camping pattern that was geared to food resources and ritual exigencies.

This mobile food-collecting unit is (was) basically made up of one or more men of a local descent group plus wife or wives (from other *gunmugugur*) and their young children. It had no fixed membership, and its numbers seem to have varied greatly according to circumstances. In the Gunwinggu area, it would never have been as large as the community, unless the community were quite small. In other words, the units of most intensive interaction included varying proportions of non-agnatic kinsmen and affines (as among the Gidjingali — Hiatt, 1962: 285), nuclear or polynuclear families varying in size from ten to thirty or more persons, moving across fairly broad regions. But this was not indiscriminate wandering. In actuality the area was arbitrarily limited, since, traditionally, seasonal and ritual demands required men to be within easy walking distance of their *gunmugugur* sites. Mobility was conditional on good, bad or indifferent seasons, and it was much more extensive in the Western Desert than in northern Arnhem Land (see R.B., 1959).

The distinction between these types of grouping is quite vital. It has been the subject of much discussion (for example, by Stanner and Hiatt, *ibid.*), and also of some confusion in usage. But, despite Stanner's apologia, this seems to be due to Radcliffe-Brown's own vague conceptualization. References to 'horde country' in the earlier and even in the recent literature (for example, Falkenberg, 1962: 124-62) usually involve: (a) the patrilineal core, associated with that country on the basis of descent; and (b) the larger population built up on that basis, mostly through wives who belong by birth to other descent groups, which normally occupies a certain stretch of country – this larger population being the *territorially based* mixed-sex grouping that has been called a community. But recognition of (a) and (b) does not automatically account for or dispose of the informal co-mobile groupings, fluctuating in size and composition, which have also been called hordes. (Substituting the term 'band' for 'horde' does not in itself clarify the community-horde distinction, because 'band' and 'band territory' have also been used in the wider as well as in the narrower sense. [See Hart and Pilling (1960: e.g., 11-14), who call a band 'the territorial group with which a man most closely identified himself', although 'he might not see many of his fellow members for weeks at a time', and who speak of the co-mobile, co-resident food-collecting group as a 'household'.])

All three kinds of unit are basic to Aboriginal organization, each being related to the land in different ways: the first through descent, direct or otherwise, and the other two through occupancy or use. Here we have, in fact, Stanner's estate and range, viewed territorially. The *gunmugugur* is the *land-owning* group, the community and the horde the *land-occupying* and *land-utilizing* groups. This division reflects two basic issues in Aboriginal social life generally – and traditionally in Gunwinggu life – the religious and economic, viewed as being interdependent. (See R. B., 1964: 264-5.) Adult men of a *gunmugugur* cared for the sites, sacred and otherwise. Some of these sites contained paintings or deposits of sacred objects, or were in themselves 'living' spiritual representations of the sacred Dreaming, and some were surrounded with tabus or restrictions. (See Chapter 3.) Many were associated with ritual, and (for example) with the fertility of the land and its inhabitants. All Aborigines, male and female, were simultaneously members of all three kinds of group. Adult men had two distinct roles. In one, as land-owners, they were *land-renewing* or *land-sustaining*, in the sense of keeping the basic machinery going. In the other, with their womenfolk, they were *land-exploiting*. (See R.B., 1964.)

Man and Man

The relationship between the local descent group on one hand, and the community and the horde on the other, is basic to the social relations of everyday life: a relatively closed, genealogically defined sub-system as against the relatively open and broadly set patterning of kin relationships in which choices operate more freely. The semi-moieties and moieties are also based on descent, in their case matrilineal, and they too are to some extent closed. On the other hand, kinship and the introduced subsection system are open-ended, and are category-oriented, as contrasted with genealogically based allocation and selectivity. In kinship, people are viewed as being and consequently used as a resource, and this is true for consanguineal as well as affinal kin.

216

The social environment is made up of a number of people who interact with one another in some way – consistently or spasmodically, depending on the relationship between them and the circumstances involved. But, whatever the range, they usually make up collectively the overall fabric within which social existence is lived out; and within the range there is a reasonable assurance that expectations between certain persons, related to one another in specific ways, will be fulfilled. Without some such assurance, even of a tentative kind, social existence would be extremely difficult. When we say 'a reasonable assurance', we mean that this may be the expectation in general terms, but that in any specific instance some variation is highly likely.

A system of kinship plots out the overall range, *in toto*, of a number of categories, each using in its construct model a consanguineally or affinally related pair as a point of reference. For example, twenty Gunwinggu terms of address are deployed in seventeen terminological dyads. Or, to put it a different way, seventeen two-way behaviour patterns are relevant throughout the range of kin: their content varies, as do the reciprocal responses. In a study of Gunwinggu behavioural patterns, one of us (R. B., 1966) tentatively classified these relationships into five primary ones (in two grades of 'primary') and two uninfluenced relationships of equality, with the residue being to some extent dependent on or influenced by the first seven, though not necessarily replicas of them.

The Gunwinggu kinship system is predominantly matrilineal and hinges on relationships between brother and sister, as illustrated in the *gagag* (MM, MMB) line with its key roles of brother-sister–nephew-niece. But there is a danger in generalizing from the system or structure itself (as Fox does, 1967: 112-13, *et seq.*): the emphasis on matrilateral linkages in kinship does not reveal the strong influence of the *gunmugugur*. It is true that, in such a matrilineal organization, males assume a significant and executive role, and in one sense the mother's brother, the *ngadjadj*, has a more important part to play in the life of his nephew than the boy's own father has. He has authority over his nephew in both the secular and ritual spheres, and influence in arranging his marriage; and, as one would expect, the relationship is tinged with some constraint and hostility. However, as we have noted, there is no avunculocal residence, and continuity is achieved through women as much as through their brothers –

except in the sphere of secret-sacred ritual.

Kinship systems are not to be understood solely in terms of their structure. Indeed, the elucidation of that structure, the inferring of relationships between parts of it, is dependent on the data we have on the relevant behavioural patterns; these give content and substance to the system and enable us to generalize more widely. It is, no doubt, something more than a useful exercise to construct a basic 'model for the understanding of the kinship-marriage system of most of the Aboriginal Australians' – and, as Fox (1967: 183-4) virtually says, it all 'boils down' to something quite simple, even though he admits that these Aborigines have introduced 'some elaborations to the basic model'. It is also true that all systems (Australian Aboriginal or otherwise) can be reduced to basic structural models – ideally, the bare bones or the shorthand statement of the total pattern: and this is useful in certain circumstances. However, model-building has an irresistible attraction for some anthropologists. One explanation for its popularity may lie in the developmental state of our discipline, and in the psychological tensions that seem to accompany technological proliferation in our kind of society. In many cases, model-building is no more than a device to keep the empirical material at arm's length. Understanding kinship rests primarily on the content of social relationships: and this is the only medium through which meaning in a broader sense can be obtained.

The focus on structure has its usefulness in, for example, understanding how exchange systems work (Fox, 1967: 183), how members of one 'family', local group or clan exchange women (or men) with another unit or with units of similar structure. Many kinship systems are constructed on this basis, on the kind of exchange taking place, whether it be direct or indirect – as Lévi-Strauss (1949) has ably demonstrated. The Gunwinggu are no exception, and emphasize the brother–sister relationship for that purpose.

There are two aspects to this as regards 'marriage exchange'. One concerns a man in relation to his sister's son and daughter (*ganggin*): he is in one sense a 'male mother', and can arrange their marriages; but, ideally, only with the sanction of his sister – in this respect, as in others, he should defer to her. Although formally a man should insist on his son marrying the daughter of an actual *ngalgurng*, Gunwinggu say also that if a man has a son, and his sister a daughter, the two may marry, but only in certain circum-stances (see Chapter 5). The other aspect concerns the exchange of sisters in marriage. This is seen in terms of balancing the exchange of wives between a man's 'side' and the 'side' of his *ngalgurng*, with his sister as pivotal and reciprocating her brother's marriage (see R.B., 1966: 22-6). Supposing a man's *ngalgurng* has a daughter, whom he marries: this is said to mean that 'a fire is burning on his side'. If his own sister has no daughter, it is said that 'no fire is burning on the *ngalgurng* side', or that 'only the brother has a fire – for nothing!' In other words, of the brother and sister's side in this case, Gunwinggu say, 'They have nothing for them' (for the *ngalgurng* side), and they have to negotiate with the mother's brother and mother of a close sister in order to achieve 'balance'. Women are thus important to their brothers through their children, because they not only reciprocate in respect of the brothers' own marriages, but also, through their sons' children, provide spouses for their brothers' sons' sons and sons' daughters; further, a woman's son's daughter could, conventionally, marry that woman's (that is, the grandmother's) brother.

Despite the undeniable importance of exchange and equivalence in the arrangement of marriages, this is not formally structured to the same extent as in a number of other societies. The formality lies in the kinship framework, which supplies rules for defining (a) who are the partners in the exchange – who is eligible, as a person or as a group, to engage in such a transaction – and (b) what is the content of the exchange – who has control over whom. But the translation of these possibilities into practice is not routinized to any extent. The machinery is there, but it is not always used, or not always used in the same way. This is partly because the Gun-winggu marriage rules, including those based on kinship, stipulate a range of preferences and prohibitions as far as eligibility to marry is concerned, whereas a man's control over his sister's daughter implies the possibility of negotiation and bargaining not only inside but also outside that range. The checks lie (i) in the kinship system and marriage rules themselves – ideally, the field is limited and bounded, confined to certain categories of people; (ii) in the conventional power of a girl's mother to block or side-track or at least to protest about an alliance she considers unsuitable; and (iii) in the fact that a father can intervene, informally but effectively, for the same purpose. (See Fig. 13, and the case associated with it, in Chapter 5, and also the case of Biliridj in Chapter 7.)

Avoidance relationships in Gunwinggu society are relevant between brother and sister (mutual); between *nagurng* and *ngalgurng*, 'son-in-law' and 'mother-in-law' (mutual); and between a man and his sister's children (partial constraint). In fact, this last is not real avoidance, but simply constraint, such as is also present in some other relationships (for instance, between a man and his father's sister, male *gagali*, male *nagurng*, and *bindoi*). Even in the brother–sister or son-in-law–mother-in-law relationships, avoidance is only partial: people calling one another by these terms may all be present in the one camp constellation. It seems fairly obvious, in this context, that any avoidance there is, is directly relevant to the brother–sister relationship and that (as noted above, in relation to marriage exchange) it is consequently associated with the *ngalgurng*. Throughout Aboriginal Australia, avoidance and constraint have been enjoined in some degree between a man and his sister, as well as between a man and his mother-in-law; and in nearly all cases this is not necessarily or basically an incest tabu. It is our contention that it is associated with social relations between brothers and sisters, and the rights of a brother over the children produced by the sister – and vice versa, from the perspective of a sister. The mother-in-law syndrome is reflective of this. This is not to say that incestuous feelings between persons in these categories do not or could not occur, and, in fact, they may be conventionalized in 'joking' between male *gagali* and in 'swearing' – but that avoidance relationships are not necessarily to be thought of as having incestuous overtones or undertones.

In Gunwinggu society, as we have seen, if any interpersonal relationship is to be singled out as dominant, it is the relationship between brother and sister (see R.B., 1966: 50 *et seq.*). Close brothers and sisters should not speak together freely, the presence of a sister makes a brother 'feel uncomfortable', and he should never touch anything which is being handled or used by his sister or is directly associated with her. This last is extended in a modified form to his sister's children, whom he must not hold even when they are babies. Indeed, his attitude toward them reflects his attitude toward their mother, although they can serve as go-betweens or mediators – for example, by giving him a present of food which actually comes, indirectly, from her.

As we have seen, a brother calls his sister by a term that can be translated as 'thing', or *ngalwari*, which can be loosely translated as 'rubbish'. This is not unlike the conventional eastern Arnhem Land term *wakinngu* (Warner, 1937/1958: 66, 110), which (according to Warner) means 'without kin', 'worthless' or 'rubbish'; or (from our own information) *mirigu*, with the same broad connotation, or *munggoiba*, the malignant spirit or bones of a dead person. The use of such terms by a brother in respect of *all* women he calls sister as well as his own or close sisters has been variously interpreted. Warner (*ibid.*: 111) suggests that it is because women at marriage are a loss to their own clans. In Hiatt's view (1964: 128), both the term and the conventional attack on a sister (see hereunder) publicly demonstrate men's revulsion at the idea of sexual intercourse between people who stand to each other as brothers and sisters. As Hiatt shows, a man can have several sisters who belong to different patrilineal clans (Gidjingali). To Makarius (1966: 151), the use of such a term implies that a sister is dangerous to her brother, and all people indulging in dangerous or forbidden acts are called *wakinngu*. He says, 'By being wakinu [i.e., *wakinngu*] – without kin – their blood ties with the rest of society are denied and they cease to be dangerous.' The word we have usually heard in this context (see R. B., 1966: 81) is *mirigu*, and when we have heard *wakinngu* it has not been translated as 'without kin'. Mostly, it has been explained in terms of the contrast between orderly human social living and a-social, non-human behaviour, such as is exhibited by wild dogs and other undomesticated creatures. Even though these have something in common with human beings, they do not have the same rules of conduct: they are 'outside' human society. In eastern Arnhem Land ('Murngin'), people indulging in dangerous or forbidden acts are not necessarily regarded as *wakinngu*, and if they are it means simply that they are foolish or ill-advised to act in that way, 'not to be taken seriously'. It is a figure of speech which implies, as one man put it, that 'one does not put one's nose into rubbish, it is wise to keep out', but not only because it may be dangerous, and certainly it is not intended to deny the linkage of blood ties. However, among the Gunwinggu, 'danger' can be associated with a sister: 'If we use something that has been in contact with her or hear bad language used in relation to her, we brothers might have an accident; something dangerous might happen to us.'

Fox (1967: 114), following Warner's explanation (above), claims that in patrilineal systems males are intact: 'they can beget their own children, but they cannot do this by their sisters any more than their matrilineal opposites'; and 'Unlike the matrilineage, the patrilineage need not be too interested in its consanguine women.' Fox adds, that 'the patrilineal tribes [*sic*] of Arnhem Land ... refer to "sisters" as "rubbish" because they cannot reproduce the group'. This, however, is not the case if marriage exchange is taken into account. In spite of Warner's comment noted above, he mentions elsewhere (*ibid.*: 66) that 'Brothers look to their sisters to supply them with wakus [*wogu*, sister's sons] for their daughters to marry'. This obligation is the crux of the brother–sister relationship. In 'Murngin' patrilineal organization, sisters are vital to men in marriage exchanges, as in other situations. They may not 'reproduce the group', but a mother's brother–sister's son relationship is especially significant, and it is incorporated in the *mari* (MMB) line which is both structurally and organizationally dominant. Further, a man's mother's brother (*ngabibi*, reciprocal *wogu*) is, ideally, expected to produce a wife for him, as matrilateral cross-cousin marriage: brothers and sisters are therefore linked in the marriage of their daughter and son respectively.

In the strongly matrilineal Gunwinggu system, the same is the case (as we have said) as far as marriage exchanges are concerned. In fact, the content of the brother–sister relationship in both of these otherwise different societies – Gunwinggu and 'Murngin' – is very similar. Both use emotionally charged terms when referring to sisters, and both have the custom of *miriri* – although the Gunwinggu have no separate word for this. Among them, such terms as *ngalwari* provide a 'front' or facade for a relationship which is quite the opposite of what the word suggests. Emotionally, it is one of the most highly charged relationships, involving dependence and obligation as well as constraint and avoidance. The term is used, men say, because 'a sister is under us': because a mother is supposed to take greater care of a male baby than of a female and because, often, a sister serves as a mother surrogate. In sibling terminology, a brother does not distinguish between younger and elder sisters; and sisters, in appropriate context, use the kin term meaning younger brother and never elder brother. The public display of disparagement is a way of stressing, by underplaying, the emotional aura surrounding the relationship, the dependence and the responsibility of mutual aid and protection; it is a conventional way of avoiding embarrassment, but this is not necessarily because the relationship is fraught with the possibility, real or imagined, of sexual relations between them. (Among the 'Murngin', the term is said to underline the need to keep away from the affairs of a sister: but this does not mean *all* of her affairs, and certainly not as far as the marriage of her sons is concerned.)

As far as we know, there are no cases of brother–sister incest among Gunwinggu, either close or 'long way'; we have encountered none since we began to record their genealogies in earnest in 1947 (after some preliminary work on them in 1945). Nor have we recorded any actual incidents of father–daughter (except among the Maung) or mother–son incest, although there are cases of long-way son-in-law–mother-in-law sexual liaisons. Local mythology provides a few examples of brother–sister incest, as well as incest between own father–daughter and grandfather(MF)–granddaughter. But we have not heard any contemporary discussions concerning sexual relations between brothers and sisters, although, of course, this does not mean that none have occurred. Brother–sister incest, if it did take place, would be regarded very seriously and most probably with abhorrence. (See R. and C.B., 1951a: 59-65.)

However, as we have said, both the Gunwinggu and the 'Murngin' do have *miriri* (see Warner, 1937/1958: 109-13; R.B., 1965a: 96), which in summary means that a brother who hears something unfavourable about his sister, any sister, or sees her behaving indiscreetly or hears someone swearing at her (or just his sister quarrelling), is 'shamed' and embarrassed; this creates a condition of *miriri*, which is distasteful and humiliating for a brother. His response is to protect her honour and his own, by making a show of attacking not only her, as the one directly or indirectly responsible for this, but all of his sisters, actual and otherwise, who are present in the camp, for example, by throwing spears at them. He does this 'because his attachment to a sister is so strong'. The focus is on the sister(s) and not on others who have been involved in the incident, even if those others have provoked it. Others are in fact, in this context, irrelevant as far as a brother is concerned. He treats a sister as a projection of himself – she must, ideally, remain circumspect, and not be embroiled in any disturbance because of its implications for himself.

These relate to his expectations as far as her children are concerned. The behaviour is peculiar to a brother, and not relevant to any other paired relationship (between father and daughter, for instance, or father and son), because the content of these other behavioural patterns differs quite considerably (see Hiatt, 1964: 125), and because no other relationship (except that between a man and his *ngalgurng*) is directly associated with marriage exchanges. To put it another way, no other relationship provides a man with the same expectations in relation to the production of children. Because the content of the relationship differs from that of others, one would not expect an emotionally charged term like *ngalwari* to be used for a father's sister or a daughter (see Hiatt, *ibid.*: 125), where it would be meaningless. We have used the word 'shame' in this context, but this is not necessarily a sexual shame due, as Hiatt suggests (*ibid.*: 128), to 'a feeling of revulsion from sexual relations' with women classified as sisters. It can be seen, no less convincingly, as an overt declaration of regard and protection. As one man put it, 'It is like a sacred relationship which means a lot to us: if we brought it into the open, it could be damaged: we react against sisters in this way to avoid a continuation of their involvement in a situation which has direct consequences for us, as brothers.' And this has nothing to do with whether the sister is in the right or in the wrong, or with who has or has not provoked her.

This may not be an entirely adequate explanation, but the sexual one (Hiatt, 1966*b*: 154) is no more compatible with the Gunwinggu or 'Murngin' facts. It also seems to us that in this relationship, as well as with the *ngalgurng*, the explanation for the special kind of avoidance behavioural pattern lies in the implications of the relationship for the brother and the sister, and for the potential or actual mother-in-law – in the sister and her children, as elements in an exchange system of marriage; in the *ngalgurng* because she has daughters who may become the *nagurng*'s wives. The *ngalgurng* relationship, as we have said, need not have any overtones or undertones of incest, because usually a man and his mother-in-law are at least several steps apart, genealogically speaking, even when she is an actual MMBD; on the other hand, she could conceivably be an actual father's sister, when this aspect would be relevant.

The Aborigines are eminently logical people and, if the intention were to erect behavioural barriers to discourage or prohibit incest, they could have done so for other relationships within the nuclear family. The Gunwinggu, and many other (but not all) Aboriginal Australians, feel just as strongly about sexual relations between a father and daughter or a mother and son as they would presumably in respect of a brother and sister, but they do not insist on full or partial avoidance between them. It seems reasonable, therefore, to infer that no such suggestion is especially or uniquely relevant to the brother–sister relationship as it is expressed among the Gunwinggu.

Man and Myth

The dependence of man on land, on his natural environment and all within it, is at a different level, the social level, equivalent to his dependence on his fellow men – on his kin, variously defined, who are arranged conventionally in a network of reciprocally dependent relationships. It is in the utilization of these resources, both human and non-human, that the lineaments of living take shape. But shape itself is not enough, much more is demanded. It is necessary to activate both these dimensions, providing a relationship between the natural and the social, establishing an interaction, and with it a familiarity and an intimacy. And it is also necessary to provide a *raison d'être*, a meaning and a pattern for social existence. Gunwinggu, like other Aboriginal Australians, saw life as a recurrent series of events stemming from the formative era, the events themselves being of a repetitive kind, set irrevocably in motion by spirit beings. The question of design is significant: as Stanner (1965*b*: 215) puts it, this is '*given* design that seemed to them to point to intent'. The rationale was that of nature itself – seasonal sequence, growth and renewal. Man was seen as mirroring this pattern, as indeed being an integral part of it. It is this emphasis on life which is perhaps the most striking feature of Aboriginal religion (a point made by Stanner, 1965*b*: 217). Even in mortuary rituals, it is life that is stressed – the past life of the deceased and his future life in a Land of the *Living* Dead, or rebirth. True, sorrow is expressed at the loss of a kinsman or friend. But the passing of man, like seasonal decay, is followed by renewal; man is not separated from nature and conditioned to different natural laws.

The stimulators and instigators, the great mythic spirit beings of the Dreaming – those who were/are responsible for both the natural and the social design – vary considerably in stature and in function. Although it is possible to separate out primary characters – Yirawadbad, Nagugur, and Lumaluma, etc. – whose actions are perpetuated in myth and enshrined in ritual, they are very numerous indeed. All, however, are connected with the land, with specific sites and with the country; some are shape-changing and some are not. The whole country is spiritually peopled. It is as if there were two *real* Gunwinggu populations simultaneously co-existing, interacting with each other, and closely bound to each other by ancestral ties. Furthermore, the 'big' myths or sagas which narrate the travels and adventures of such beings cover wide areas, and these too are linked. Just as the essence of Dreaming resides in each human being, male and female, and is activated through ritual, so every element in the natural environment has this same quality – a sacred quality, since sacredness in the Gunwinggu sense is derived from the Dreaming and the spirit beings; it is pervasive, part of life and of living.

Although man's association with the Dreaming is ensured by his being, in effect, *of the same order* as his natural environment and the creative and spirit beings responsible for it, that connection is, further, mediated through what has been called 'totemism' (see Lévi-Strauss, 1962; R.B., n.d.[1]). This concept has been variously described (for example, by Elkin, 1938/1964: 164-87; R. and C. B., 1964: 186-98; Stanner, 1960: 255-6, 1965b: 223-37), and the present volume is not the place to discuss it in any detail. However, it is essential to bear in mind that, if the term 'totemism' is to be used at all, it should be thought of as being well entrenched in the Dreaming and as establishing in a symbolic fashion – that is, through providing a series of signs in Stanner's sense (1965b: 214-16) – spiritual relationships, expressed in tangible terms, between man and the non-empirical. The signs which are chosen for expressing this symbolic association are varied, as we have seen: they are not necessarily confined to natural species or to attributes or parts of the spirit beings themselves; the selection superficially appears to be arbitrary. This is not the case, however. They are part of the overall patterning of symbolic design, part of the total framework of man's attempt, not only to give meaning to the social order in which he lives, but to link him securely to what can be regarded as the purpose and reason of living. In this way, is enshrined a series of binding and perpetual and, in the Gunwinggu sense, inherited relationships which give man the illusion (from our point of view, but not from the Gunwinggu, since this relationship justifies or substantiates the purpose) that he is not only in direct contact with the spirit beings, but can control or influence them. In other words, 'man must play his part'. In the Aboriginal view, such beings came into existence in the first place, and continue to exist, *because* of this symbolic relationship, or network of symbolic relationships; the cycle of life, seasonal fluctuation, the increase of natural species – in fact, the socio-natural order of things – is maintained through the performance of ritual. Man is not separated from this mytho-ritual or Dreaming stream, which provides him with physical and emotional security. It should also be remembered that not all of this is necessarily secret-sacred – much is sacred in a broader fashion and is not hedged in with restrictions.

A case could probably be made for speaking of Gunwinggu religion as 'polytheistic', provided we do not read into this too much of worship or reverence or awe. The spirits symbolize various aspects or attributes of natural and social life, but Australianists have hesitated to call them deities. At one time, they searched in Aboriginal cultures for male High Gods or Supreme Beings or, as Eliade (1966-7) calls them, Primordial Beings. In one sense, in the Gunwinggu situation, the Fertility Mother in her many manifestations is primary. But although she is symbolized in all the major rituals in one way or another, in her guise of the humanized Waramurungundji, the Rainbow Snake, or Kunapipi, and although her presence is invoked and symbolized, she is often in the background and the mythic substantiation of a particular ritual sequence rests on other characters who serve as intermediaries. A direct relationship between the Mother and sacred rites is not so apparent among the Gunwinggu as it is in eastern Arnhem Land (see R.B., 1951a, 1952a). It is usually a matter of beings like Yirawadbad, Nagugur and Lumaluma first performing ritual symbolic of the Mother, and giving this to man.

The emphasis on the Mother is widespread, and not necessarily linked with an emphasis on matriliny (see R. and C. B., 1964:

227

234-45), although Meggitt (1966: 84-5) has shown that the Gadjari or Big Sunday of the Walbiri, equivalent to the Kunapipi, has been brought 'into line with the "indigenous" desert type *ngallungu* ritual that is most clearly exemplified in the Ingkura of the Aranda'. (See also Strehlow, 1947: 100-12.) As we saw earlier (Chapter 2), the Rainbow is predominantly a male figure among the Maung – even though, structurally speaking, Maung and Gunwinggu are very close indeed; they have the same matrilineal moieties, semi-moieties and subsections, and the same kind of named patrilineal descent group. And farther east, again, the Rainbow or Rock Python is more obviously male and more obviously a phallic symbol, although the Wawalag myth can actually be seen as a 'transition myth' between the cultures of western and eastern Arnhem Land. We could relate the Rainbow, in any of these three situations, to the seasonal fluctuation between dry season and north-west monsoon, with the concomitant changes in terrain from dry land to flood-plains, and so on. (See Lévi-Strauss, 1962; also C. B., n.d. [3]). This last also brings in the *threefold* contrast noted in Chapter 3, between dry rocks and wet or potentially wet ground, with con-sistently habitable 'bush' as the desirable medium – and leads on to the contrast between symbolically high ground and symbolically low, in the ritual sense, with the implication that ordinary living needs to take into account both extremes but should not have an excess of either: that it needs to include both secret-sacred *and* mundane, not exclusively one or the other. In this respect as in others, Gunwinggu themselves recognize contrasts and oppositions; but they also recognize gradations in between – they dramatize these for certain purposes, but qualify and amplify them for others.

Among the Gunwinggu, the 'indigenous' fertility constellation was reinforced by the incoming rites from the east and south-east. However, we should not think of only one Mother, but keep in mind that there are many manifestations. Also, she is not envisaged as being alone, either in myth or in ritual. She is seen and thought of as interacting with others, over and above her relations with ordinary human beings – with male postulants and novices, and with women in certain circumstances. And this is true too for other spirit beings – they are not alone. The Mother does, however, epitomize the basic elements that are needed to maintain con-tinuity and design: it is her *intent* which is at stake in, for example, ritual.

All myth is, of course, contemporary. Although Gunwinggu myths tell of origins, they do so in non-empirical terms. They are also more concerned with the social picture and with the institution of socio-cultural features as perceived in today's terms and as having present-day relevance. Although myth is presented as a series of statements hallowed by time, changeless, within the perspective of the Dreaming, it is in fact subject to both variation and interpretation. Most Gunwinggu myths, including the sacred and more portentous, exist in many versions and are not relevant only to one sex.

The myths clustered around the Fertility Mother Waramurungundji, Ngaljod the Rainbow Snake, and Kunapipi do not imply that there is 'some kind of "immemorial misdirection" in human affairs, and that living men are committed to its consequences' (see Stanner, 1960: 260 *et seq.*). Although the content differs, the Murinbata myth of the Old Woman set out by Stanner (*ibid.*: 260-2) is roughly similar to the Mara version of the Kunapipi 'Old' Woman (R.B., 1951*a*: 148-52). Gunwinggu mythology has nothing resembling this. It is true that Lumaluma is killed. Also, the 'Mother as Rainbow Snake' has two primary manifestations, one as what can virtually be spoken of as the 'good' Mother, and the other as the 'bad' Mother; and it is the second of these who brings disaster and, in myth as in pseudo-historical accounts, is often 'killed' by human beings. There is nothing to suggest mythic 'misdirection' which cannot be remedied. The only instance of this is the well-known myth which tells how death came into the world: it could have been averted, but it was not. Natural disasters like flood, fire, death by lightning, and so on, are viewed as being a part of the natural order of things, even though they may be directly associated with mythical beings, and even though in any specific instance they are traced to a mistake or a wrong or foolish action. The Rainbow Snake is an agent of destiny (see Chapter 2), but not to the exclusion of 'free will' or choice on the part of the mythical characters she encounters. *If* these First People had not taken a wrong turning or allowed the Orphan to cry or cooked a goanna or possum in a sandy spot by the water, and so on, or *if* Djabo (etc. – see Chapter 6) had taken Moon's advice – then they would have avoided suffering the penalty. The Rainbow is not a moral watchdog, however. It is such things as the crying of the child or the sizzling of the possum or the loss of her/his egg (sacred stone) which precipitate the catastrophe, and not any breach of the social/moral rules among the First People themselves. For instance, it is not the fact that the Orphan was neglected, but the fact that he cried. There is no *supernatural* moral retribution for offences such as incest.

Nevertheless, in almost every case where a narrative sequence is spelt out or implied, the final climax follows (comes as a result of) some action that is defined as wrong. This happens even in the case of Wuragag, who managed his own metamorphosis without the help of the Rainbow: and Lumaluma's death was a direct consequence of wrongdoing. Yirawadbad killed his wife and her mother for the same reason – they did not conform with the rules. (For one way of looking at this, in summary, see Fig. 21.) But Wuragag and others like him became *djang*, Lumaluma gave people the sacred *maraiin* and other rites, and Yirawadbad instituted the sacred *ubar* on the basis of the hollow log in which he hid before killing the women. In other words, out of the wrongdoing came good – the *djang*, and the most sacred rites. There is no explicit statement that 'mythically speaking, wrongdoing is a necessary prelude to good'; but the shape that dramatic conflict takes in Gunwinggu mythology emphasizes, not 'bad from bad', but *'good* from bad'. Pessimism is certainly the prevailing mood at the climax of the *djang* stories, but in the long term the outlook is optimistic.

to page 233

Key to figure 21

mri, mrii = marriage rules	O^1 = Yirawadbad's mother-in-law, living
fa = emphasis on female authority	$●^1$ = Yirawadbad's mother-in-law, dead
ma = emphasis on male authority	O^2 = Yirawadbad's wife, living
(r) = reaffirmed	$●^2$ = Yirawadbad's wife, dead
Rr = ritual rule	⬧ = (Yirawadbad as) snake
Nr = natural rule	♀ = female as Mother
O = female	X X = rejection
△ = male	✳ = breach
$△^y$ = Yirawadbad	⊔ = marriage

230

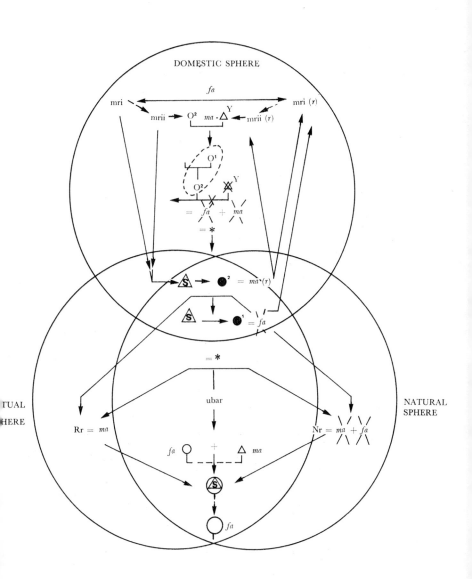

Fig. 21. The Yirawadbad myth.

Notes on Fig. 21:

1. The main Gunwinggu marriage rule (mri) is a kinship rule. It emphasizes female authority (*fa*): specifically, of mother-in-law in relation to son-in-law; and of mother over unmarried or newly married daughter.

2. The main Gunwinggu *marital* rule (under the general heading of 'marriage rules', and therefore shown as mrii) emphasizes male authority (*ma*): specifically, of husband over wife.

3. Yirawadbad's wife commits a breach of both rules, mri and mrii. She rejects her husband (rejects him as a person) and his authority over her, and refuses to stay with him. She rejects her mother's authority too, but remains in her company, forming a female (mother-daughter) pair or, from Yirawadbad's point of view, a female coalition against him.

4. In killing his wife, Yirawadbad reaffirms mrii (*ma*) and, indirectly, mri; but,

5. In killing his mother-in-law and rejecting *fa*, Yirawadbad himself commits a breach of mri – even though, in a sense, he thereby reaffirms the rule (mri) by punishing someone who has either broken it or, in this case, apparently condoned the breach. (The mother-in-law did not exercise enough authority to force her daughter to accept Yirawadbad as a husband, and did not punish her severely enough for rejecting him.)

6. Yirawadbad's breach (5) is expressed as (mediated through) a ritual killing, and

7. Has ritual implications and consequences: (*a*) 'new' ritual (10, below); (*b*) 'new' ritual rule (*ma* dominant) – women are excluded from the male coalition in secret-sacred rites, just as Yirawadbad was earlier excluded from the female (mother-daughter) coalition.

8. Blame for (5) and for (4), above, as well as for (3), is ascribed to Yirawadbad's wife, not to Yirawadbad himself.

9. Retaliation for (8) is transferred from the purely human sphere to the sphere of man-in-nature (nature in relation to man): Yirawadbad-as-snake, in the *natural* sphere, rejects *all* human authority (both *fa* and *ma*) and is hostile to human beings. (The sorcery aspect is relevant here, but we shall not follow it up. See the Yirawadbad myth itself, and the sorcery discussion in Chapter 7.)

10. Compensation for (4), (5) and (9) above is transferred to the sphere of sacred ritual: Yirawadbad as a symbolic snake in a ritual context can bring benefits (life, not death) to human beings. In the human sphere, in his story, Yirawadbad's marital union was either unconsummated or not satisfactorily consummated; and it was infertile. In the ritual sphere, he influences seasonal and natural (and human) fertility: (*a*) through symbolic union between male and female – snake in hollow log. (In the myth, Yirawadbad's wife and mother-in-law are both close kin to him, but in both cases the marriage/affinal link is emphasized.) And (*b*) through composite or merging or shifting sex identification, blurring or uniting male and female, *and* male and female authority – the *ubar* snake as Rainbow Snake (male and/or female); and the Ubar Woman as the mother of all human beings, but also described as the symbolic wife of male *ubar* participants, especially young initiands, on the secret-sacred ground – a combined kin (descent) and marital relationship of a sort that is quite outside the range of everyday acceptability.

This could be set out a little differently in another diagram, which we have not included here. The central theme, or core, begins with the action that precipitates the main sequence – the rejection of Yirawadbad by his promised wife. The union is incomplete, and infertile: no new life results from it; at the same time, no offspring from it died or were killed, and so in that respect it could be described as entirely negative. The progression then, stated very briefly and without elaboration, is: (i) Yirawadbad kills his wife and mother-in-law – snake in hollow log brings death (to females); (ii) Yirawadbad retains his snake form in the natural sphere – snake in nature, alone and without log connection, brings death (to everyone, but 'especially hostile to girls'); (iii) Yirawadbad joins other males, asserting male control of secret-sacred ritual – snake in hollow log brings death (to females and to uninitiated males); (iv) Yirawadbad is partly identified with other mythical beings, including the Rainbow (male *and/or* female) and the Ubar Woman – snake in hollow log brings life and fertility (to everyone, male and female). And so on.

Finally: if Yirawadbad's wife was, ultimately, responsible ([8], above) for the train of events that followed her first 'offence' ([3], above), this responsibility must extend to the ritual as well as to the natural sphere. In other words, as far as the Yirawadbad myth is concerned, without her action – specifically, without her rejection of her husband – there would have been no *ubar* ritual at all.

Here we come back to women's reference (see Chapter 7) to the Ubar *woman* – as mother, not wife: in women's accounts, except for the human *ubar* participants, she has no husband. Whether or not we bring in the issue of matrilineal emphasis, this could be the beginning of a more complex analysis; but such an analysis would also have to include other versions of the *ubar* and related mythology, from both men's and women's points of view.

Stanner (*ibid.*: 276-7) speaks of Murinbata religion as affirming 'a necessary connection between life and suffering', involving the 're-enactment of the primordial tragedy [the myth of the Old Woman who is eventually killed]', with the Mother's blood as 'a symbol both of life and of suffering'. Among the Gunwinggu, no sacred ritual re-enacts tragedy *per se*: it may certainly re-enact death (not the death of the Mother), but not in terms of an explicit statement with social and/or personal implications. The emphasis is rather, as already noted, on birth and rebirth. Symbolic actions and signs indicate the spiritual presence of the Mother. Postulants enter her uterus, and in doing so they become as one with her, either in their own or in totemic form; novices also enter the Mother or are swallowed by her only to emerge or be vomited out, 'reborn', renewed, resurrected. Many myths contain 'primordial tragedies', but these reflect the personal tragedies which continue to occur in ordinary contemporary life, as part of the expected life-pattern. In Gunwinggu religious ideology, in its myth, ritual and symbolism, it is difficult to distinguish what can be regarded as 'suffering', even in abstract. It is true that these are often focused on life-crises and on birth and rebirth, with the intermediate state of death; but this is not suffering, unless the term is interpreted very loosely indeed.

The Mother's blood, in the Gunwinggu sense, has nothing to do with this: when blood is used in, for example, *kunapipi* or *maraiin* rites it is simply an adhesive for feather-down, and it symbolizes life – 'they are smeared with blood as they leave the womb of the mother' or, in decoration, 'the blood activates the postulant, he becomes (is) the being or creature his decoration is intended to convey'. This is not sacrifice in Stanner's terms (1959: 109), not from the point of view of Gunwinggu – although there is evidence that it may be elsewhere.

The Gunwinggu cultural area, as we have seen, is remarkably free from physical operations such as accompanied initiatory rites in other parts of Aboriginal Australia. The focus is, instead, on the discipline of the food tabu. In one sense, the Gunwinggu are intensely materialistic, and the emphasis on food tabus is but one expression of this. In one sense, too, in spite of what can be regarded as transcendental, the final mystery – even though it is couched in symbolic terms of complex imagery – is no more and no less than the basic elements of social existence. The 'mystery' underlines a belief in life, in the well-tested lessons from the past, which are just as relevant now as they always have been and will be for the future – but lessons placed within the design which is inspired by the Dreaming and guided by the invisible presence of the significant spirit beings.

Much of Gunwinggu ritual has specific and detailed mythical support, but some of it does not. Conversely, many myths have no ritual expression. The problem of explanation is not an especially difficult one at the empirical level, since most actions have meanings that are often expressed in mythic terms. The problem really lies in the realm of inferred explanations, because in actual fact much of Gunwinggu ritual bears a close resemblance to ritual in other parts of Arnhem Land as well as in other parts of Aboriginal Australia. Explanations in broader terms can be arrived at only by detailed comparative analysis, which we are unable to attempt here. Gunwinggu ritual is divided up and seen as a series of stages or progressions, with novices beginning at the first and moving through in a fairly uniform fashion, at least traditionally, as part of the socialization process, each subsequent ritual being regarded as a reinforcement of the last, but at the same time adding something more, extending the range of knowledge. This ritual stream runs, in a complementary way, alongside of *other*, non-ritualized, activity, not separated from it (except on formal occasions) but actually a part of it. It is this understanding of Gunwinggu religion which is contrary to Durkheim's concept of the sacred and profane. As Stanner (1960: 278) has rightly remarked, 'the relation between the religious and the mundane life is continuous'. And this is certainly so in the Gunwinggu case. (See also C.B., 1965: 238-81.) The division of labour between the sexes which is relevant in 'secular' or mundane life is relevant also in the sacred life. The executive role of men in ritual action, on the secret-sacred ground, is contrasted with the executive role of women in relation to that ground and in relation to what the men are doing: this may involve ritual action on their own part or in conjunction with men – and it too is sacred, even if it is not performed on that secret-sacred ground. The same is the case with myth: each sex may be in possession of differing versions associated with the same characters.

The division of labour in ritual poses some intriguing problems, however, and not least in respect of the overall question of men's position and roles vis-à-vis women. The sequence of the Yirawadbad myth, for instance, not only points to woman-as-the-offender (and, like Eve, responsible for a venomous snake's hostility to humankind). It also suggests that women's exclusion from the domain of the secret-sacred was more than punishment or revenge, that the way Yirawadbad *could* have put it was: 'If we men can't be certain of our control over women in ordinary life, in matters of betrothal and marriage, let us try to ensure that we have one sphere in which we can be dominant. Let's keep them out of some areas of sacred ritual – and these will be the most important parts . . . .' The ramifications of this myth alone, and its practical implications, need to be looked at further. And, at this point, we merely underline the point that all sacred ritual involves men and women in differing degrees, all are committed, and Gunwinggu religion is relevant to the society as a whole.

To some extent we have been selective in reviewing these three aspects, Land, Man and Myth. There are others too on which we could have focused. However, these constitute major categories under which much else can be subsumed. They should be thought of, not so much as a triad, as embracing a totality, a multi-faceted wholeness, which spells out the design of which we have spoken. Further, they represent basic ingredients of socio-cultural living.

In the *man–land* dimension, the focus is on the sensible and skilful exploitation of the natural environment, on material survival, and on the organization of human resources in order to achieve this satisfactorily. It is on this basis that territorial and local associations provide the fabric of socio-economic life.

In the *man–man* dimension, linked as it is with the first, is a network of social relations which binds persons together into cooperative and mutually dependent groups, in an endeavour to achieve social security. This underlines the obvious fact that man cannot be independent, whether this be in matters of food collection or in making decisions – others must always be taken into account. The Gunwinggu, like all other Aboriginal Australians, are kin-oriented. Their relations with others (and these are always significant others) are couched in terms of responsibilities and reciprocal obligations: not as a game or an exercise or a desirable but unattainable ideal, but as a necessity.

In the *man–myth* dimension, which is inseparable from the last two, are expressed in a multitude of symbolic ways (through myth, totemism and rite) the meaning and intent of socio-cultural living. It is as if the first two dimensions were combined and re-sorted, and provided with a series of explanations and relevances. Or, to put it in another way, the man–land and man–man dimensions constitute the empirical, the man–myth the non-empirical. The first is the area of acting, of getting things done; the second is the area of thinking, and of meaning, and of explanation. It is true that such a distinction is not really satisfactory, that in fact it is not possible to separate things out in this way, and that a proto-scientific approach is evident in the mundane taxonomic classification of the natural environment, just as in ritual the emphasis is on 'getting things done', and on controlling and influencing the 'theo-mythic' spirits for the benefit of man. Nevertheless, it is in the realm of myth and ritual, in the symbolic expressions and allusions, that final answers are sought to the eternal question concerning the mystery of life and of living.

Appendix I

Gunmugugur territorial units

Note: In the following table we have included some variant forms, although these need more discussion; for instance, in a number of cases they represent different statements from men on one hand, women on the other.

Gunmugugur name	*Igurumu*	Approximate location
Barbin	Nabambidmag (or Nayunban)	Gumadir and Margulidjban
Born	Nagolgborn (or Djudu Garamira)	Gumadir and Margulidjban
Dangulu	Wabuwi	Margulidjban; also Gumadir
Danig (or Wurin)	Badjulaidj (or Badjanangu; or Magaliraga)	Gumadir; also Gogalag and Maburin
Djelama	Magaliraga (or Belwari)	Two main divisions: Gurudjmug; also Sandy Creek area to Tor Rock; includes Maung
Djorg	Waiin(i)ngura (or Nagamu)	Gumadir and Margulidjban
Durmangga	Neiilibidj	Gumadir and Margulidjban; and Dangbun
Gadbam	Miranggangu	Gumadir, and rocky stretch inland from Sandy Creek
Gamurgban	Gurbilamar	Three main divisions: two coastal (Gunbalang and Yiwadja) and one inland (Dangbun)
Gunumbidj	Nagurula	Margulidjban

237

Gunmugugur name	*Igurumu*	Approximate location
Gurwala (or Guruwala)	Ganamul	Coast, Gunbalang and fringe Gunwinggu
Madbadji (or Malbari)	Gumunggudu (or Mararumbu)	Coast and inland, mainly Gunbalang; Margulidjban; but actually three divisions, including mouth of King River on coast
Madjawar	Djambunu (or Nabamgarg)	Nimbuwa area
Maiirgulidj	Nagurulg (or Marangu Gurindjil)	Three main divisions: part of South Goulburn Island and adjoining coast (Maung); Gumadir; and Margulidjban. (Maung name: Merwulidj, m.; Berwulidj, f.)
Mandjulngoin	Miranggangu (or Gabudaid Magaliraga; or Mabinngul)	Three main divisions: Mangerdji, originally around Oenpelli; inland Gunwinggu, 'mixed with' Gadbam; and Gunbalang side toward Sandy Creek and Cooper's Creek
Maningererbi	Mangigi	Margulidjban, and coast east of Liverpool River, including Gunbalang
Maninggali	Mardjaleiala (or Nabambidmag)	Tor Rock area and coast westward; mixed Maung-Yiwadja and fringe Gunwinggu; Marganala
Marin	Nagulban (or Gumbaldja)	Gumadir and Margulidjban
Mirar (or Miar)	Neiilibidj (or Nabamgarg)	Three main divisions: Oenpelli area (Mangerdji) and Gunbargid; Tor Rock area to Marganala; and inland (Maiali-Djeibmi, and toward Djauan)
Munari (or Munwari)	Gaddura	Gumadir, Gunwinggu and Maung
Murwan	Djambunu (or Nabamgarg: 'same as Madjawar')	Four main divisions: two coastal (Maung; Yiwadja), and two inland (Gunbargid; and Gunwinggu, in Fish Creek area)
Ngalngbali	Namalinggunja	Gurudjmug, Gumadir and Gudjegbin
Nguluminj	Wainmargi (or Badjanangu)	Inland, Gogalag

Gunmugugur name	_Igurumu_	Approximate location
Wadjag	Alamin-gunumbu	Gunwinggu-Dangbun, including Djalbangur area
Wurig	Guwadu	Gurudjmug, Margulidjban, Gumara (includes small country, Nabarbinwer ?meng, in Mandaidgaidjan); mixed Gunbalang
Yagidjagid	Magaliraga	Gumadir; and coast (Gunbalang)
Yilugidj (or Yigilugidj)	Marinbal	Gurudjmug

Other main 'Gunwinggu-fringe' units are, on the eastern side, Bingururu, Bobereri, Bulngu, Djindibi, Gadjarngu, Girarbi, Giwilu, Gularama or Gulmaru, Gurulg, Marawaindja, Miwi, Morg, Walmindju, and Wunal; and, on the Maiali and Dangbun sides and into Djauan territory, Badmadi, Baraba or Burabu, Baraid, Bedbed, Bidjamiran, Bolmo, Bulaldja, Buru, Djori, Djorolam, Djulbin, Gungomgu, Guraidjarlngo, Gurgbaba, Lambira, Madalg, Maradidj, Margu, Mingalgen or Midngalgen, Murgana, Rul, Waraingo, Waramal, Wogmarain, Worgorl, Wurban, Yamarg and Yil?main.

Appendix II

Ordinary Terms of Reference

Note: The numbers correspond to those in the list of terms of address in Chapter 5. Only a few of the terms are translated here, without going into any detail.

The sign + indicates an inflected form that varies for person and number, etc. The masculine prefix *na-* is not included in all masculine forms, but *ngal-* is a feminine prefix. To make these forms easier to read, the prefixes are hyphenated here. Some ordinary vocative terms can be used in reference as well, usually preceded by ngadug, 'my'; other forms are more impersonal.

1. a. garad, garad ngadug, 'my mother'.
   b. +ngal-baidjan, ngal-badjan (*baidjan,* 'big'); first person singular agent, nga-baidjan.
   c. [ngalbu] +ngan-jaumei (ngan-yaumei), '[she who] got me as jau' (see 8); +nga-jaumei, 'I got [him, her] as jau', etc.

2. As 1.

3. a. ngaba, ngabad, ngadug ngabad, 'my father'.
   b. gongomu (*gom,* 'neck' or, specifically, 'throat'): reference to carrying child on his shoulders, astride his neck.
   c. [nawu] +ngan-bonang, '[he who] saw me [in spirit]'; first person singular agent, nga-bonang. (Restricted to own or very close father.)

4. 5. 6. a. +ngane-dangin (two), ngari-dangin (more than two), etc., 'we [who] stand [together]'. Also used in direct address – ngune-dangin, 'you two . . . ', etc.

   b. In impersonal reference – na-walawalag (m.), ngal-walawalag (f.), younger, youngest, same-sex sibling; na-wenwari (m.), ngal-wenwari (f.), elder, eldest, same-sex sibling.

   c. na-rangem, 'brother' (term used by a woman speaking to her daughter about the girl's close or full brother).

   d. ngal-dalug (*dalug*, ordinary Gunwinggu word for 'woman'), 'sister' (term used, for example, by a woman speaking to her son about his close or full sister).

7. bewud (m.), ngal-bewud (f.); wud, an ordinary term for a child from before its birth until a little before puberty, can mean 'offspring', and is used in *gundebi* forms (see Chapter 5).

8. jau (m.), ngal-jau (f.) (yau, ngalyau); general term, wudjau.

9. baidjan, badjan: see 1.
   baidjan-rangem, 'baidjan as brother', emphasizing his double role as not only an uncle but also a MB.

10. a. ngal-gongomu: see 3.
    b. [ngalbu] +ngan-bonang: as for 3, but feminine referent.

11. a. ngal-ginbalen.
    b. [nawu, ngalbu] +ngan-djumdoi, +nga-djumdoi (from perspective of younger and elder members of gagag dyad, respectively).

12. a. na-mainmigen, ngal-mainmigen.
    b. [nawu, ngalbu] +gebmainmeng, +nga-gebmainmeng, etc. (*geb*, 'nose' or, by extension, 'face').

13. [nawu, ngalbu] +ngan-gebmawaʔmeng, +nga-gebmawaʔmeng, etc.

14. [nawu, ngalbu] +ngan-gebmagaʔmeng, +nga-gebmagaʔmeng, etc.

15. +ngan-doidoiʔmigen, +nga-doidoiʔmigen, etc. (sometimes identified with 11).

16. [nawu, ngalbu] +nga-jaumei (nga-yaumei), etc.

17. mudjalgdoi; +ngane-mudjalgdoren, 'we two . . . ', etc.

18. a. na-gobeng, ngal-gobeng.
    b. na-ganjulg, ngal-ganjulg; na-mamam, mamam.

20. +ngan-doibun, +nga-doibun, etc.

For 19*a* and 19*b*, and 21*a* and 21*b*, see Table 4 in Chapter 5.

Appendix III

'Tribal' or language names in Gunwinggu perspective

Note: The prefix *gun-* before a name in this context refers to language. The numbers refer to the locations marked on Fig. 22.

1. Adawuli
2. Amurag
3. Awur
4. Balang, Gunbalang (Maung name: Walang or Wolang)
5. Bargid, Gunbargid
6. Dangbun, Gundangbun
7. Djauan, Djawun, Gundjauan
8. Djeibmi, Gundjeibmi, Gundaidnjebmi (alternatively, 'b' is replaced by a glottal stop, for example, Djeiᵖmi)
9. Eri
10. Gadjalibi
11. Garig
12. Gunavidji, Gunyibidji, Yibidji
13. Gundjirbara
14. Gungurugoni
15. Gunwinggu, see Winggu
16. Guru, Gungurulg
17. Kakadu, Gagudju, Kakudju
18. Magabala, Gabala, Gungarigen
19. Maiali, Gunmaiali
20. Mangawulu
21. Mangeri, Mangerdji
22. Margu
23. Maung (Maung name), Marung, Gunmarung
24. Nagara
25. Naragani
26. Ngunbudj
27. Rembarnga, Rembranga
28. Waramungguwi
29. As 15. Winggu, Gunwinggu (Maung name: Neinggu)
30. Woraidbag, Woraidbug
31. Wuningag
32. Wurilg
33. Wurugu
34. Yilga
35. Yiwadja, Yibadja, Jiwadja, Juwadja

Notes on the list of names and the map on page 242-43:

    (a) For comments on the location of these names, and others, see Chapter 1.

    (b) No. 5 is a collective name, that includes 2, 3, 9, 17, 21, 28, 30 and 31, and therefore does not appear on the map.

    (c) Numbers in brackets signify tentative location.

    (d) No. 10 is a Gunwinggu name for the Gidjingali. (See Hiatt, 1965: 2.)

    (e) In the list, Gunwinggu are indicated by Nos. 15 and 29. In the map only the number 15 is used.

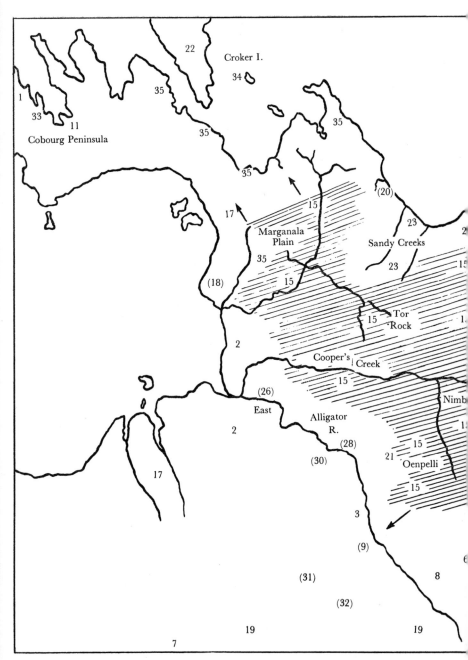

Fig. 22. Map of western Arnhem Land: Approximate positioning of main 'tribal' territories, showing spread of Gunwinggu influence (shaded area, plus arrows).

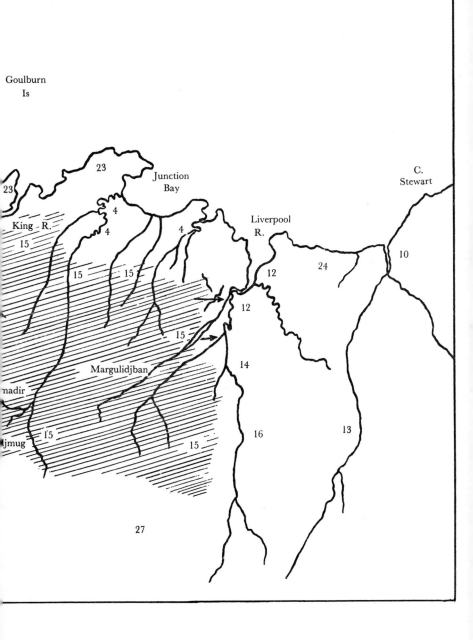

Glossary

This glossary includes the main Gunwinggu words mentioned in the text. It does not include ordinary names for birds, animals, etc., or foods (see Chapter 3, for example, list of main root foods), or kin terms (see Chapter 5, Table 4, and Appendix 2), or subsection terms (see Chapter 4), or seasonal names (see Chapter 3).

baidjan: Big, in sense of important; alone, or with prefixes na- or ngal-, specific kin term; with prefix man-, ritual connotation.

balanda: European.

-bang: Dangerous, strong, bitter, risky; used of foods (manbang), persons (for example, nabang, ngalbang), etc.

bengwabun, bengwabom: Victim of temporary upset or lapse: 'mind going round'.

bengwar (ngalbengwar, female): 'Deaf', stupid or silly person.

binin: Man, human being, Aboriginal person.

-bolg: *See* gunbolg.

dagwar: Food restricted to male participants in maraiin ritual.

dalug: Woman.

djamala: Part of Kunapipi singing.

djamalag: Ceremony, with trade as one feature.

djambuldjambul: Post-platform used in maraiin ritual. (Also, mandjanngarl.) Pandanus tree or 'forked post'.

djamun: Set apart, forbidden, tabu, or (especially with prefix man-) sacred.

djang: Spirit being or mythical character associated with specific site or territory.

djarada, tjarada: Love-magic rites, songs.

djebalmandji, djebanbani: Post structure used in Kunapipi ritual.

djirg: Leader in maraiin ritual. (Also, gandjari.)

djuandjuan: 'Stick' figure of paperbark or twine, placed by mortuary platform.

djumanggal: Post used in ubar ritual

djunggawon: Lorgun mortuary ritual; eastern Arnhem Land circumcision ritual.

djuruwari: Sweetheart relationship between persons calling each other gagag.

dua: Patrilineal moiety name, introduced from eastern Arnhem Land.

dudji: Bundle of sacred maraiin objects.

gadgad: Message-stick, used in lorgun ritual.

gagawar: Kunapipi messenger.

gaingen: Creature or plant associated with a child's pre-natal spirit.

ganala: Trench used in Kunapipi ritual.

gandjari: Leader in maraiin ritual. (Also, djirg.)

-gang: 'Took', etc.; in reference to country, 'came from', 'originated in'.

gawoˀnan: Ordinary word meaning 'looks after', 'cares for', etc. (third person singular, present tense); hence used in sense of ordinary, non-ritual leader.

-gid: Sorcerized, not truly alive.

-gobeng: 'Spouse'; also kin term.

-gom: Throat (*see* nagomdudj, etc.); also kin term, gongomu.

guin: Kangaroo (general term).

gulbagen: Betrothed wife.

gun-: Prefix categorizing, for example, language, various natural features, etc.

gunabibi: *See* Kunapipi.

gunbolg, gubolg: Land, country.

gundebi: Set of polite kin-reference terms.

gungamag: 'Good thing'; in ritual context, ritual performance.

gungurng: Special vocabulary used between 'mother-in-law' and 'son-in-law'.

gunmud: *(a)* named matrilineal unit(s): moieties, semi-moieties, subsections; *(b)* animal fur or hair. *See also* namud.

gunmugugur: Named patrilineal descent unit associated with specific territory. (Also, ngwoia; *and see* igurumu. Maung term: namanamaidj.)

gunmurng: Bone, skeleton, hard core or basis.

gunred, gured: Camp, territory, nest.

igurumu: Named patrilineal descent unit associated with specific territory; linked with gunmugugur.

jariburig
jarigarngurg   — Semi-moieties, matrilineal descent.
jarijaning
jariwurga

-jau: 'Small'; also kin term.

jelmalandji: Pole used in Kunapipi ritual.

-jime, -jimi: Say, make, do.

-jimeran: Become, 'make oneself' into; specifically, refers to *(a)* mythical beings, *(b)* participation in sacred ritual.

jira: Rain-restraining songs.

jiridja: Patrilineal moiety name, introduced from eastern Arnhem Land.

jurmi: Exchange commodity, in marriage negotiations.

kudjiga: Section of Kunapipi ritual.

kunapipi: Sacred ritual involving mythical character of that name.

laidgurunga, laidgurunguni: Maraiin novice.

largan: Mortuary ritual, jiridja moiety.

lida: Snail-shell rattles used in ubar ritual.

limbid: Lorgun novice.

lorgan, lorgun: Mortuary ritual.

maam: Malignant spirit, ghost. *See also* namandi.

madgu: Name of one matrilineal moiety. (*See* ngaraidgu.)

madjidji: Women's maraiin dancing.

magarada, makarata: Eastern Arnhem Land peace-making ritual. *See also* maneiag.

magu: Drone-pipe, didjeridu.

maiˀ: Creature, animal; but ngalbu maiˀ, Rainbow Snake.

malaidj: *See* namalaidj.

malbinbin: Message-stick in ubar ritual.

mamberiwul: Stone, used in ubar ritual, symbolizing Ngaljod's head (*see below*).

mamurung: Ceremony, with trade as one feature.

man-: Prefix categorizing, for example, vegetable foods; but specifically, in ritual contexts, referring to ritual affairs and personages, etc.

manbaidjan: *See* baidjan.

manberg: Bush country, dry land, mainland.

mandjamun: *See* djamun.

mandjanngarl: Post-platform used in maraiin ritual. (Also, djambuldjambul.)

maneiag: Peace-making ritual; western Arnhem Land version of magarada.

mangindjeg: Ritual associated with food of that name.

mangorang: Sorcery, sorcerer.

manme: General term for vegetable foods.

mar: Primeval, truly indigenous; of spiritual association with some natural feature, etc.

maralbibi: Kunapipi headband.

maralbindi: Kunapipi bullroarer.

mararaidj: Sweetheart.

margidbu: Native doctor, 'powerful' man.

mari: Eastern Arnhem Land kin term (for MM, MMB).

marlwa: Spirit being, sometimes malignant.

midjan: Ceremony, with trade as one feature.

mimi, mi?mi: Spirit beings, and rock art associated with them.

mindiwala: Men's circumcision dancing.

mirigu: Eastern Arnhem Land word; derogatory term, suggesting a-social behaviour.

miriri: Eastern Arnhem Land term for conventional discipline-and-constraint behaviour of a brother in relation to a sister.

-mud: *See* gunmud, namud, ngalmud.

mulu: Message-stick in maraiin ritual.

mumana: Kunapipi bullroarer. (Also, ngalmamuna.) *See also* maralbindi.

munggoiba: Eastern Arnhem Land word; derogatory term, suggesting a-social behaviour.

-murng: *See* gunmurng.

na-: Prefix categorizing, for example, masculine or male persons, creatures, etc.

nabiningobeng: Husband.

nabolggandjeri: Leader in ubar ritual. (Also, gandjari.)

nadulmi: Messenger in ubar ritual.

nagobeng: *See* nabiningobeng.

nagomdjangnan
nagomdudj (ngalgomdudj)
nagomjag } Ubar novice. (*See also* -gom.)
nagomgerngi

nagomgare: Ubar initiate.

namadgu: See madgu.

namalaidj: Orphan, fatherless boy.

namandi: Malignant spirit, ghost, corpse, *See also* maam.

namud: Circle of kindred.

nangaraidgu: *See* ngaraidgu.

nanggaru: Hole in Kunapipi ritual ground.

nara: Eastern Arnhem Land sacred ritual.

ngabibi: Eastern Arnhem Land kin term (for MB).

ngal-: Prefix categorizing, for example, feminine or female persons, creatures, etc.

ngalbu: *See* ngal-.

ngaldalug: Term used to or concerning a brother in reference to his sister.

ngalbiningobeng: Wife.

ngalgobeng: *See* ngalbiningobeng.

ngaljod: Rainbow Snake.

ngalmud: Rainbow Snake.

ngalwari: Quasi-derogatory term used by or to a brother about his sister.

ngaraidgu: Name of one matrilineal moiety. (*See* madgu.)

ngurlmag: Eastern Arnhem Land ritual. In western Arnhem Land, term used in Gunwinggu gungurng (q.v.) vocabulary for ubar and lorgun rituals.

ngwoia: Named patrilineal descent unit associated with specific territory. (Also, gunmugugur; *and see* igurumu.)

njalaidj: Ceremony, with trade as one feature.

rom: Ceremony, with trade as one feature.

ubar: Sacred ritual involving sacred object of that name. (Maung name: uwar.)

wakinngu: Eastern Arnhem Land word; derogatory term, indicating a-social behaviour.

waku, wogu: Eastern Arnhem Land kin term (S or D, *f.s.*; ZS or ZD, *m.s.*).

walalala: Mortuary ritual, dua moiety.

walg: Kunapipi novice.

wangaridja: Shade or bush hut, in ubar ritual.

warimulunggul: Part of Kunapipi singing.

wawul: Post used in lorgun ritual.

wud: Child. (Also, wudjau.) Also used in kinship terms.

wurbu: Ceremony, with trade as one feature.

Bibliography

BARNES, J. A., 1967. Genealogies, in *The Craft of Social Anthropology* (A. L. Epstein, ed.). Social Science Paperbacks, Tavistock, London.

BERNDT, C. H., 1951. Some figures of speech and oblique references in an Australian language (Gunwinggu), *Southwestern Journal of Anthropology*, Vol. 7, No. 3.

BERNDT, C. H., 1961. The quest for identity: The case of the Australian Aborigines, *Oceania*, Vol. XXXII, No. 1.

BERNDT, C. H., 1962. The arts of life: An Australian Aboriginal perspective, *Westerly*, Vol. 1, Nos. 2 and 3.

BERNDT, C. H., 1964. The role of native doctors in Aboriginal Australia, in *Magic, faith, and Healing* (A. Kiev, ed.). The Free Press, Glencoe.

BERNDT, C. H., 1965. Women and the 'secret life', in *Aboriginal Man in Australia* (R. and C. Berndt, eds). [Small section referring to western Arnhem Land.]

BERNDT, C. H., n.d. (1). Children's Stories from Western Arnhem Land. (Cyclostyled.) Western Australian Education Department, Perth. [Also as *Land of the Rainbow Snake*. Revised and enlarged version. Ure Smith, Sydney (forthcoming).]

BERNDT, C. H., n.d. (2). Marriage and Family in Western Arnhem Land. (Manuscript volume.)

BERNDT, C. H., n.d. (3). Monsoon and honey wind, in 'Claude Lévi-Strauss Festschrift' (J. Pouillon and P. Maranda, eds). Paris (forthcoming).

BERNDT, C. H., n.d. (4). Myth and mother-in-law: A question of meaning and interpretation in myth. Paper presented at the VIIIth International Congress of Anthropological and Ethnological Sciences, Tokyo, 1968. [Summary to be published in the relevant *Proceedings*.]

BERNDT, C. H. and R. M., 1951. An Oenpelli monologue: Culture contact, *Oceania*, Vol. XXII, No. 1.

BERNDT, R. M., 1951a. *Kunapipi*. Cheshire, Melbourne.

BERNDT, R. M., 1951b. Ceremonial exchange in western Arnhem Land, *Southwestern Journal of Anthropology*, Vol. 7, No. 2.

BERNDT, R. M., 1951c. Aboriginal ochre-moulded heads from western Arnhem Land, *Meanjin*, Vol. X, No. 4.

BERNDT, R. M., 1952a. *Djanggawul*. Routledge & Kegan Paul, London.

BERNDT, R. M., 1952b. Subincision in a non-subincision area, *American Imago*, Vol. 8, No. 2.

---

1 Not all references set out here are noted in the main text.

BERNDT, R. M., 1952c. Circumcision in a non-circumcision area, *International Archives of Ethnography*, Vol. XLVI, No. 2.

BERNDT, R. M., 1958a. Some methodological considerations in the study of Australian Aboriginal art, *Oceania*, Vol. XXIX, No. 1.

BERNDT, R. M., 1958b. The Mountford volume on Arnhem Land Art, Myth and Symbolism: A critical review, *Mankind*, Vol. 5, No. 6.

BERNDT, R. M., 1959. The concept of 'the tribe' in the Western Desert of Australia, *Oceania*, Vol. XXX, No. 2.

BERNDT, R. M., 1962. *An Adjustment Movement in Arnhem Land*. Cahiers de l'Homme, Mouton, Paris and The Hague.

BERNDT, R. M., 1964. The Gove dispute: The question of Australian Aboriginal land and the preservation of sacred sites, *Anthropological Forum*, Vol. I, No. 2.

BERNDT, R. M., 1965a. Marriage and the family in north-eastern Arnhem Land, in *Comparative Family Systems* (M. F. Nimkoff, ed.). Houghton, Mifflin, Boston.

BERNDT, R. M., 1965b. Law and order in Aboriginal Australia, in *Aboriginal Man in Australia* (R. and C. Berndt, eds).

BERNDT, R. M., 1966. Dominant social relationships among the Gunwinggu and 'Murngin' of Aboriginal Australia. Wenner-Gren Foundation for Anthropological Research, Burg Wartenstein, Symposium No. 35. Replicated paper for distribution to participants: pp. 1-114, with diagrams. [To be published, 1970, in an enlarged version as Social relationships in two Australian Aboriginal societies of Arnhem Land: Gunwinggu and 'Murngin', in a volume of the Symposium's Proceedings, *Kinship and Culture* (F. L. K. Hsu, ed.). See also F. L. K. Hsu, 1967.]

BERNDT, R. M., n.d. (1). Two in one, and more in two, in 'Claude Lévi-Strauss Festschrift' (J. Pouillon and P. Maranda, eds). Paris (forthcoming).

BERNDT, R. M., n.d. (2). The sacred site: A western Arnhem Land example. General meeting of the Australian Institute of Aboriginal Studies, 1968. Occasional Papers in Aboriginal Studies, 1969. A.I.A.S., Canberra.

BERNDT, R. M. (ed.), 1964. *Australian Aboriginal Art*. Ure Smith, Sydney.

BERNDT, R. M., and BERNDT, C. H., 1944-6. Native employment and welfare in the Northern Territory and survey of Army-controlled settlements. (Unpublished, duplicated reports.)

BERNDT, R. M., and BERNDT, C. H., 1951a. *Sexual Behavior in Western Arnhem Land*. Viking Fund Publications in Anthropology, No. 16, Wenner-Gren Foundation, New York. (Reprinted: Johnson Reprint Corporation, New York 1963.) [*Note:* The native words in this volume contain a number of typographical errors which we have not had an opportunity to correct.]

BERNDT, R. M., and BERNDT, C. H., 1951b. The concept of abnormality in an Australian Aboriginal society, in *Psychoanalysis and Culture* (G. B. Wilbur and W. Muensterberger, eds). International Universities Press, New York.

BERNDT, R. M., and BERNDT, C. H., 1952/1967. *The First Australians*. Ure Smith, Sydney. Walkabout Pocket Book edition, 1969.

BERNDT, R. M., and BERNDT, C. H., 1954. *Arnhem Land, Its History and Its People*. Cheshire, Melbourne.

BERNDT, R. M., and BERNDT, C. H., 1964. *The World of the First Australians*. Angus & Robertson, London; Ure Smith, Sydney. (Reprinted 1965, 1968.)

BERNDT, R. M., and BERNDT, C. H. (eds) 1965. *Aboriginal Man in Australia*. Angus & Robertson, Sydney.

CAPELL, A., 1940. The classification of languages in North and North-west Australia, *Oceania*, Vol. X, Nos. 3 and 4.

CAPELL, A., 1942. Languages of Arnhem Land, North Australia, *Oceania*, Vol. XII, No. 4; Vol. XIII, No. 1.

DOUGLAS, W. H., 1964. An Introduction to the Western Desert Language. *Oceania Linguistic Monographs*, No. 4. University of Sydney, Sydney.

ELIADE, M., 1966-7. Australian religions: An introduction. Parts I and II. *History of Religions*, Vol. 6, Nos. 2 and 3.

ELKIN, A. P., 1938/1964. *The Australian Aborigines*. Angus & Robertson, Sydney. (Reprinted 1966.)

ELKIN, A. P., 1950. The complexity of social organization in Arnhem Land, *Southwestern Journal of Anthropology*, Vol. 6, No. 1.

ELKIN, A. P., 1961. Maraiin at Mainoru, 1949, *Oceania*, Vol. XXXI No. 4; Vol. XXXII, No. 1.

ELKIN, A. P., and BERNDT, R. and C., 1950. *Art in Arnhem Land*. Cheshire, Melbourne.

ELKIN, A. P., and BERNDT, R. and C., 1951. Social organization of Arnhem Land I: Western Arnhem Land, *Oceania*, Vol. XXI, No. 4.

FALKENBERG, J., 1962. *Kin and Totem* .... Oslo University Press, Oslo (and Allen & Unwin).

FOX, R., 1967. *Kinship and Marriage*. Penguin Books (Pelican), Harmondsworth.

HART, C. W. M., and PILLING, A. R., 1960. *The Tiwi of North Australia*. Case Studies in General Anthropology (G. and L. Spindler, eds). Holt-Dryden, New York.

HIATT, L. R., 1959. Social control in central Arnhem Land, *South Pacific*, Vol. 10, No. 7.

HIATT, L. R., 1962. Local organization among the Australian Aborigines, *Oceania*, Vol. XXXII, No. 4.

HIATT, L. R., 1964. Incest in Arnhem Land, *Oceania*, Vol. XXXV, No. 2.

HIATT, L. R., 1965. *Kinship and Conflict*. Australian National University, Canberra.

HIATT, L. R., 1966a The lost horde, *Oceania*, Vol. XXXVII, No. 2.

HIATT, L. R., 1966b A spear in the ear, *Oceania*, Vol. XXXVII, No. 2.

HSU, F. L. K., 1967. Symposium on kinship and culture, *Current Anthropology*, Vol. 8, No. 5: pp. 512-17.

KYLE-LITTLE, S., 1957. *Whispering Wind*. Hutchinson, London.

LÉVI-STRAUSS, C., 1949. *Les Structures Élémentaires de la Parenté*. Presses universitaires de France, Paris.

LÉVI-STRAUSS, C., 1962. *La Pensée Sauvage*. Plon, Paris.

LÉVI-STRAUSS, C., 1963. *Totemism* (R. Needham, trans.). Beacon Press, Boston. (First published in 1962, as *Le totémisme aujourd'hui*. Presses universitaires de France, Paris.)

LINDSAY, D., 1883-4. Mr. D. Lindsay's Exploration through Arnheim's Land, *Proceedings of the Parliament of South Australia, 1883-4*, Paper No. 239. (Also, An expedition across Australia from south to north ... in 1885-6, *Journal of the Royal Geographical Society*, London, 1889, Vol. XI; and Explorations in the Northern Territory, *Proceedings of the Royal Geographical Society of Australasia, South Australian Branch*, 1887-8.)

MAKARIUS, R., 1966. Incest and redemption in Arnhem Land, *Oceania*, Vol. XXXVII, No. 2.

MCARTHUR, M., 1960. Food consumption and dietary levels of groups of Aborigines living on naturally occurring foods, in C. P. Mountford (ed.), 1960: pp. 96-135.

MCCARTHY, F. D., 1957. *Australia's Aborigines, their Life and Culture.* Colorgravure Publications, Melbourne.

MCCARTHY, F. D., 1958. *Australian Aboriginal Rock Art.* Australian Museum, Sydney.

MCCARTHY, F. D., and MCARTHUR, M., 1960. The food quest and the time factor in Aboriginal economic life, in C. P. Mountford (ed.), 1960: pp. 145-94.

MEGGITT. M. J., 1966. Gadjari among the Walbiri Aborigines of Central Australia. *Oceania Monographs*, No. 14. University of Sydney, Sydney.

MOUNTFORD, C. P., (ed.), 1956. *Records of the American-Australian Scientific Expedition to Arnhem Land*, Vol. 1: Art, Myth and Symbolism. Melbourne University Press, Melbourne.

MOUNTFORD, C. P. (ed.), 1960. *Records of the American-Australian Scientific Expedition to Arnhem Land*, Vol. 2: Anthropology and Nutrition. Melbourne University Press, Melbourne.

OATES, L. F., 1964. A Tentative Description of the Gunwinggu Language (Western Arnhem Land). *Oceania Linguistic Monographs*, No. 10. University of Sydney, Sydney.

O'GRADY, G. N., WURM, S. A., and HALE, K. L., 1966. Aboriginal Languages of Australia (map). Department of Linguistics, University of Victoria, Victoria, B.C.

PRICE, A. G., 1930. *The History and Problems of the Northern Territory, Australia.* The John Murtagh Macrossan Lecture for 1930, University of Queensland. Acott, Adelaide.

SEARCY, A., 1905. *In Northern Seas.* (Reprinted from "The Register" [newspaper] by authority of the South Australian Government.) Thomas, Adelaide.

SEARCY, A., 1909. *In Australian Tropics.* G. Robertson, London. (Second edition.)

SHEILS, H. (ed.), 1963. *Australian Aboriginal Studies.* A symposium of papers presented at the 1961 research conference (W. E. H. Stanner, convenor). Oxford University Press, Melbourne, for the Australian Institute of Aboriginal Studies.

SPENCER, B., 1913. Preliminary report. On the Aboriginals of the Northern Territory, *Bulletin of the Northern Territory*, No. 7. Department of External Affairs, Melbourne.

SPENCER, B., 1914. *Native Tribes of the Northern Territory of Australia.* Macmillan, London.

SPENCER, B., 1928. *Wanderings in Wild Australia.* Vols 1 and 2. Macmillan, London.

STANNER, W. E. H., 1959. On Aboriginal religion, I: The lineaments of sacrifice, *Oceania*, Vol. XXX, No. 2. [See Stanner, 1959-63.]

STANNER, W. E. H., 1959-63. On Aboriginal religion, *Oceania* Vol. XXX, Nos. 2 and 4; Vol. XXXI, Nos. 2 and 4; Vol. XXXII, No. 2; Vol. XXXIII, No. 4; Vol. XXXIV, No. 1.

STANNER, W. E. H., 1960. On Aboriginal religion, III: Symbolism in the higher rites, *Oceania*, Vol XXXI, No. 2. [See Stanner, 1959-63.]

STANNER, W. E. H., 1965*a*. Aboriginal territorial organization: Estate, range, domain and regime, *Oceania*, Vol. XXXVI, No. 1.

STANNER, W. E. H., 1965*b*. Religion, totemism, and symbolism, in *Aboriginal Man in Australia* (R. and C. Berndt, eds).

STREHLOW, T. G. H., 1947. *Aranda Traditions*. Melbourne University Press, Melbourne.

WARNER, W. L., 1937/1958. *A Black Civilization*. Harper, New York.

Index *

Abnormality, in Gunwinggu terms 153, 156–57, 171

'Aboriginality', emphasis on 203, 209

Administration/Government: attitudes to Aboriginal culture 128, 203; of Northern Territory xvi, 3, 4; settlements 5, 6, 104, changes in Aboriginal residence patterns at 104 (*see also* Maningrida)

Archaeology xv–xvi

Arnhem Land, eastern 4, 10, 57, 60, 67, 70, 85, 97, 110, 120, 121, 122, 124–25, 128, 133, 135, 136, 138, 139, 177, 194, 195, 198, 199, 205, 221, 222, 223, 227, 228

Art, styles in 192, 194. *See also* Painting(s)

Assimilation: as official policy 199, 209; opposition to 199

Australian Institute of Aboriginal Studies 202

Authority, traditional: based ultimately on 'supernatural' sanctions 149, 182; loss of, with advancing age 185, 186; of brother over sister 86, 165, 166, 169, 181, 222, 223–24, men over women 110, 186, 232, 235, mother over daughter 232, older men over younger men 150, 186, older women over younger women 115, 150, 186; vested in headmen and elders 150, or ritual leaders 149, but not simply on basis of age 150. *See also* Leaders; Mother's brother

Avoidance or constraint: between man and father's sister 86, 189, 220, own children 86, 189, sister 80–81, 84, 160, 220–25, in terms of address 78, 81; between man and sister's children 217, 220, sister's husband

---

* We thank Mrs. Veronica MacKenzie for helping with the Index, and Mrs. Eve Hewett for so conscientiously and patiently typing the manuscript.

221, wife's mother, *see* Mother-in-law; in mourning 93; learning about, by children 160

Barnes, J.A. 71, 73

Basket(s), bag(s): as female symbol 186, mythical origin of 118; sacred or containing sacred material 23, 39, 137; varieties of 23, 33, 38, 39, 41, 47, 121, 134, 135, 165

Bathing: ritual, associated with *maraiin* 137, with mortuary rites 93, 165

Bathurst and/or Melville Island(s) 1; Gunwinggu trade with 40; mythical characters coming via 12, 13, 118

Beings, creative, mythical, totemic: as creative spirits 113, 225, 226, 233, instituting sacred ritual 114, 122, 133, 230; coming from other areas 124, 205 (*see also* Myth(s)); connected with specific sites 113, 226 (*see* Sites); human influence over 227; indestructible 113. *See also Djang; Myth(s)

Berndt, R.M. and/or C.H. 2, 2*n*, 4, 54, 66, 71, 78, 81, 119, 120, 121, 122, 133, 139, 142, 144, 145, 147, 177, 194, 200, 201, 204, 208, 212, 214, 215, 216, 217, 219, 220, 221, 223, 226, 227, 228, 229, 235

Betrothal 91, 105; and rearing of wife 96; disputes over 97–99, 101, 152–53, 166, 167, 197; ideal age at 95–96, 100, 161, 167, not always achieved 167; mission attitudes to 103, 200–01; notions of balancing/exchange in 95, 96, 97, 103, 179, 218–22, 224; part played in by kin 94, 101, 168, girl's father 95, 97, 197, mother 95, 97, 100, 101, 165, 218, 219, mother's brother 86, 95, 97, 100, 172, 217, 218; rejection of, by girl 144, 167–68 (*see* Yirawadbad). *See also* Marriage; Mother-in-law

Birth 17, 26, 49, 91, 105, 145, 167, 174, 191, 202, 225, 233; symbolic 131, 148, 233, 234 (*see* Rites, initiation)

Blood: afterbirth, and betrothal 96, 191; attracting Rainbow Snake 180–81; drawing of, in mourning 93; mythical, ritual, symbolic associations of 123, 141, 182, 233, 234

Cahill, P. 5, 7

Capell, A. 2*n*

Ceremonies: exchange of gifts at 21, 46; multipurpose 147, focusing on trade and exchange 56, 146, 147. *See* Rites

Children: affection for 162; and choice between mother's and father's language 9, 87, 159; disciplining of 151, 163, 164, 165, 183; event-centred food tabus observed by 46, 160, 161 (*see also* Initiation; Food(s); Tabu(s); Rites); expected to support parents 97, 162; games of 33, 35, 159–60, 165, 179; 'illegitimate' 201; indulgence of 23, 49, 162; learning about avoidance and constraints 159, 160, betrothal and marriage 97, food collecting 30, 33, food tabus 160–61, kin terms and/or behaviour 89, 91, 155, 158, natural environment 30, 33, own pre-natal spirit 156, respect for sacred 138, sex roles 28, 33, 159, 165, 187, social categories 53, 159, 202; mistreatment or neglect of, in myth 21–23, 56, 153; phases in life-cycle of 105, 155; rebirth of 174; responsible for younger siblings 160, 165–66; songs of 5, 32–33, 206; spirit children, including pre-natal spirits 26, 27, 85, 156 (*see* Djang); toilet training 155; weaning 158. *See also* Parents; Socialization

Chinese, on Cobourg peninsula 5

Circumcision: not traditionally Gunwinggu practice 115, 139, 187, 195, reasons for, in myth 27, 123–24

Community 203, 212–16

Conformity: not excluding innovation 151, 187; overt, in religious sphere 112. *See* Myth

Croker Island 3, 5, 7, 8, 9, 14, 31, 32, 45, 107, 171, 193, 198–99, 202–03

Cross-cousin(s): and marriage preferences 80, 85, 99–100, 218–19, in relation to age at betrothal 100

Dances, dancing: associated with girls

129, men 131, 137, 141, 142, women 132, 134, 135; in myth 21, 22, 120, 123

Darwin: Aboriginal orientation toward or visits to 6, 105, 198; Gunwinggu in 3, 7

Dead: and native doctors 145, 146, songmen 146; spirits of 38, 81, 134, 145, 146, 187, 206, 221; tabus associated with personal names of 61, 88

Death: attributed to Kunapipi 182–83, to neglect 174, to sorcery 144–45, 177, 182; beliefs regarding 18, 27, 133, 135, 152, 173–74, 191, 225, 229, 233; food tabus associated with, *see* Food(s); foreshadowing rebirth 174; importance of kin obligations at *see* Obligations; movement to new site following 92, 165; search for scapegoat following 173–74, 176

Descent: balance between matrilineal and patrilineal 53, 57, 111, 113, 159, 204–05, 212; matrilineal, as major emphasis among Gunwinggu 53, 54, 60, 67, 95, 109, 212, 217, and moieties 60, semi-moieties 60, 61, 216, subsections 67–70, in relation to 'Mother' 227; patrilineal, as major criterion of local descent group (*see* Gunmugugur), and territorial rights 53, 54, 55, 111, 205, 212, 214 (*see* Gunmugugur), and sources of personal names 55, 161, 162, importance of, in religious ritual 57, 66, 70, 111, 113, 117, 205, 213–16, moieties 55, 57, 60, 64, 70, 205, traditionally unnamed 57, 67, 70. *See also* Marriage

Destiny, inherent, as mythical theme 19, 113, 205, 229

Didjeridu (drone-pipe), creation of, in myth 119

Disease, sickness 7, 14, 38, 45, 91, 145, 146, 176, 197–98, 199

Division of labour: economic 33–4, 52, 91, 109, 110, 115, 116, 148, 235, 236 (*see* Food(s); Woman); mortuary, *see* Obligations; ritual, *see* Rites; Woman

Djang 18–27, 49, 51, 66, 75, 109, 189, 192, 230; as ancestors 113, 118; associated with sickness 197; bound to specific localities 17, 18, 19, 21, 22, 23, 25, 26, 42, 44, 45, 46, 47, 49, 56, 58–59, 64, 107, 113, 178; destruction of, in myth, followed by disaster 27, 56, 152; increase rituals at *djang* sites 143; meaning of term 18, 19, 75. *See* Myth(s); Rainbow

Doctor(s), native (*margidbu*) 145–46, 150, 157, 173, 186, 207; associated with inquest following death 176, with Rainbow Snake 146, 152; contrasted with sorcerer 145; in myths and stories 146

Dogs 35, 106, 155, 166, 187, 189; in myth 13, 23–24, 41–42, 45, 56, 64, 119, 129

Douglas, W.H. 72

Dreaming, dreamtime 227; Aboriginal words translated as 75; as formative period 216, 226; as source of sacred 226, 229

Dream(s): allocating responsibility for death 176; and revelation of sacred objects 138; as source of songs 146. *See* Spirit(s)

Durkheim, E. 235

Education (European), and schools for Aboriginal children 198–99, use of English in 199, and Gunwinggu 204; possible effect on marriage 201

Eliade, M. 227

Elkin, A.P. xvi, 54, 71, 226

Elopement 103, 168, 169–70, 172, 185, 186; and care of children 193; and conformity with marriage rules 170; and punishments by sorcery 173 or spearing 167; as source of quarrels 166, 169–70; in myth 16, 191; increasing tolerance of 170–71

Employment: and sacred rites 125; for wages 201; in buffalo camps 5, 202

Environment, natural: attempts to influence by ritual/supernatural means 108, 143 (*see* Rites); range of or contrasts in 1, 30–32, 50–51, 107, 204, 228; religion closely associated with 12, 27, 51, 52, 13–14, 207, 225–27 (*see* Myth); utilization of resources in 38–41, 52, 206–07, 225, 236

Europeans, impact of: and broader 'Aboriginal' social identification 15, 203, 208–09; and depopulation, *see* Population; creating new 'needs' 7, 201, 205; initial, on Gunwinggu 198 (*see also* Gunwinggu); on Aboriginal social relations 104; on marriage/ betrothal partners 200, 201. *See also* Education; Employment; Missions

Exchange: of gifts at ceremonies 21, 146–47, between sweethearts 168; of goods at mortuary rites 135, Kunapipi rites 142, *ubar* rites 132. *See also* Betrothal

'Explorers' in western Arnhem Land 5

Extra-marital relations 90, 101, 110, 166, 214; attitudes toward 90, 101, 168, 185–86, 201. *See* Sweetheart(s)

Falkenberg, J. 215

Fertility: and human beings 144; as emphasis in sacred ritual 114, 142, 143, 144, 147, 227, 228, 232 (*see also* Kunapipi; *Lorgun; Mangindjeg; Maraiin; Ubar*); in songs 122, 138, 144

Fights, fighting, quarrels 39, 40, 61, 92, 96, 97, 165, 166–87; and police intervention 177; between women 165, 166–67, 184; in myth and story 13, 47, 167. *See also* Jealousy, Warfare

Food(s): contrast between coastal and inland 47, 48; cooking, preparation of 33–35, 36, 39, 42–44, 45, 46, 47, 50, 118, 133, 166, 206, 207; division of labour in gathering 33, 34, 109–10 (*see also* Woman); emphasis on sharing 44–5, and domestic quarrels 166; giving of, in betrothal 95, 96, 97, 168; groups involved in collection 33, 52, 104–06, 108–110, 150, 208, 213, 215–16, 220; introduced 201, 205; left by mythical beings 13, 14, 18, 24, 26, 41, 45–47, 118; varieties of 24, 33, 34–38, 39, 43, 45, 50, 51, 131, 178, 201

Food restrictions and/or tabus 35, 37, 52, 66, 93, 96, 115, 165, 180, 181; associated with initiation 115, 116, 131, 132, 134, 136, 137, 138, 234 or other religious 35, 49 or mortuary rites 93, 134, menstruation 49, pregnancy 49, 156, 180, specific localities 23, 24, 26, 49, 50; between brother and sister 160, 220–21; children's 46, 49, 161, 162; in myth and story 21, 23, 27, 45, 49, 197; symbolizing social and ritual status 49, 52, 115. *See* Tabu(s)

Fox, R. 217, 218, 222

Genealogical relationships, actual or implied, as basis of kinship reckoning 76–77, 86–88, 90, 216. *See* Kinship

Genealogy, genealogies: and personal names 162; material on xv, xvi, 88–89, 99, 103, 176; teaching children about 159; variation in individual knowledge of 88–89; versus category, as basis of affiliation 162, 163, 216

Goulburn Island(s) xiv, 3, 6, 7, 11, 31–2, 40, 107, 125, 128, 177, 198, 202. *See* Maung

Grievances, settlement of 169, 182,

183–85; through *maneiag* 92, 177, in mythology 178; raiding parties in 178. *See* Fights, Spearing

Gunbalang (Walang), in relation to Gunwinggu xvi, 8, 9, 13, 26, 67, 103, 107, 194, 195

Gunmugugur, Igurumu, Ngwoia 54–64, 71, 88–89, 111, 122, 134, 156, 214, 237–39; and 'correct' marriage 57, 71, 94, 109, 111, 214, 215; and personal names 55, 161, 162; and territorial ties 9, 54, 55, 57, 64, 87, 107, 113, 212–16; and 'tribal' affiliation 111, 196; as pointers to actual regional distribution 107, 213–16, but not necessarily to language 54, 196; boundaries of 213; children's knowledge of affiliation 202; meaning of 9, 54, 217; numerical size of 55; ties, emphasized in ritual 57, 71, 117, 134, 136, 137, 138 and in acquisition of *margidbu* power 146

Gunwinggu: and Maiali 10, 11, 46, 107, 139, 174, 192, 210; and Maung, *see* Maung; and question of separate identity xv, 1, 2, 3, 10–11, 65, 194–96, 207–08, 210, 211; as innovators and adapters 147, 187, 199, 205, 211; as *lingua franca* 7, 8, 195–96, 203–04; composite culture identified as 203; differences within 2*n*, 8, 10, 11; emergence of 196, 197; expansion into other areas 5–7, 75, 104, 199, 211, 241; language as basis of identification 1–2, 6, 7, 8, 11, 195–96, 210–11; traditional territory of, *see* Land

Hale, K.L. 2*n*
Hart, C.W.M. 1, 215
Hiatt, L. 72, 194, 212, 213, 214, 215, 221, 224
Horde(s) 213, basis of formation 215; relationship to land 216 and *gunmugugur* 216. *See also* Food(s), groups involved in collecting

Incest, quasi-incest 223, 225; in myth and story 23, 28, 47, 153, 223; punishment for 23, 230
'Illegitimacy' 201
Indonesia ('Macassar'); as origin-place of mythical characters 4, 12, 42, 117, 118, 123, 124; associations with in myth and story 13, 14, 197; traders from, on coast 4, 5, 8, 19
Initiation, *see* Rites
Intermarriage and language divisions 51–52, 197; and 'tribal' identity 7, 197, 208

Jealousy: between husband and wife 110, 168–69 (*see* Extra-marital relations; Fights), in myth 16, 197; between co-wives 200, sweethearts 168; on part of Mother or *Ubar* Woman 116, 121
Joking, formalized 90, 159, 220; children learning rules associated with 159
Jurawadbad *see* Yirawadbad

Kinship: and circle of close kin (*namud*) 75, 76, 77, 158, 174, 183, 184, expectations associated with 89, 183–84, 185, 217; and establishing relationship with strangers 75, 77, 89; and marriage stability 94, 101; and range of potential spouses 80, 90, 93–94, 95, 99–100, 184, 218–19; and subsection system, *see* Subsection(s); and study of marriage exchange systems 218–19; as basis of interpersonal relationships 75, 76, 89, 91, 154, 183, 202, 236; role of close kin in preventing social disruption 101, 183–85
Kinship obligations 76, 89, 91, 161, 185, 188, 225, 236 (*see also* Obligations); changes in through outside contact 201–02; children learning about 89, 91, 154–5; in mortuary arrangements, *see* Obligations; in ritual performance 116–17, 129–30, 132, 133–35, 137 reciprocal 183, 184, 202, 236; varying in accordance with kinship distance 88, 89, 91, 93, 183–84
Kinship terminology: as guide to behaviour 81, 86, 89, 217, but only partial 86; as guide to degree of relationship 77–78, 80; distinction between terms of address and reference 78–80; *gundebi* 77–78, 86, 188; Gunwinggu 81–87, 239–40, as pointer to potential marriage partners 85, 90, indicating distinction between close and more distant kin 86, 87–88, 188, but not necessarily 87; indicating generation levels 80; learning of, by children 89, 155, 158, 202; more than one term for relationship 77–78, 81; territorial bonds and 87
Kunapipi, Gunabibi, *kunapipi*: as initiation rite for girls 142; discouraged by missions and Administration 128;

initially owned by women 123; mother (Creative Mother) in 16, 117, 147, 227; not traditionally associated with Gunwinggu 135, 139, 182–83, 187, 195; partially closed to women and children 123; Rainbow Snake and 16, 123, 139, 141; 'risks' of participation in 123, 182–3; rites 16, 126–27, 138–42, 147, 174, 234; ritual exchange of wives or plural intercourse at 142; songs 17, 141–42; territorial spread of 122–24

Land, territory: alienation of 128, 203, 204; emotional attitudes to xiv, 17, 109, 135, 207, 208, 213–14; Gunwinggu, terms for 11–12, traditional 2, 2n, 3, 9, 21, 24, 32, 40, 204, 210, movement away from 40, 104, 105, 187, 213 after European contact 197–98, 213; patrilineal ties with 9, 17, 24, 27, 53, 54, 55, 57, 64, 66, 87, 106, 107, 109, 111, 212–16; quarrelling over 187, in myth 13; related to religion 106, 107, 114, 207, 208, 213, 214; validation of ownership in myth 206, songs 138. See Environment; *Gunmugugur*; Sites
Language: and bilingualism 7, 87, 195; and dialects 195; and marriage preference 94; and overall orientation 207–08; as basis of identification *see* Gunwinggu; changing, in myth 13, 14, 26; children's learning of 11, 155, 203–04; choice between father's and mother's 9, 87, 159; divisions, coinciding with territorial divisions 8, 9, 10, 54, 87, 196–97 but not always 54, or overlapping 9, 11, 26; divisions, in myth 11, 13, 14; Gunwinggu, *see* Gunwinggu; Gunwinggu 'tribal' or language names 240–41; styles in, and alternatives in vocabulary 189, 190, difference in status 189, diffidence 189, figures of speech 190, 191, but not exclusive to Gunwinggu 192. *See also* Mother-in-law
Leaders, leadership, in religious sphere 112, 115, 128, 130, 135, 138, 142, 143, 149–51; not always impartial 182; not simply on basis of age 149, 150, 186; ritual-ceremonial 117, 128, affected by outside contact 150
Lévi-Strauss, C. 73, 218, 226, 228
Lorgun, lorgan 143, 203; as mortuary rite 92, 117, 125, 133–35, 202; as sacred-secret rite of initiation 116, 125, 133–35, 161

Lumaluma the Whale 123, 137, 151, 182, 226, 229; and abuse of sacred food tabus 45, 230; instituting sacred ritual 45, 122, 152, 227, 230, especially *maraiin* 121, 122, 230

Magic: as distinct from religion 27, 143; love magic 128, 144; rain-restraining 144. *See also* Sorcery
Magico-religious 29, use of term 112
Makarius, R. 221
Mangindjeg 24, 37, 46–47, 124, 125, 131; ritual 132–33, 143
Maningrida 3, 6, 104, 193–94, 203
Maraiin rites 45, 116, 117, 121–22, 124, 125, 128, 134, 135–38, 143, 147, 161, 178, 181, 182, 234; and *gunmugugur* 136, 137; and inter-moiety cooperation 136; and objects 21, 121, 122, 123, 128, 134, 136, 137, 138; songs 138; Mother in 147; origin of 121; question of whether traditionally Gunwinggu 125, 195; sequence of, in initiation rites 126–27
Marriage(s), Gunwinggu: and case history material 89–90, 97–99, 101–03, 105, 167–68; and European-type schooling 201; and settlement living 201; arranged at ceremonial gatherings 146; as universal expectation 95; expected age at, *see* Betrothal; 'ideal' 68, 80, 94–95, 168, 184, 201, but alternatives 69, 80; mission attitudes to 103, 200; in relation to moieties 61, 70, 71, 90, 94, 194, semi-moieties 61, 64, 94, 170; not necessarily monogamous 95, 101; polygynous unions 95, 106, 110, 190, 200; preference for younger women as wives 80, 186; proportion of conventionally wrong 89, 100; role of kin in arranging 86, 94, 95, 111, 167–68, 217, 219, and maintaining 94, 101, 165 (*see also* Betrothal; rules and preferences relating to 57, 61, 64, 68, 69, 80, 94–95, 99–100, 101, 135, 169, 201, 219, 232, with kinship as major factor 94–95. *See also* Cross-cousin(s); Extramarital affairs; *Gunmugugur*; Subsection(s)
Maung xvi, 1, 2, 2n, 16, 183, 193; culture, decline of 7; identity, emphasis on 7, 203, 204; in relation to Gunwinggu 7, 8, 9, 11, 13, 14, 20, 26, 40, 54, 60, 67, 79, 81, 103, 107, 119, 153, 159, 194, 195, 201, 204, 208, 228

McArthur, M. 36

Meggitt, M. 228

Melville and/or Bathurst islands, *see* under Bathurst

Men: formal authority vested in 110, 150–51, 181, 217 (*see* Authority); initiated, controlling major rituals, *see* Rites

Menstruation: marking girl's transition to adult status 161; tabus associated with 49, 180, 191, instituted by mythical beings 119, not always observed in contact situation 181

Messenger: carrying news of death 91, 92, 93, 134, 197; summoning men to fight 178–79; summoning visitors to ceremonies 21, 147 or sacred rites 116, 128–29, 134, 135, 139. *See also* Rites

Military activities and/or Army settlements xiv, 4, 5, 6, 8, 10

Mission(s) 181, 199; and tourism 203; attitudes toward Aboriginal culture 7, 125, 128, 200, including marriage 61, 103, 200–01; settlements, Aboriginal residence patterns at 104, 205; sponsoring Aboriginal art 193

Moiety, moieties 60–61; affiliation fixed before birth 73; and marriage rules 61, 64, 70, 71, 90, 94, 170, 194, 195; and matrilineal descent 60, 216, 228, and patrilineal descent 55, 57–58, 64, 67, 70, 205, importance of, in ritual 57, 70–71, 116–17, 135–36; and territorial affiliation 56, 57, 205; cooperation between, in ritual 116–17, 136; names as basis of identification 61

Mortuary paraphernalia 40, 92, 106, 122, 134, 135, 165, 195; decline in making and use of 202

Mortuary rites 12, 117, 165, 195, 202, 225; absence of 182; and mourning 91, 92–93, 174; exchange of goods at 135; now rarely performed 128, 202; tabus associated with 92–93, 134. *See also Lorgun;* Obligations

Mother, Creative, Fertility 16, 20, 117, 118, 119, 121, 142, 227, 228, 229. *See* Kunapipi; Rainbow; *Ubar;* Waramurungundji

Mother: expected behaviour of 86, 165; personal bond between child and 86, 165, 111, daughter and 109, son and 132, 158; role in daughter's marriage arrangements 95, 96, 111, 219. *See also* Orphan

Mother-in-law, relations between man

and 94–97, 101, 160, 194; avoidance behaviour between 81, 100, 101, 200; gifts to, by son-in-law 95, 96, 97; in myth 152–54 (*see also* Yirawadbad); use of special vocabulary between 77, 85, 96, 100, 125, 160

Mother's brother, authority of: over sister's daughter 165–66, 189, in marriage arrangements 100 (*see* Betrothal); over sister's son 165–66, 189, 217, in regard to extra-marital affairs 169, marriage arrangements 86, 95, 217, ritual 86, 217

Mountford, C.P. 36

Myth(s) and stories: and circumstances of telling 17; and creation of landscape 18, 27, 38, people, 19, 20, 117–18; and erotic stimulation 28, 153; and marriage preferences 28–29, 95, 152; and origin of death 27, 133, 146, 173, 229, 233, fire 27, 42–43, sorcery 144–45; and semi-moiety connections 66; as basis of language divisions 13, 14; as basis for magico-religious rites 16, 112, 147, 234–36 (*see* Rites); as guide to correct social behaviour 28–29, 151, 152, 153, but also 'good' coming from 'bad' 151–52; 230, 232; as guide to local resources and natural environment 33, 34, 35, 38, 39, 40–50 106, 107, 108, 113, 206, but no longer adequate 45, 207; as source of general explanation of human situation 27–29, 33, 112, 113, 154, 206, 234, 236; 'bad example' in 23, 28, 144, 151–53, 154; changes in telling of, in contact situation 28, 206; criteria of 'correct' versions 16, 17; decline in women's knowledge of 16–17, 66; diffusion of 147; metamorphosis in 12, 13, 19, 20, 21, 22, 23, 24–25, 26, 42, 45, 46, 47, 56, 114, 118, 122, 152; range of knowledge of 16–17; revealing narrator's interests/attitudes 47–48; sharing of, between 'tribes' 107, 228; snake characters in 16, 20, 119, 123, 125, 154, 228, 233 (*see* Rainbow; Yirawadbad); spatial mobility in 12, 13, 17, 18–19, 20, 23, 24, 26, 41–42, 43, 44, 59, 106–09, 119, 121, 124, 212, 226; territorial associations of 17, 25, 40–41, 125, 147, 189, 205, 226, 234 (*see Djang*); validating claims to land 14, 206; variation in 13, 16, 17, 20, 21, 22–23, 24, 49, 119–20, 122, 229, between men's and women's versions 17, 117, 122, 235. *See also* Mother, Creative; Rainbow; Rites

Mythical characters: as creators of human beings 19, 20, 26–27, 117–18, 119, of natural environment 18, 27, 28, 38, 39; bringing fire 42–43; coming from north-west 14, 118 (*see* Bathurst; Indonesia); leaving behind domestic equipment 42, 45, 47, 118; terms for 15. *See also* Food(s)

Mythical characters: Barramundi fish 15, 17, 27; Crow 15; Leech 13, 25; Louse 25, 26; Nabiridauda 41; Nadjarami wild bee 13; Nadulmi (Narol' mi) 119, 120, 128, 129, 131; Nagugur 122, 123, 133, 142, 226, 227; Nawulabeg 41, 46; Nimbuwa 12, 13, 46; Waralag Brothers 39, 48; Yiriu 13, 42, 154. *See* Lumaluma; Orphan; Rainbow; Waramurungundji; Wawalag Wuragag, Yirawadbad

Names: avoided in conversation 61 (*see also* Dead) and in 'gossip' songs 103; joking or nicknames 61, 81, 161, 162; personal 15, 55, 61, 161, sources of 16, 55, transmission of 162

Oates, L.F. 2

Obligations: associated with death 91–93, 133, 134, 135 now less relevant 202, with initiation 116, 117, 129–30, 132, 137, with ritual 116; changing content of 201. *See also* Kinship

Oenpelli xiv, 13, 15, 23, 124, 125, 128, 142, 168, 170, 174, 181, 182, 193; archaeological material at xvi; as meeting place for Gunwinggu and other 'tribes' 6, 107; changes at 5–6, 198; mission 3, 6, 97, 104, 193, 198–99, 200–01, 203; movement of Aborigines to 6, 104; school at 198, 202, 203–04; tourism at 203

O'Grady, G.N. 2*n*

Old age 161; ambivalence regarding 163, but loss of status in 185–86; care of old 163, 174; children expected to support parents in 162

Orphan and Rainbow story 21–23, 56, 59, 143, 152, 153, 206, and adults' affection for children 162; and special bond between mother and son 23, 158; outcome of, as penalty for wrong-doing 21–23, 229–30

Painting(s): bark 192–94; rock and cave 27, 192, 193; and tourism 203;

associated with magic and sorcery 144, 192, and/or myth 27, 46, 192

Parents: and mourning for child 91, 93, 165; contributing to child's growth 155, before birth 156; dependence on children 111, 162; man not competing for wives with father 101; no equivalent term in Gunwinggu 85; socialization of children by 158, 159, 160, including discipline 163–65; special bond between prenatal spirit and father 156; terms of address and reference for 78–79, 82, 84, 85, 86, 87–88, 239; wife homesick for, in myth 23. *See also* Children; Descent; Obligations

Payments, gifts: between sweethearts 168; for assistance or participation in rituals 116, 142, 146; to wife's parents, especially mother-in-law 95, 96, 97

Phratry, *see* semi-moiety

Pilling, A. 1, 215

Population, in Western Arnhem Land, estimates of, references to 3, 3*n*, 55, 104, 106, 194, 204, 214; depopulation, in myth 167, 197; growth of 8, 199, after earlier decline 7, 211

Puberty rites of girls, 161, 202. *See also* Initiation

Python, as male symbol 20, 228. *See* Rainbow; Yirawadbad

Radcliffe-Brown, A.R. 71, 215

Rainbow in Snake manifestation 19–24, 38, 75, 114, 190, 195; as agent of punishment for breach of tabus 20, 21, 23, 27, 28, 42, 132 or 'wrong' behaviour 22, 44, 45, 152, but not agent of supernatural moral retribution 230; as agent of transformation into *djang* 19, 20, 21, 22, 24; as creator 20, 27, 118, of human beings 20, 117–18; as male figure 20, 228; as manifestation of Mother 20, 117, 147, 227, 229; associated with disaster and storm 20, 22, 50, 144, 207, 229, with native doctors or sorcerers 145, 146, 152, with songmen 146; care taken in precautions concerning 195; coming from the east 121; dangerous to children 180; in Kunapipi ritual 123, 139, 141, 142; in *maraiin* ritual 138; in *ubar* ritual 130, 131, 132, 232; 'killing' of, in myth 20, 229; swallowing by 20, 21, 22, 23, 24, 42, 44, 45, 48, 49, 56, 132, of novices 131, 132, 139, 141

Social Service Benefits, as cash income 202

Socialization of children: 23, 30, 33, 138, 151, 154–56, 158–59, 160–61, 162, 163, 165–66, 202, 234, 235

Songmen 146, 169, 186, 191–92

Songs: associated with rites 17, 114, 115, 133, 134, 138, 139, 141, 142, 146, 148; children's 5, 32–33, 206, as means of instruction 33; concerned with fertility 138, 144; dealing with marriage exchange 103, seasonal changes 132, 138, sorcery 144, territorial ownership 138; *djarada* 144; erotic stimulation in 144, 153; 'gossip' 103, 144, 146, 169, 186; indirect allusions in 191–92; rain-restraining 143–44

Sorcerer, sorcery 144–46, 173, 181, 189, 207; accusations and search for a scapegoat 93, 174, 176; and bark/cave paintings 144, 192; and camp hygiene 155; as revenge 157, 173, 176–77, 191; death as 'proof' of 144, 173; in myth and story 119, 144, 173, 182, 197; materials used in 176–77; rare among close kin 184

Spear(s), spearing 40, 120, 133, 167, 177, 178–79, 182; and small boys 33; and threat of police action 177; conventional symbol(s) of maleness 186; in expressing grief 93; in myth 122, 191. *See* Fight(s)

Spelling of Aboriginal words xvi, 64

Spencer, B. 5, 124, 133, 135, 138

Spirit(s) 20, 51; children 26, 27, 156; Dadube 18; familiar or assistant, of native doctor or songman 146, 186; indestructible 27; *maam* 20, 47, 133; malignant, 18, 157; *marlwa* 20; *mimi* 18, 51, in rock paintings 192; Nagidgid 18, 51 (*see* Sorcery); *namandi* 20. *See also* Dead, *Djang*

Stanner, W.E.H. 212, 213, 214, 215, 225, 226, 229, 233, 234, 235

Stealing 45, 187

Strehlow, T.G.H. 228

Subincision: associated with Kunapipi 139; not traditionally Gunwinggu practice 115, 139, 195

Subsection(s), subsection system 10, 66–75, 79–80, 90, 195, 202, 204; affiliation fixed before birth but subsequent change possible 73, 90; and marriage rules 67, 68–70, 71, 74, 90, 94; as means of incorporating outsiders into kinship system 8, 67, 75, 76, 77, 89, basis of descent in 60,

74, matrilineal 66–67, 71–72, 205, patrilineal 67, 69–71, connected with moiety/semi-moiety system 60, 70

Suicide: confined to myth 27, 152

Sweetheart(s): and response of spouse(s) 168–69; as long-standing tradition 201; increase of 'wrong' liaisons 89; recognized code of behaviour between 168, 190; relationship in myth and story 16, 154, 168–69, 191. *See also* Extra-marital affairs

Tabu(s), restrictions 50–51; associated with certain sites 14, 22, 23, 24, 25, 26, 27–28, 42, 44, 45, 50, 107, 162, 216, with initiation of boys, *see* Food(s), also observed by female kin 132, 137, with menstruation 49, 119, 180, 191, with pregnancy and childbirth 155–56, 180; personal names of dead 61, other mortuary 92–93, 134

Tabu(s), restrictions: breaches of, infrequent 28, 166, 180, leading to fights 166, punished by death 173, responsible for abnormalities in children 156–57; types of sanction resulting from 181

Tabu(s), restrictions: observance of, and control by initiated men 185–86

Time: categories 31, 108, reckoning 32; views regarding 15, 18, 111, 112

Totems, totemism, totemic 113, 226, 233; and pre-natal spirit child 156; and semi-moieties 65, 66; 'conception' or pre-natal totemism 66, 191; emblems, *see* Sacred Emblems/Objects

Tourism 203

Towns, cities: Aboriginal contacts with 6, 7, 105, 198, 202. *See also* Darwin

Trade, trading 39; as feature of ceremonial/ritual gatherings 128, 146, 147; between 'tribes' or local groups 40, 195, 197; providing links outside 'tribal' territory 52, 212. *See also* Exchange; Indonesia

'Tribe(s)': increasing importance of 'tribal' identification 9, 11, 208; intermarriage among 7, 11, 197, 208; 'tribal' names, range of, from Gunwinggu angle 8–11, 240–41; use of term xv, 2, 7

Ubar (*Uwar*) gong, myth(s), rites, songs 16, 43, 59, 116, 117, 120, 121, 123, 124, 125, 126–27, 128–32, 134, 139, 161, 195, 232–33, confined to

Western Arnhem Land 124; food tabus connected with 131; Mother in 16, 116, 129, 130, 131, 217; parts not to be seen/heard by women and children 120, 123; origin of 119, 128; role of women in 129, 131–32; seasonal performance of 128; *Ubar* Woman 121, 129, 233. *See also* Rainbow; Yirawadbad

Values 112, 149, 151. *See* Myth(s)

Vocabularies, special, complete or partial: alternatives in Gunwinggu 189–90; between man and mother-in-law 120, 125, 160

Waramurungundji (mythical First Woman) 12, 16, 118, 123; as creator of menstrual tabus 119, institutor of girls' puberty rites 119, manifestation of Mother 118, 227, 229

Warner, W.L. 124, 125, 135, 139, 177 221, 222, 223

Wawalag (Sisters) 20, 121, 122, 124, 125, 133, 138, as 'transition' myth 228

White, C. xvi

Widow, widower 12, 92, 109, 110, 181; as sorcery suspect 93

Wife, wives: 'lending' of 101, 172; and tabus at husband's initiation 116, 138, 142; preference for younger women as 80, 186; rejection of husband by, *see* Yirawadbad. *See also* Elopement; Extra-marital-affairs; Marriage; Woman

Woman, women: and/or children,

excluded from secret-sacred myth, ritual, sight of certain objects 120, 123, 138, 235, reasons for, in myths 120, 232–33, 235; and division of labour in food-collecting 33–34, 39; and own territory 109; as original owners of sacred myths, objects, rites, grounds 116, 120, 123; authority of, in immediate family 163, 232 (*see also* Socialization), older over younger 186; contributing greater part of food supply 109; fighting between 166–67, 184; food tabus of, *see* Food(s); old, place of in ritual affairs 116, 163; role in performance of rites 17, 112, 125, 129, 130, 131, 132, 134, 137, 148, 235

Wuragag, Tor Rock 9, 12, 13, 16, 33, 42, 107, 119, 152, 230; as bringer of fire 42–43; metamorphosis of 13, 118, 230

Wurm, S.A. 2n

Woraidbag, Woraidbug 13, 23, 42

Yirawadbad (Yirabadbad) 2n, 184, 226; as 'bad' example 153; creator of *ubar* ritual 119–20, 227, 230 and ground 129; coming from 'Macassar' 124; in snake form 154, 233; myth 119, 186, 235, as reflection of attitudes to marriage 28, as support for established marriage rules 154, 168–69, 184, 232–33, reenacted in *ubar* rite 130; using sorcery in revenge 173

Yiwadja 8, 9, 11, 13, 14, 20, 40, 45, 48, 61, 67, 193, 194, 195–96, 201